TOP
10
LISTS

BOOKS

OVER 100 TOP 10 LISTS

BOOKS

OVER 100 TOP 10 LISTS

FID & SUE BACKHOUSE

&B Bounty
BOOKS

Publisher: Samantha Warrington
Editorial & Design Manager: Emma Hill
Designer: Eoghan O'Brien
Senior Production Manager: Peter Hunt

First published in 2014 by Bounty Books,
a division of Octopus Publishing Group Ltd
Endeavour House,
189 Shaftesbury Avenue,
London WC2H 8JY
www.octopusbooks.co.uk

An Hachette UK Company
www.hachette.co.uk

ISBN: 978-0-753728-58-1

A CIP catalogue record for this book is
available from the British Library

Printed and bound in China

CONTENTS

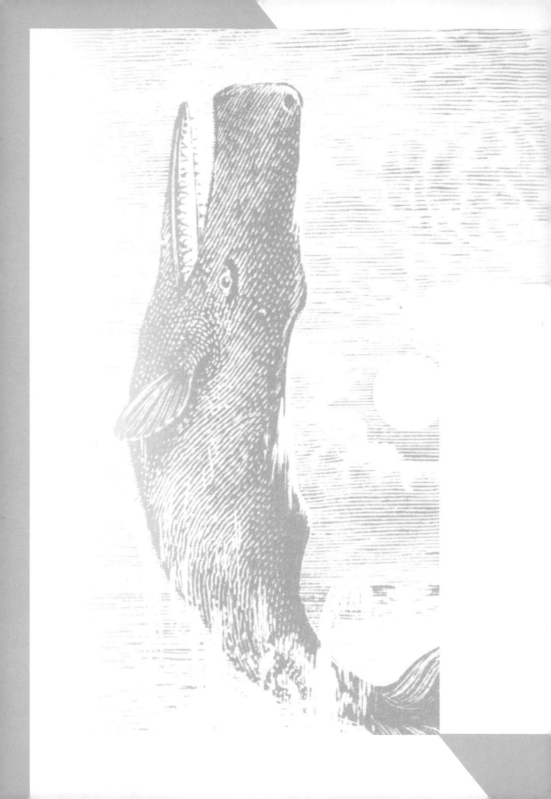

INTRODUCTION

Where to start? That's a pretty tough question when it comes to compiling a book that lists a selection of other books, especially when there is only space to include just over a thousand of them. After all, the size of the task is emphasized by the fact that a certain well-known on-line book store proudly boasts that it has over two million titles to choose from on its physical and electronic shelves (no names, but think BIG South American river). Of course one obvious answer to the question is that anyone can take a deep breath, then just wade in and start doing it. But such an exercise – whoever undertakes it – is obviously so subjective that, even if every reader in the world had a go, no two people could ever come up with the same selection in a thousand years.

Still, needs must. A constructive way to begin is by dividing up the task into broad chapters. We've chosen six, as follows: World of Books (featuring assorted genres and styles); Compelling Characters (showcasing memorable fictional individuals); Out of this World (covering sci-fi, fantasy & horror); Relativity (dealing loosely with human relationships); Imagine That (stimulating books for kids & teens); Page-turners (exciting escapist action & adventure). Of course there's inevitably plenty of overlap between the various chapters, but a certain order does start to emerge that allows the fun to begin. And it's not only fun to do, but exciting, because anyone who loves books cannot fail to enjoy choosing Top 10 lists featuring their own favourite reads.

That said, few book lovers can claim extensive knowledge across the full publishing spectrum   and that's the very rationale behind the creation of this book. For in compiling over a hundred Top 10 lists we have reviewed the entire field, and hope that in so doing our readers will be encouraged to try some interesting titles that have

previously slipped under their radar, or alternatively dip into an area they have not hitherto explored. But there's more! Another facet of our grand design is to create a little creative controversy by providing readers with the opportunity to disagree with our choices, on the perfectly valid basis that they know better. You understand the form (and can shortly start playing the game with relish): Why on earth did they include that one? Rubbish! How dare they leave out that one? Scandalous!; Was this list compiled by a five-year-old? Ridiculous! And that's just for starters. Don't hold back, because we can take it. Indeed, we welcome it and if anyone is moved to compile their own alternative Top 10 lists, so much the better. To help the process along, we asked each of our two compilers to choose one personal special Top 10 list from all the wonderful titles featured in this book, just to get you going. Here goes . . .

The one who likes rather weighty reads chose these:

10 *The Age of Innocence*, Edith Wharton
9 *Death in Venice*, Thomas Mann
8 *The Rings of Saturn*, W G Sebald
7 *A Thousand Splendid Suns*, Khaled Hosseini
6 *The Worst Journey in the World*, Apsley Cherry-Garrard
5 *The Diaries of Jane Somers*, Doris Lessing
4 *Sophie's Choice* by William Styron
3 *The Alexandria Quartet* by Lawrence Durrell
2 *Perfume* by Patrick Suskind
1 *Vanity Fair* by William Makepeace Thackeray.

And the one who veers towards books-as-entertainment picked these:

10 *The Adventures of Sherlock Holmes* by Arthur Conan Doyle
9 *The Talented Mr Ripley* by Patricia Highsmith
8 *The Long Goodbye* by Raymond Chandler
7 *A Clockwork Orange* by Anthony Burgess
6 *Notes from a Small Island* by Bill Bryson
5 *Catch-22* by Joseph Heller
4 *The Silence of the Lambs* by Thomas Harris
3 *Clear and Present Danger* by Tom Clancy
2 *The Girl with the Dragon Tattoo* by Stieg Larson
1 *The Day of the Jackal* by Frederick Forsyth.

As we said, it's all very subjective, but enjoyable. Over to you happy reading!

CHAPTER 1

COMPELLING CHARACTERS

What makes any book special? Nine times out of ten it is fascination with characters that populate the pages, springing to life from the writer's imagination and in turn firing the interest of readers. So this book about books can justifiably pick out and list some of the best and most interesting characters ever created (along with the odd surprise).

Those who say romance is dead in the modern world of social media and 'computer says' must surely be confounded by the enduring popularity of classic romantic heroes and heroines (we'll get to the ladies next), often from times past when life was very different. Different it may have been, but the appeal of those long-ago love stories never dims.

ENDURING **ROMANTIC HEROES**

10 ORLANDO
Although he's over 400 years old (albeit wearing well), Orlando still cuts a dash as a romantic hero in Shakespeare's *mêlée* of chaotic cross-dressing love stories. Suffice to say that the boy finally gets his adored Rosalind.

9 IVANHOE
Upstanding Ivanhoe's love for Rowena is the actual romance, but what could be more romantic than the mysterious Black Knight who intervenes positively at critical moments in the turbulent narrative, only to be revealed as (spoiler alert) King Richard the Lionheart!

8 DANIEL DERONDA
This chap is on the worthy side, but his initial (unrequited) love for Gwendoline remains true, and even as he eventually marries another he gives her hope, after she has ruined her own life. That's romance, folks, Victorian style!

7 TOM JONES
The lusty foundling nurtured by kind Squire Allworthy is not as good as he should be, but Tom is redeemed by love (which, needless to say, doesn't run smoothly) for virtuous Sophia Western.

6 RHETT BUTLER
He's romantic, he's dashing, he's wealthy, he's passionate, he's a little dangerous - so what's not to like? Ask the tempestuous Scarlett O'Hara, who somehow manages to mess up her marriage to the aforementioned Rhett.

5 HEATHCLIFF
Both hero and villain, this gypsy foundling is the archetypal tortured romantic. He loves Catherine, who loves him back but accepts a 'suitable' marriage. Heathcliff takes cruel revenge on those who wronged him, but happily the lost lovers do get buried side by side.

4 SYDNEY CARTON
As romantic heroes go, Sydney is flawed - a

brilliant but drunken lawyer cursed by self-doubt and unlucky in love (for Lucie Manette loves his client, Darnay). So how romantic is it when he goes to the guillotine instead of Darnay, finally reconciled with himself?

3 EDWARD ROCHESTER

The brooding Rochester might be a man of destructive secrets, whose aborted marriage to Jane Eyre sent our heroine into a sad spiral of circumstantial decline, but he finally came good and this darkly romantic hero got the girl.

2 FITZWILLIAM DARCY

Has there ever been a more romantic hero than the initially aloof Mr Darcy? It seems not, as his happy-ending love story is constantly voted a favourite read (and filmed every week or so, if memory serves).

1 ROMEO MONTAGUE

Romeo and his Juliet are inescapably star-crossed. Their ultimately tragic love match has universal appeal, and the word Romeo has come to symbolize an ardent male lover (not always, admittedly, as noble as young Montague).

TOP 10

Modern women may shudder at the inferior status of women and painful chauvinistic excesses of times past, but the pages of literature are actually full of romantic heroines who were often (though not, in truth, inevitably) striking characters by any standards. Here are ten such, all of whom (whether happy, sad or tragic) can stand tall in their own right.

ENDURING **ROMANTIC HEROINES**

10 DAISY MILLER
The flirtatious Annie 'Daisy' Miller is very appealing, but not the most upstanding of heroines. Her romantic entanglement with Winterbourne swiftly stalls, before she defies convention by falling in love with the dashing but unsuitable Giovanelli. Then she tragically dies.

9 ANNE ELLIOT
It's 1818, so how can a confirmed spinster of 27 become a romantic heroine? Trust Jane Austen – Anne's unhappiness at long ago turning down that unsuitable young naval officer she once loved passionately is tempered when he returns, rich and successful. Love rules!

8 BATHSHEBA EVERDENE
The independently minded Bathsheba rejects sturdy Gabriel Oak, and it takes a no-good husband, possessive older suitor, mayhem and murder before the destined-for-each-other couple finally get together.

7 EMMA BOVARY
Heroines could be scandalous, even in 19th-century France, and Madame Bovary fits that job description to perfection. Boring marriage, unwanted child, betrayed by dashing lover, secret affair, ruination, suicide. Tragically romantic, or what?

6 DOROTHEA BROOKE
The idealistic Dorothea marries an unsuitable older man, and it takes an entire book set against the rich tapestry of Middlemarch town before she renounces her dead husband's fortune and marries her true love. All together now – ahhhh . . .

MADAME BOVARY

COMPOSITIONS DE ALFRED DE RICHEMONT
GRAVÉES A L'EAU-FORTE
PAR
C. CHESSA

PRÉFACE PAR LÉOS HENRIQUE

PARIS
LIBRAIRIE DES AMATEURS
A. FERROUD — F. FERROUD, SUCCESSEUR
127, BOULEVARD SAINT-GERMAIN, 127

1905

5 TESS DURBEYFIELD
What's romantic about the hangman's noose? Well, think journey rather than ending. Tess's status (though blameless) as a fallen woman blights her life. When she stabs her D'Urberville seducer and gains the forgiveness of beloved husband Angel, the tragic die is cast.

4 ANNA KARENINA
Heroines often overcome daunting obstacles before reaching a happy ending – or not, in Anna's case. Suicide after the failure of her relationship with the dashing Count Vronsky again proves that romantic heroines and tragedy can walk hand in hand.

3 JANE EYRE

The heroine created by Currer Bell (okay, Charlotte Brontë) set the scene for countless future novels featuring unfolding consciousness. But Jane's developing moral sensibilities don't stop her being the better half of one of fiction's classic triumph-over-tragedy love stories.

2 ELIZABETH BENNET

How refreshing – not marrying for money and status! How shocking that initial rejection must have seemed to Regency readers, but how delightful when the principled Elizabeth finally marries the oh-so-eligible (and decent) Mr Darcy.

> "FOR NEVER WAS A STORY OF MORE WOE THAN THIS OF JULIET AND HER ROMEO"
>
> **– PRINCE ESCALUS OF VERONA**

1 JULIET CAPULET

Their love was true, but warring families meant its course would be tragic. Despite a secret marriage (and covert consummation) it duly ended badly, with Romeo and Juliet dead by their own hands. As scant consolation, the Montagues and Capulets were reconciled.

10 DAISY MILLER
Daisy Miller
Henry James

9 ANNE ELLIOT
Persuasion
Jane Austen

8 BATHSHEBA EVERDENE
Far From The Madding Crowd
Thomas Hardy

7 EMMA BOVARY
Madame Bovary
Gustave Flaubert

6 DOROTHEA BROOKE
Middlemarch
George Eliot

5 TESS D'URBERVILLE
Tess Of The D'urbervilles
Thomas Hardy

4 ANNA KARENINA
Anna Karenina
Leo Tolstoy

3 JANE EYRE
Jane Eyre
Charlotte Brontë

2 ELIZABETH BENNET
Pride And Prejudice
Jane Austen

1 JULIET CAPULET
Romeo And Juliet
William Shakespeare

As one of Britain's (no, make that the world's) greatest writers, the genius of Charles Dickens was to comment powerfully on the towering iniquities of 19th-century society, and miserable lot of the deprived, by creating riveting stories populated by memorable characters. Almost by definition most were flawed and many were bad. Here are ten that had telling tales to tell.

MEMORABLE **DICKENS CHARACTERS**

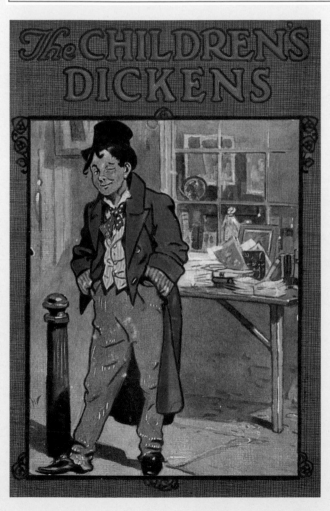

10 JENNY WREN
Although not the largest loomer among memorable Dickens characters, the disabled teenager (just) makes the list as a shining example of the author's sentimentality, also representing his acute observational insights. Happily, this 'good girl' finds love.

9 FAGIN
The unforgettable Fagin, though humorously portrayed, is a very bad man. Constantly referred to as 'The Jew' (Dickens claimed with no anti-Semitic intent), this 'kidsman' (user of children to steal) is a larger-than-life grotesque who gets his just desserts.

8 SARAH GAMP
Anyone who becomes a synonym for 'umbrella' because she

carries one has to have captured the public imagination, which for an alcoholic midwife and layer-out of the dead was quite a feat, perhaps inspired by visionary conversations with an imaginary friend.

7 WILKINS MICAWBER
The embodiment of the human penchant for (often wrongly) assuming that everything will be all right on the night ('something will turn up'), Mickawber's bankruptcy doesn't stop him from eventually becoming a successful banker.

6 URIAH HEEP
The snakelike Heep is the very incarnation of that which is inelegantly described today as 'brown nosing' – the ignoble art of obsequiously seeking to impress as a spineless yes man, whilst deviously plotting. Don't worry, he gets transported to Australia.

5 SAM WELLER
The hilarious interaction between crafty cockney Sam Weller and his unworldly master Mr Pickwick captured the reading public's imagination and catapulted

Dickens towards fame and fortune.

4 MISS HAVISHAM
This tragic figure excites both pity and revulsion. Still wearing her now-tattered wedding dress, the desiccated spinster has spent her life in torment after being jilted, and seeks revenge on men through her ice-hearted ward Estella.

3 DANIEL QUILP
One of the author's most evil creations, moneylender Quilp is the deformed dwarf who maliciously destroys the

life of Little Nell and her grandfather after evicting them from the Old Curiosity Shop. Nell expires, and it is scant consolation that nemesis Quilp also perishes.

2 EBENEZER SCROOGE
Bah! Humbug! Thus did the Victorian world meet Ebeneezer Scrooge. But wait! After ghostly visitations to the miserable miser, the sentimental seasonal story failed to end in tears as Scrooge turned cuddly, and Tiny Tim feasted on Christmas turkey.

1 JACK DAWKINS
Who? Well, he didn't make number one for his given name, but for his universal *sobriquet* - the Artful Dodger. This endearing urchin leads Fagin's gang of junior thieves and befriends Oliver Twist. But ultimately he wasn't artful enough - transported for snuff-box theft.

"GOD BLESS US, EVERYONE"

– TINY TIM

10 JENNY WREN
Our Mutual Friend

9 FAGIN
Oliver Twist

8 SARAH GAMP
Martin Chuzzlewit

7 WILKINS MICAWBER
David Copperfield

6 URIAH HEEP
David Copperfield

5 SAM WELLER
The Pickwick Papers

4 MISS HAVISHAM
Great Expectations

3 DANIEL QUILP
The Old Curiosity Shop

2 EBENEZER SCROOGE
A Christmas Carol

1 JACK DAWKINS
Oliver Twist

TOP
10

Of course all the world likes a goodie, but writers often decide that good goodies must have flaws, and even so are sometimes rather less interesting than good baddies. Hence the number of thoroughly reprehensible characters that have lied, cheated, connived, deceived and bullied their way onto this list, testifying to the fact that in many books, bad is good.

SUPER **BADDIES**

9 MILO MINDERBINDER
Every conflict spawns wheeler-dealers who exploit the chaos for personal gain, and Milo is the most famous fictional war profiteer of them all – the author's stinging symbolic slap on the wrist for capitalism.

8 STEERPIKE
As cunning as they come, this murderous former kitchen boy worms his way up the Gormenghast tree, exploiting a Machiavellian ability to present himself as personable even as he feathers his own nest.

7 MRS DANVERS
Manderley's sinister housekeeper remains devoted to her dead former mistress (though Rebecca cared not a jot for her). After failing to destroy her master's new bride, Danvers does what thwarted housekeepers do – burns the place down.

5 MR HYDE
He may have had a good side, but that didn't stop this pioneering example of a schizophrenic antihero doing some awfully bad stuff. Luckily, he had a friend called Dr Jekyll with deep pockets to clear up after him.

6 CRUELLA DE VIL
Cruel devil indeed! Although you might not think there's a huge demand for fashion items made from the soft fur of Dalmatian puppies, the evil dognapper begs to differ. But then anyone expelled from school for drinking ink must be a pretty bad lot.

10 SATAN
Bad guys don't come much badder, and the fallen angel who seeks to debase the world looms large in Milton's 17th-century epic poem, as he tempts Adam and Eve to stray from the straight and narrow.

4 ERNST STAVRO BLOFELD
Treat anyone with a fluffy white cat on their lap with extreme suspicion - it could be Number One, the evil genius bent on world domination who heads the sinister SPECTRE organization. Worry you not - James Bond will soon be along.

3 PROFESSOR JAMES MORIARTY
The fiendishly clever criminal mastermind is (nearly) a match for Sherlock Holmes, and but for that unfortunate tumble down the Reichenbach Falls which he didn't miraculously survive, this 'Napoleon of crime' would have continued to dog the (reborn) supersleuth's life.

2 LORD VOLDEMORT
Tom Marvolo Riddle is the last descendent of sinister wizard Salazar Slytherin, and the Dark Lord will surely conquer and unite the worlds of muggles and wizards, to the general detriment of human/wizardkind. But wait, here comes Harry Potter!

1 HARRY PAGET FLASHMAN
The bully we first met in *Tom Brown's School Days* went on to fame and glory - but only because he wrote the script, to cunningly disguise the fact that he was the worst kind of cowardly cad.

10 SATAN
Paradise Lost
John Milton

9 MILO MINDERBINDER
Catch-22
Joseph Heller

8 STEERPIKE
Gormenghast Series
Mervyn Peake

7 MRS DANVERS
Rebecca
Daphne Du Maurier

6 MR HYDE
Dr Jekyll And Mr Hyde
Robert Louis Stevenson

5 CRUELLA DE VIL
101 Dalmation
Dodie Smith

4 ERNST STAVRO BLOFELD
Thunderball
Ian Fleming

3 PROFESSOR JAMES MORIARTY
The Adventure Of The Final Problem
Arthur Conan Doyle

2 LORD VOLDEMORT
Harry Potter And The Philosopher's Stone
J K Rowling

1 HARRY PAGET FLASHMAN
The Flashman Papers
George Macdonald Fraser

TOP
10

Hunched over their computers, they listen to the world's telecommunications, steal the electronic secrets of their enemies (and, impartially, friends too), prowling hidden places and guarding their nations using all sorts of devious means. But all that is in real life. On the pages of books, espionage is an altogether more exciting business, as this selection of not-so-secret servants confirms.

SECRET SERVANTS

10 SIR WALTER BULLIVANT

He's included as the first 'head of service' in a long line of fiction's dedicated spymasters, including Ian Fleming's 'M'. Sir Walt appears in *The Thirty-Nine Steps* and tasks Richard Hannay with a dangerous mission in *Greenmantle*.

9 QUILLER

Adam Hall (actually Elleston Trevor) created an enigmatic Cold War operative who worked alone. Who needed help? Quiller's a karate king, qualified pilot, advanced driver, deep diver and linguist. Better yet, he's reliable under torture.

8 FELIX LEITER

Let's hear it for the little guy, who has secondary roles in James Bond's many adventures – never in charge but frequently saving our hero's bacon. The shark attack was unfortunate.

7 RONALD MALCOLM

Who? Don't be confused, it's just that Ronald didn't do it for Robert Redford in the movie version, where he became Joe Turner. The real Ronald (codename Condor) was a bookish CIA office type who had to acquire superspy cunning to defeat a rogue faction.

6 ROSA KLEBB

As vicious spies go, lesbian Colonel Klebb of the deadly SMERSH agency is queen. As James Bond's arch enemy she (nearly) wins. Her poisonous pointy shoe killed Bond in *From Russia with Love*, but he was resurrected by commercial demand.

5 ALDEN PYLE

This young CIA agent operates in 1950s Vietnam, when the French were doing the fighting. Pyle needs advice from a journalist but steals his live-in lover, before being assassinated by the journo, who gets his girl back. Win some . . .

4 JASON BOURNE

Jason's back story is complicated, so just enjoy the journey as the amnesiac operative finds out he's really David Webb, although not before some extraordinary feats of derring-do. And yes, he does finally get Carlos the Jackal.

3 THE MAN WITH NO NAME

He had no name in the atmospheric books, but anonymity would never do on the silver screen – so the cockney with culinary skills became Harry Palmer, who joined the iconography of memorable spies.

2 JACK RYAN
After dropping in on runaway sub Red October, Ryan's career took off. The ex-Marine became an academic, then a CIA operative who became Deputy Director. Oh, and he ended up as President of the USA.

1 GEORGE SMILEY
The greatest fictional spy of all time? You bet! Once described by his bosses as 'having the cunning of Satan and the conscience of a virgin', Smiley roots out moles, recruits top defectors and ends up running 'The Circus'. Pity about the wife.

10 SIR WALTER BULLIVANT
The Thirty-Nine Steps
John Buchan

9 QUILLER
The Berlin Memorandum
Adam Hall

8 FELIX LEITER
Casino Royale
Ian Fleming

7 RONALD MALCOLM
Three Days Of The Condor
James Grady

6 ROSA KLEBB
From Russia With Love
Ian Fleming

5 ALDEN PYLE
The Quiet American
Graham Greene

4 JASON BOURNE
The Bourne Identity
Robert Ludlum

3 THE MAN WITH NO NAME
The Ipcress File
Len Deighton

2 JACK RYAN
The Hunt For Red October
Tom Clancy

1 GEORGE SMILEY
Call For The Dead
John Le Carre

TOP 10

Men behaving badly? Perish the thought in these enlightened modern times. But boys will sometimes still be boys, growing up into men who like doing things their way. Their way may sometimes leave lots to be desired (no pun intended), but that doesn't deflect these masterful males. Love 'em or hate 'em, here are ten of the best (or worst).

MASTERFUL MALES

10 REGINALD JEEVES This awesome valet makes the list on the grounds of delicious irony. Without his calm and collected servant, the hopelessly incompetent Bertram Wilberforce Wooster would be lost – so who was the real master there?

CARRY ON, JEEVES

When the jolly old storm-clouds rolled up, Bertie Wooster turned instinctively to his man, Jeeves. Bertie's friends likewise. Jeeves's judgment was infallible, likewise his taste in neckwear. By P.G.Wodehouse.

9 JUDGE HOLDEN The hairless Judge was certainly masterful,

standing seven feet tall. His gang slaughtered people along the Texas-Mexico border – lots of them, including women and children. But was he a supernatural entity, or (as some say) did he really exist?

8 FRANCIS URQUHART The scheming Brit politician was a hit with readers, especially after a lauded TV series popularized Urquhart's memorable catch phrase – then the political shenanigans transferred to Washington.

7 COUNT DRACULA The blood-sucking Count shocked Victorian readers, but after cutting a swathe through numerous tasty females, this Gothic tale ended with the demonic Transylvanian

crumbling to dust. But (surprise!) that wasn't quite the end of him . . .

6 WINDSOR "WIN" HORNE LOCKWOOD III If you're an ex-basketball pro with a bad knee who's prone to getting into fearful scrapes (called, say, Myron Bolito), it helps to have a rich, ruthless best friend who zaps baddies for breakfast. Yup, Win's a winner.

5 RICHARD SHARPE Anyone who can rise from private to Lieutenant Colonel in Napoleonic times, fight countless battles and skirmishes and say 'I know the Duke of Wellington' gets promoted to the list instantly.

4 TARZAN He's a noble savage who rules his own

animal kingdom, but also happens to be British aristocrat John Clayton. And when already extraordinary powers are boosted by a drug that makes him immortal, he becomes masterful forever.

3 JOHN RAMBO
His name was Rambo, and he was just some nothing kid for all anyone knew – thus was the future hero of a thousand films (or does it just seem like that?) erroneously evaluated after he made his modest entry, before the bullets started flying.

2 CHRISTIAN GREY
Partners into a bit of slap and tickle (emphasis on 'slap') will appreciate the masterful qualities of Mr Grey. Apart from being fabulously rich, he's seriously into BDSM (that's bondage and domination, sadism and masochism). Just keep wearing the collar.

1 JAMES BOND
Bond's casual attitude to the fair sex (though to be fair, some of the fiercer females he encounters are distinctly unfair) puts him top of the Mr Masterful list, as the thought of a mere woman (or serious baddie) besting him would surely bring the ageing spy out in hives.

10 REGINALD JEEVES
Thank You, Jeeves
P G Wodehouse

9 JUDGE HOLDEN
Blood Meridian
Cormac Mccarthy

8 FRANCIS URQUHART
House Of Cards
Michael Dobbs

7 COUNT DRACULA
Dracula
Bram Stoker

6 WINDSOR "WIN" HORNE LOCKWOOD III
Deal Breaker
Harlan Coben

5 RICHARD SHARPE
Sharpe's Tiger
Bernard Cornwell

4 TARZAN
Tarzan Of The Apes
Edgar Rice Burroughs

3 JOHN RAMBO
First Blood
David Morrell

2 CHRISTIAN GREY
Fifty Shades Trilogy
E L James

1 JAMES BOND
Casino Royale
Ian Fleming

TOP 10

If the men are sometimes caught behaving badly, there are plenty of feisty fictional females around who can give the guys a serious run for their money. And that's not just true of the empowered heroines of liberated 21st-century literature, as some of our chosen Top Ten have been throwing their weight about (metaphorically speaking, of course) since the mid 1700s.

FEISTY FEMALES

10 HARRIET VANE
Independently minded Harriet scandalously (for the 1930s) lived with her lover, but did the talented crime writer poison him after their split? Don't answer – suffice to say that she subsequently gives the romantic run-around to aristocratic sleuth Peter Wimsey.

9 MOLL FLANDERS
After cutting a 70-year swathe through 17th-century England (and America), scattering lovers, husbands and abandoned children like confetti in her wake, the determined and ever-resourceful Moll finally finds fortune and true love.

8 LADY BRETT ASHLEY
World War I's 'Lost Generation' fascinated Hemingway and he created a formidable denizen in the alluring and promiscuous Lady Ashley (twice divorced), icon of 1920s sexual liberation, who gets four disparate/desperate men to fight over her.

7 BECKY SHARPE
Sharp by name, sharp by nature. Thackeray's penniless anti-heroine has to take on the world using no more than God-given assets, as she cheats and schemes her way up the social ladder. She was supposed to attract opprobrium, but readers loved her.

6 EMMA WOODHOUSE
She's handsome, clever and rich, but that doesn't stop Emma meddling mercilessly in other people's lives. But her messianic 'Emma knows best' attitude mellows, and everything comes right in the end.

5 HOLLY GOLIGHTLY
Flighty, flirty Holly was the epitome of 1940s New York café-society chic – a country girl who took to city life like a duck to water (as memorably portrayed by Audrey Hepburn on the silver screen), while she twirled wealthy men around her little finger.

4 HERMIONE GRANGER

Bookish Hermione has it all – intelligence, wizardry, good looks and courage. She's initially cool towards Harry Potter and future hubby Ron Weasley when meeting them on the Hogwarts Express, though they eventually become buddies in educational adversity.

3 LOLITA

Dolores Haze (aka Lolita) was the under-age victim of Humbert Humbert, but she was no innocent herself, manipulating her obsessed lover in return for sexual favours. But she eventually left him for a (doomed) shot at a normal life.

2 ELINOR DASHWOOD

She's 'sense' personified, and as the family (mum and flighty sister Marianne) fall on hard times it's Elinor's steely resolve and determination to maintain standards that sees them through and (happy ending!) she even attains some 'sensibility'.

1 LISBETH SALANDER

If you value your secrets, fortune and even your life (should you behave really badly), don't get on the wrong side of the super-resourceful girl with a dragon tattoo. When it comes to feisty females, even when beaten she's . . . unbeatable!

---

10 HARRIET VANE
Strong Poison
Dorothy L Sayers

9 MOLL FLANDERS
Moll Flanders
Daniel Defoe

8 LADY BRETT ASHLEY
The Sun Also Rises
Ernest Hemingway

7 BECKY SHARPE
Vanity Fair
George Eliot

6 EMMA WOODHOUSE
Emma
Jane Austen

5 HOLLY GOLIGHTLY
Breakfast At Tiffany's
Truman Capote

4 HERMIONE GRANGER
Harry Potter Series
J K Rowling

3 LOLITA
Lolita
Vladimir Nabokov

2 ELINOR DASHWOOD
Sense And Sensibility
Jane Austen

---

1 LISBETH SALANDER
The Millenium Trilogy
Stig Larsson

TOP 10

There have been junior heroes and heroines around forever, but literature featuring engaging youngsters has really come of age in recent years. Many fascinating characters have emerged, and it must be said that some of them are not always quite as well behaved as their parents might wish. Strangely, that seems to make them even more appealing to young readers.

YOUNG ONES

10 PENELOPE TREDWELL
Orphan heiress Penelope is 13, and has inherited lurid mag *The Penny Dreadful*. Victorian readers don't know our spirited heroine pens macabre tales that thrill them – and she's soon involved in terrifying real-life adventures.

9 LYRA SILVERTONGUE
Officially Lyra Belacqua, this rebellious 12-year-old tomboy in a parallel universe is very good at making up convincing lies – most helpful when she's dragged into the cosmic war between The Authority and Lord Asriel.

8 PIPPI LONGSTOCKING
Long before Scandi thrillers hit the headlines, children were delighted by the nine-year-old Swedish heroine with superhuman strength (you try lifting a horse one-handed!). Any pompous adult behaving badly should fear Pippi's wrath.

7 TOM SAWYER
Tom and his pal Huck Finn enjoyed the sort of freedom denied to many of today's kids, roaming wild along the banks (and surface) of the Mississippi River as they dodge bad guys and search for treasure. Tom even finds time to fall in love with new-girl-in-town Becky.

6 MATILDA
Now why on earth might the story of a wee lassie with magical powers, whose rich but stupid parents just can't see how extraordinary she is, appeal to youngsters? Pity those self-same parents

and Miss Trunchbull, the headmistress from hell.

5 COLIN MUDFORD
Australians behaving badly in London aren't unheard of, but rampaging 12-year-old Aussie boys are less common. Meet Colin Mudford. He's accompanying a brother being treated for cancer, and Colin's angry frustrations lead to interesting encounters.

4 TRACY BEAKER
Tracy's in care, and a 10-year-old wild child. But then any youngster abandoned by her mum in a care home called the Dumping Ground is entitled to be bolshie – and strong-willed Tracy is happy to oblige. Loved by kids, not so much by parents.

3 ALEX RIDER
A teenage James Bond without the dry martinis and, er, steamy encounters with the opposite sex. How clever is that? Very, according to the legion of fans who adore this clever, all-action young British spy.

2 KATNISS EVERDEEN
America has become a dystopian wasteland where young Katniss must use survival skills to play the deadly Hunger Games, where reps of the 12 districts fight until only one is left standing. Does Katniss make it? Take a guess!

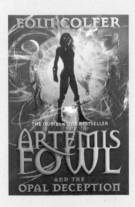

1 ARTEMIS FOWL II
The teenage criminal mastermind seeks to rebuild his family's fortunes by kidnapping a female Fairy, Holly Short. But as events unfold over eight books, Artemis co-operates with the Fairy People – and finally becomes a new man after the concluding cataclysm.

TOP 10

Oh my, how can any ten be chosen to stand out from the extraordinary and vivid canvas of compelling characters so skilfully woven by the Bard either side of 1600, as subsequently recorded in the First Folio? Someone has to do it, but all you fans of Romeo and Juliet, Othello or Macbeth (et al) must feel free to differ!

SHAKESPEAREAN GREATS

10 THE BEAR
The world's most famous stage direction reads 'exit, pursued by a bear'. Did Shakespeare use a real animal from London's notorious bear pits? Well, the great playwright was a canny showman. Ursine!

9 BEATRICE & BENEDICK
Rambunctious comedy accompanies these two bright young things from elegant verbal sparring to trickery that reveals their true love. Amazingly, everyone is still standing at the end. Uplifting!

8 KING LEAR
Never was human frailty so frail. Old King Lear is flattered into giving his realm to two of his three daughters, disinheriting the good one. The consequences are fearsome – Lear goes mad, mayhem erupts and everyone pretty much kills everyone else, or themselves. Tragic!

7 PROSPERO
The rightful duke, Prospero, and daughter Miranda survive the usurper's attempt to drown them in a storm. But they're marooned on an island and Prospero learns sorcery to survive, mastering monstrous Caliban along the way. Magical!

6 VIOLA
Shipwrecked Viola masquerades as eunuch Cesario and enters Duke Orsino's service. She carries messages between the Duke and his squeeze, Olivia. Viola falls for the count and Olivia falls for Viola (thinking her a man). Olivia marries Sebastian (Viola's lost twin) and the Duke (discovering Cesario's a woman) marries him/her. Love rules!

5 RICHARD III
Crookback's famous plea for transport after being unhorsed at the Battle of Bosworth Field went unanswered, and he was soon bloodily slain. Ironically, his 21st-century bodily remains were found beneath a council car park in Leicester. Grave!

4 IAGO
Disgruntled Iago plans to destroy his master, Othello, by persuading him wife Desdemona is having an affair with Iago's rival Cassio. Two birds with one stone is the plan, and it almost comes off. But Othello and Desdemona end up dead and Cassio emerges as top banana. Duplicitous!

3 FALSTAFF

Weightwatchers hadn't been invented, but the jovial Sir John probably wouldn't have signed up. The fat buffoon appears in three plays as vain and cowardly light relief. Hilarious!

2 LADY MACBETH

She persuades husband Macbeth to kill King Duncan, then (in agonies of guilt at the monster she's unleashed) sleepwalks memorably ('Out, damned spot!') before committing suicide off stage. Somnambulistic!

1 HAMLET

Your dad (the king) has been murdered by your uncle (the new king) who has married your mum. A ghost (your dad?) reveals all and tells you to kill your step-dad in revenge. People think you've gone raving mad, you have a chat with a skull and everyone dies. Ethereal!

The Tragicall Historie of
HAMLET
Prince of Denmarke.

Enter two Centinels. {now call'd Bernardo & Francisco—

1. STand : who is that?
2. 'Tis I.
1. O you come most carefully vpon your watch,
2. And if you meete *Marcellus* and *Horatio*,
The partners of my watch, bid them make haste.
1. I will : See who goes there.
        Enter Horatio and Marcellus.
Hor. Friends to this ground.
Mar. And leegemen to the Dane,
O farewell honest souldier, who hath releeued you?
1. *Barnardo* hath my place, giue you good night.
Mar. Holla, *Barnardo.*
2. Say, is *Horatio* there?
Hor. A peece of him.
2. Welcome *Horatio*, welcome good *Marcellus.*
Mar. What hath this thing appear'd againe to night.
2. I haue seene nothing.
Mar. *Horatio* sayes tis but our fantasie,
And wil not let beliefe take hold of him,
Touching this dreaded sight twice seene by v>,
                    B   There-

---

10 THE BEAR
The Winter's Tale

9 BEATRICE & BENEDICK
Much Ado About Nothing

8 KING LEAR
King Lear

7 PROSPERO
The Tempest

6 VIOLA
Twelfth Night

5 RICHARD III
Richard III

4 IAGO
Othello

3 FALSTAFF
Henry Iv I & 2, The Merry Wives Of Windsor

2 LADY MACBETH
Macbeth

1 HAMLET
Hamlet

"A HORSE, A HORSE, MY KINGDOM FOR A HORSE!"

– RICHARD III

For those why cry 'Why no Black Beauty?', suffice to say that a diligent search will find the put-upon mare elsewhere in these pages. That still leaves a wonderful choice of animals to adore, anthropomorphically or as themselves, allowing this list to confirm the enduring appeal of all sorts of animals as the stars of books we love to read.

APPEALING ANIMALS

10 **BUCK**
Stolen from California, Buck is taken to the Yukon to work as a sled dog during the Klondike gold rush. Overcoming privation and careless owners, he finds and loses a good master before reverting magnificently to the wild.

9 **BR'ER RABBIT**
This crafty but likeable rabbit appears in tales of the Old South told by freed slave Uncle Remus in the 1880s. The African-American folklore features 'trickster' tales starring Br'er (Brother) Rabbit and the likes of Br'er Fox and Br'er Bear.

8 **MACAVITY**
This master canine criminal never left evidence, and the ginger menace (known as The Mystery Cat or Hidden Paw) baffled Scotland Yard and the secret service. He went on to star in the musical *Cats*.

7 **BABE**
The heartwarming tale of a pig that wins a sheepdog trial, after making himself indispensible as the only porker on a sheep farm where animals talk to each other, and saving the flock from thieves.

6 **AKELA**
He's the resourceful leader of the wolf pack that adopts lost child Mowgli, and defends him against enemies like deadly tiger Shere Khan. He leaves the pack (his name means 'Lone Wolf'), before returning to die in its defence.

5 **WINNIE-THE-POOH**
This anthropomorphic bear and friends (named after the stuffed toys of author's son Christopher Robin) have been delighting kids (and others) since the 1920s, helped by the evocative illustrations of E H Shepherd.

4 **MR TOAD**
With lots of parp-parping, this engaging amphibian drives (dangerously) into the lexicon of great children's

TDHL-01

literature, along with equally engaging Mole, (Water) Ratty and Badger. After trials and tribulations, reformed Mr Toad and his pals drive wicked weasels, stoats and ferrets out of Toad Hall.

3 THE CHESHIRE CAT
Is it a smile to die for, or a tad creepy?

As Alice adventures through Wonderland, she can't decide. When sentenced to beheading by the Queen of Hearts, Cheshire's body vanishes, and eventually everything but that enigmatic grin dematerialises.

2 PETER RABBIT
Born in 1902 and still going strong, Peter and his family (Mum Josephine and sisters Mopsy, Flopsy and Cotton-tail) have become enduring favourites – except with the irascible Mr McGregor, whose vegetable garden invariably gets plundered.

1 JOEY

Farm horse Joey becomes War Horse Joey in World War I. Even as young Albert dreams of bringing his beloved horse back home, the unfolding horrors of war are seen through Joey's eyes. But at war's end (tissues out) he's reunited with Albert and returned to England.

10 BUCK
The Call Of The Wild
Jack London

9 BR'ER RABBIT
Uncle Remus
Joel Chandler Harris

8 MACAVITY
Old Possum's Book Of Practical Cats
T S Eliot

7 BABE
The Sheep-pig
Dick King-Smith

6 AKELA
The Jungle Book
Rudyard Kipling

5 WINNIE-THE-POOH
Winnie-the-pooh
A A Milne

4 MR TOAD
The Wind In The Willows
Kenneth Grahame

3 THE CHESHIRE CAT
Alice In Wonderland
Lewis Carroll

2 PETER RABBIT
The Tale Of Peter Rabbit
Beatrix Potter

1 JOEY
Warhorse
Michael Morpurgo

TOP 10

Mad, bad and dangerous they may be, but somehow these seriously salacious characters have a naughty but compelling appeal to readers (and sometimes, to be fair, these badly flawed types do have the occasional redeeming feature). But actually it matters not what you think of them, for antiheroes old and new are here to stay, as our chosen ten testify.

ANTIHEROES

10 ROBERT LOVELACE The one thing an 18th-century girl should never do is elope – especially not with a rascally type like dissolute aristo Robert Lovelace, who'll imprison her in a brothel and rape her when she refuses to surrender her virtue. Poor Clarissa!

9 ALEX In a dystopian Britain, Alex leads his droogs on ultra-violent sprees. Eventually Alex is convicted of murder, but his life becomes even more horrendous (and complicated) when society tries to reform him – violently.

8 DEXTER MORGAN Do dozens of wrongs (lots of dead baddies) add up to a right (lots of dead baddies)? Try asking personable Dexter Morgan, the serial slaughterer who believes you can kill only if you prove the target is a killer (and leave no evidence).

7 MADAME DEFARGE In revolutionary France, Madame Thérèse Defarge is a hellion seeking revenge on aristocrat Charles Darnay, though he is innocent of wrongdoing. Worse, she means to dispose of his wife and child and will stop at nothing.

6 PINKIE BROWN A Catholic who believes he's original sin incarnate, teenager Pinkie is sexually repressed. Up-and-coming gangster 'Boy' is also a sociopathic killer who terrorises friend and foe alike as he slashes his way to the top of Brighton's seedy underworld.

5 TOM RIPLEY Con artist Ripley soon discovers that identity theft (after disposing of the rightful owner) pays handsome dividends. Any complications like suspicious friends also bite the dust, as the amoral antihero develops his new career.

4 SEVERUS SNAPE
Former pupil Snape becomes Headmaster of Hogwarts School. Addicted to the Dark Arts, he joined the Death Eaters with fellow Slytherans and, as a skilled poisoner, became a member of the evil Slug Club. Ultimately redeemed.

3 SCARLETT O'HARA
This headstrong Southern Belle did what she had to do to survive in the aftermath of the American Civil War, with little thought for the grief imposed on unfortunate husbands littering her wake (and emotional cruelty to the one who survived).

2 SAM SPADE
Created for iconic *noir* thriller *The Maltese Falcon*, Spade was the template for all subsequent hard-boiled, cynical private detectives. No better than he had to be, but ranks highly as a classic example of the really-rather-appealing antihero.

1 HANNIBAL LECTER
If there was ever a more evil, complex and compelling baddie than Hannibal Lecter, he would be a fiend indeed. The cultured master of psychology and cannibalistic killer is regularly voted best antihero of all time – so here he is at number one.

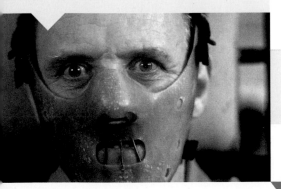

10 ROBERT LOVELACE
Clarissa
Samuel Richardson

9 ALEX
A Clockwork Orange
Anthony Burgess

8 DEXTER MORGAN
Darkly Dreaming Dexter
Jeff Lindsay

7 MADAME DEFARGE
A Tale Of Two Cities
Charles Dickens

6 PINKIE BROWN
Brighton Rock
Graham Greene

5 TOM RIPLEY
The Talented Mr Ripley
Patricia Highsmith

4 SEVERUS SNAPE
Harry Potter Series
J K Rowling

3 SCARLETT O'HARA
Gone With The Wind
Margaret Mitchell

2 SAM SPADE
The Maltese Falcon
Dashiell Hammett

1 HANNIBAL LECTER
The Red Dragon
Thomas Harris

Creatures, creatures everywhere. And every one of them is both mythical and magical, greatly enriching the world of Harry Potter and company with their extraordinary capabilities and amazing antics. The task of choosing ten among so many is almost impossible, but everyone's invited to have a go. Feel free to disagree, but here is our best shot . . .

HARRY POTTER CREATURES

10 **NEARLY-HEADLESS NICK**
Representing four resident House Ghosts, this poor fellow is forced to haunt the corridors of Gryffindor with a loose head. Five centuries ago the executioner's blunt axe failed to sever it in 45 attempts.

9 **NAGINI**
She may be female, but she's no lady. She's Lord Voldemort's long green snake, whose venom helps him to rebirth after his first downfall. Sadly for ophiophilists, Nagini is eventually slain by Neville Longbottom, wielding Godric Gryffindor's sword.

8 **GRIPHOOK**
The goblin with gainful employment at Gringotts Wizarding Bank, before going on the run following the wizardly takeover. After initially helping Harry Potter, he absconds with Godric Gryffindor's sword and is slain by one of Lord Voldemort's Killing Curses.

7 **PROFESSOR FIRENZE**
Rejected by the Forbidden Forest Centaur colony after saving Harry Potter from Voldemort by carrying him to safety (centaurs never act as beasts of burden), Firenze becomes a Divination teacher at Hogwarts before being reconciled with the colony.

6 **KREACHER**
As inheritances go, ancient house-elf Kreacher (left to his godson by Sirius Black) disappointed Harry Potter, especially when giving him maggots for Christmas. Put to work in the Hogwarts kitchens, Kreacher fights back when the Death Eaters attack.

5 **PEEVES**
Poltergeist Peeves has been making trouble at Hogwarts for a thousand years and (despite helping to eject the unloved Dolores Umbrage and fighting Voldemort's Death Eaters at the Battle of Hogwarts) intends to go on rocking the boat for another millennium.

4 **DOBBY**
A house elf treated badly by the Malfoys, Dobby is freed at Harry

Potter's instigation and works in the Hogwarts kitchens. A loyal friend, he is sent by Dumbledore to save Harry and his companions from Death Eaters at Malfoy Manor, dying in the process.

3 CROOKSHANKS
The leonine ginger Crookshanks (half cat, half Kneazle) belongs to Hermione Grainger, and this super-intelligent feline keeps a stern eye on Peter Pettigrew, disguised as Ron Weasley's pet rat Scabbers. Enjoys chasing gnomes, attacking chess pieces and catching spiders.

2 HEDWIG
A gift from Rubeus Hagrid, Hedwig the Snowy Owl became Harry Potter's close companion during dark days *chez* Dursley, fetching and carrying messages and generally supporting her master. Harry's devastated when she's killed at the Battle of the Seven Potters.

1 FAWKES
Albus Dumbledore's defender and companion, this highly intelligent phoenix helped Harry Potter vanquish Salazar Slytherin's basilisk and stood wing to shoulder with Dumbledore in the Battle of the Department of Mysteries. Devastated when Dumbledore died.

10 NEARLY-HEADLESS NICK
House Ghost

9 NAGINI
Snake

8 GRIPHOOK
Goblin

7 PROFESSOR FIRENZE
Centaur

6 KREACHER
House Elf

5 PEEVES
Poltergeist

4 DOBBY
House Elf

3 CROOKSHANKS
Kneazle-cat Hybrid

2 HEDWIG
Snowy Owl

1 FAWKES
Phoenix

TOP 10

War can take a terrible toll on those exposed to its horrors, which perhaps explains why writers have found war-damaged characters so compelling. Exposed to the awful stresses and strains of combat and the surrounding trauma, the human psyche can react in unpredictable ways. But as this list confirms, few are lucky enough to escape unscathed – physically, mentally or both.

WAR-DAMAGED CHARACTERS

10 CHRISTOPHER TIETJENS
Brilliant evocation of senseless slaughter, revolving around the psychodrama of a government statistician who chooses to fight in World War I – whilst coping with a flighty wife, a child that may not be his and unconsummated love for another.

9 TOM CUNDALL
Based on the author's experiences, Tom Cundall's description of air warfare over the trenches is grimly authentic, and the men themselves (author and character both) were traumatized by losing all their friends, and the enduring aftertaste of war.

8 BILLY LYNN
Bravo Squad are famously filmed heroes of the Iraq War, but when paraded as their 'Victory Tour' reaches the packed Dallas Cowboys stadium young Specialist William Lynn reflects on the realities of war – realities that will leave him a changed man.

7 CAPTAIN CLEVE CONNELL
As with many moving war stories, the hero and author talk with one voice about true-life experiences, but pilot Cleve Connell didn't make it back from the Korean War after the stresses of combat slowly destroyed him.

6 JAMIE GRAHAM
Yet more autobiographical fiction, for Jamie Graham follows the footsteps of author J G (as in James Graham) Ballard through a Japanese internment camp in World War II. A masterclass on the impact of war and privation.

5 WAINO MELLAS
Take a highly decorated US Marine vet, let him write about the impact of combat on young college graduate Waino Mellas as he leads Bravo Company into messy combat – then wait 36 years for a publisher to recognize a Vietnam War classic novel.

4 WITT & WARDEN
Two for the price of one as buddies W & W battle across the Pacific in World War II, showing along the way how war cruelly brutalizes combatants. And yes, author James Jones was there.

3 STEPHEN WRAYSFORD
Back in World War I (again), Stephen Wraysford's journey from pre-war love affair to fierce combat on the Somme turns him from optimist to cold fighting machine, though he comes to dread the deadly work he must do.

2 PAUL BAUMER
World War I was a two-edged sword, and no character more clearly illustrates the fact that soldiers are just people, as Paul Baumer describes the mental and physical trauma of German soldiers, and the difficulty of readjusting to civilian life.

1 JOHN YOSSARIAN
If ever there was a manual on the mad, bad, anarchic craziness of war and the destructive consequences it imposes, Yossarian wrote it. This is the ultimate expression of human survival instinct.

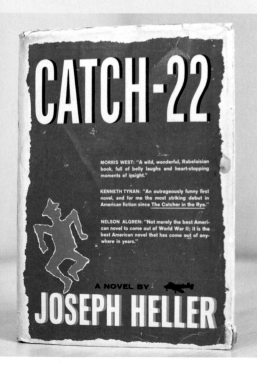

TOP 10

It's surprising how few books by creative writers are actually intended to amuse, and quite often those that do raise a smile have a hard satirical edge that darkens the humour. Happily there are also some genuine sidesplitters that are designed to give readers of all ages a good laugh, and this list contains a quirky selection of both types.

SIDESPLITTERS

9 BILLY PILGRIM
The satirical humour in *Slaughterhouse-Five* is darker than a moonless midnight, as time-traveller Billy becomes unhinged by the stresses of war and begins a bizarre journey that takes him to an alien planet (among other places) while his reason disintegrates.

8 THE CAT IN THE HAT
In the 1950s classic, the top-hatted and bow-tied Cat in the Hat (created by the wonderfully named Dr Seuss, actually one Theodor Geisel) makes the sort of anarchic mayhem children adore, but rarely found in books back then.

7 SKULLION
He may sound like a zombie, but Skullion is actually the self-important porter and self-appointed guardian of the louche traditions of Cambridge's most corrupt college, Porterhouse. Hilariously, after a combative journey he somehow ends up as Master.

6 CHARLES POOTER
This middle-aged City of London clerk has ideas way above his station, with catastrophic results, in one of the funniest comic novels ever written – not only in its own late Victorian context, but also that of pompous self-deluders everywhere.

5 IGNATIUS J REILLY
Published 11 years after its author's suicide and becoming an American Pulitzer-winning classic, A Confederacy of Dunces features the shambolic Ignatius, an overweight Don Quixote who rails

10 ALFRED JINGLE
Dickens didn't make a habit of trying to split sides, but made a very good effort when he dreamed up Alfred Jingle. A cheat and trickster, the strolling player nonetheless delights with his extraordinary tales and amusingly mangled use of the English language.

at rednecks and tilts entertainingly at modern culture. Brilliant!

4 BILL BRYSON AS HIMSELF
With the keenest of eyes, Anglophile American Bill Bryson has a genius for seeing the humorous side of life – and turning those observations into a sidesplitting commentary on human nature and the nature of human life.

3 ADRIAN MOLE
Teenage angst isn't amusing at the time – but after dissection by the late Sue Townsend as she peered into Adrian Mole's secret diary, his coming-of-age traumas certainly seem funny to us (but please don't tell Adrian).

2 BERTIE WOOSTER
This unemployed (and unemployable) member of the Drones Club luckily has private means, which enable him to employ the imperturbable Jeeves, who persistently rescues his brainless master from all sorts of laughable scrapes.

1 GEORGE W BUSH
For the most powerful man in the world, the USA's 43rd President (aka George W Bush, taking over the family business) showed a truly awesome non-grasp of the nation's mother tongue (no, not Spanish – yet). Enjoy!

10 ALFRED JINGLE
The Pickwick Papers
Charles Dickens

9 BILLY PILGRIM
Slaughterhouse-five
Kurt Vonnegut

8 THE CAT IN THE HAT
The Cat In The Hat
Dr Seuss

7 SKULLION
Porterhouse Blue
Tom Sharp

6 CHARLES POOTER
Diary Of A Nobody
George And Weedon Grossmith

5 IGNATIUS J REILLY
A Confederacy Of Dunces
John Kennedy Toole

4 BILL BRYSON AS HIMSELF
Notes From A Small Island
Bill Bryson

3 ADRIAN MOLE
The Secret Diary Of Adrian Mole Aged 13 ¾
Margaret

2 BERTIE WOOSTER
Thank You, Jeeves
P G Wodehouse

1 GEORGE W BUSH
The Ultimate George W Bushisms

John Ronald Reuel Tolkien was a soldier, professor, philologist (student of languages to you and me), writer and poet – but this Renaissance man is remembered for a story written for his children. *The Hobbit* wasn't intended for publication, but was 'discovered' in 1936. *The Lord of the Rings* and *The Silmarillon* followed ... and the rest is history.

TOLKIEN CHARACTERS

10 BEREN
If your prospective father-in-law requires you to bring back a Silmaril (think certain death), he doesn't want you to marry his daughter. Come back with one (minus a hand) and it will still end badly – you'll get killed and she'll die of a broken heart. Yet Tolkien still chose the name Beren for his tombstone, and Lúthien for his beloved wife.

9 BOROMIR
Heir to Denethor II, last ruling Steward of Gondor, the commanding Boromir was a great warrior who led resistance to Sauron's dark forces.

8 GOLLUM
How could he be so careless? The small and slimy Gollum (aged nearly 600) managed to lose The Ring that guaranteed his longevity, and failed to kill and eat Bilbo Baggins when the adventurous hobbit found it.

7 MELKOR/MORGOTH
The immortal Ainur spirit Melkor turned to the dark side and became Morgoth Bauglir. His evil influence lingered after he was cast into the outer void, a salutary reminder that greed and lust for power are destructive (and self-destructive) forces.

6 LEGOLAS
A valued part of the Fellowship of the Ring, the high-born Elf is a Prince of the Woodland Realm. He's a dab hand with a great war-bow - a skill proving vital during the Fellowship's quest to destroy the One Ring.

5 SAMWISE GAMGEE
Where would the heroic Frodo Baggins have

been without sidekick Samwise? He saved Frodo more than once and briefly became Ring-bearer, ultimately being rewarded with a wife and thirteen children.

4 ARAGORN II
As befits a great warrior, the 16th Chieftain of the Dúnedain of the North gained rapid promotion. So let's hear it for King Elessar Telcontar, 26th King of Arnor, 35th King of Gondor and First High King of the Reunited Kingdom.

3 SAURON
A fallen Maia and eponymous Lord of the Rings, Sauron was evil Morgoth's number two, taking over after his master's fall and battling on until his ultimate defeat in the Third-Age War of the Ring.

2 BILBO BAGGINS
Tolkien modestly credited Bilbo Baggins as author of The Hobbit (as well as the book's star), and at Gandalf's direction the middle-aged hobbit led his companions on the dangerous quest to retrieve the Lonely Mountain's treasure from dragon-guardian Smaug.

1 GANDALF
The fantasy world of Arda and Middle-earth is populated by countless memorable characters, but Gandalf is one of the most iconic. His legendary wisdom elevated wizardry to a high art, while Dark Lord Sauron couldn't have wished for a worse enemy.

"HOBBITS CAN PASS UNSEEN BY MOST IF THEY CHOSE WHICH GIVES US A DISTINCT ADVANTAGE"

– GANDALF

10 BEREN
Hero & Adventurer

9 BOROMIR
Steward Of Gondor

8 GOLLUM
Ring Holder

7 MELKOR/MORGOTH
Dark Lord

6 LEGOLAS
Elf Of Gondolin

5 SAMWISE GAMGEE
Hobbit Of The Shire

4 ARAGORN II
Chieftain Of The Dunedain

3 SAURON
Lord Of The Rings

2 BILBO BAGGINS
Hobbit At Large

1 GANDALF
Wizard

TOP
10

Family life brings out the best in us . . . when it works well. But the reverse is also true. Flawed families adversely affect children who can pass on the baggage to their own youngsters, creating a depressing cycle of despair. Needless to say, writers have found more to interest them in the latter, as these unhappy examples confirm.

UNHAPPY FAMILIES

10 THE KARAMAZOVS
Dad's a wastrel with three sons from two marriages (plus an illegitimate fourth), who fights eldest son Dmitri for the same woman as the latter demands his inheritance. Ivan's remote and aloof. Young Alexei is nice, but polluted by the rest. Russian angst personified!

9 THE DOLLANGANGERS
Gothic! Four siblings are imprisoned in the attic by mum and horrible gran. They eventually escape, but not before the eldest (Cathy and Chris) fall in love and brother Cory is poisoned by mum, causing his twin Carrie to be struck dumb.

8 THE LAMBERTS
Take a repressed Midwestern family (tyrannical dad Alfred, long-suffering mum Enid). Add three kids who have fled, only to find they haven't left their troubles behind. Then bring them together for a traumatic Christmas. Happy families it ain't.

7 THE WORMWOODS
Wormwood is notoriously bitter, a fact obviously known to Roald Dahl when he named one of the most memorable families in children's literature. Young Matilda is the shining exception, but her parents are deadly.

6 THE GLASSES
Where to begin? With the Australian-Jewish entertainer father? The worried Irish matriarch? The seven children, all troubled more than somewhat by the realities of life? Or with Buddy Glass, Salinger's *alter ego*? You work it out!

5 THE VANGERS
It's one thing having all the cash in Sweden, quite another living happily ever after. Was Henrik's great-niece Harriet murdered by a family member? If only that were the most sinister of the Vangers' worries, but . . .

4 THE CORLEONES
Any family where Puzo's filmic Godfather has his brother shot for being a loose cannon (while he watches) can fairly be described as dysfunctional, but then again the moral compass of Mafia families is notoriously wobbly.

3 MCCOURT FAMILY
Ouch! If this were fiction the author would be criticized for creating

an unbelievably awful vision of life, and a much-too-painful storyline. But unhappily this isn't fiction, but true-life human trauma.

2 THE DURSLEYS
Vernon and Petunia regard Harry Potter as the cuckoo in their nest, despising his special powers and thoroughly spoiling their dear boy Dudley, while Vernon's moustachioed sis Marge makes Harry's life hell. But guess who has the last laugh?

1 THE LANNISTERS
Be very suspicious of any family with golden hair and emerald eyes. Should it be the Lannister family gaming for a throne you'll be in the very worst of company, what with all that devious scheming, violence, incestuous parenting and death.

10 THE KARAMAZOVS
The Brothers Karamazov
Fyodor Dostoyevsky

9 THE DOLLANGANGERS
Flowers In The Attic
V C Andrews

8 THE LAMBERTS
The Corrections
Jonathan Franzen

7 THE WORMWOODS
Matilda
Roald Dahl

6 THE GLASSES
Nine Stories
John Salinger

5 THE VANGERS
The Girl With A Dragon Tattoo
Stig Larsson

4 THE CORLEONES
The Godfather
Mario Puzo

3 MCCOURT FAMILY
Angela's Ashes
Frank Mccourt

2 THE DURSLEYS
Harry Potter Series
J K Rowling

1 THE LANNISTERS
A Song Of Ice And Fire
George R R Martin

TOP
10

Time to put pen to paper and create your own top 10 list of crime novels...

10
9
8
7
6
5
4
3
2
1

TOP 10

The pages of popular fiction are populated with a host of great detectives. All have quirks (an essential part of the job description), and mostly (after a labyrinthine investigation) they get the men (or women) responsible for an infinite variety of dark deeds. With apologies to all those qualified super-sleuths who didn't make it, here are ten of the best.

GREAT DETECTIVES

10 C AUGUSTE DUPIN
Poe's intuitive crime-solver was created before the word 'detective' was even thought of, so those early Victorian murders in the Rue Morgue (where else?) saw the birth of a whole new genre of fiction, which is alive and well to this day.

9 LORD PETER WIMSEY
The piano-playing, war-veteran second son of the Duke of Denver (helped by talented valet Mervyn Bunter) is the very epitome of the English gentleman detective – but will he ever get the girl, crime writer Harriet Vane?

8 FATHER BROWN
As dumpy Roman Catholic priests go, Father Brown had a somewhat evil turn of mind – asking himself how he would have committed the murder, at which point the solution usually became obvious. Confessions a specialty!

7 JULES MAIGRET
Even on the Riviera, the pipe-smoking French detective wore a heavy overcoat that gave away his status as a policeman, but he still solved many more cases than Hercule Poirot, in a career lasting from 1931 until 1972.

6 V I WARSHAWSKI
Chicago's answer to Miss Marple packs more punch than St Mary Mead's most famous resident and much, much more than your average male PI. For those who don't know her personally, it's Vic (Victoria Iphigenia to her late mum).

5 PHILIP MARLOWE
If you're ever feeling cynical, tired of life and ready with a memorable wisecrack that makes the point abundantly clear, forget it. Philip Marlowe has been doing that since 1938, and nobody will ever do it better.

4 INSPECTOR MORSE
Beer, opera and *The Times* crossword may not seem ideal weapons for a police detective as the Oxford body count soars, but with a little help from level-headed Sergeant Lewis everything turns out right on the night.

3 LINCOLN RHYME
For a quadriplegic ex-cop, Rhyme (felled in the line of duty) is an amazing investigator. But if you're thinking of following Lincoln's career path, just be really careful that your carer doesn't turn out to be a murderous psychopath.

2 HERCULE POIROT
Invariably topping any list of famous Belgians, the clever little detective waddled onto the crime scene in 1920 and died in 1975 – but happily his famous 'little grey cells' were miraculously resurrected 40 years on.

1 SHERLOCK HOLMES
The words 'Elementary, my dear Watson' most certainly summarize the mighty magic of the world's most famous sleuth, whose formidable powers of observation and deduction would put a suspicious wife to shame. Unfortunately, Sherlock himself never uttered them.

"ELEMENTARY, MY DEAR WATSON"

– (NOT) SHERLOCK HOLMES

10 C AUGUSTE DUPIN
Edgar Allan Poe

9 LORD PETER WIMSEY
Dorothy L Sayers

8 FATHER BROWN
G K Chesterton

7 JULES MAIGRET
Georges Simenon

6 V I WARSHAWSKI
Sara Paretsky

5 PHILIP MARLOWE
Raymond Chandler

4 INSPECTOR MORSE
Colin Dexter

3 LINCOLN RHYME
Jeffery Deaver

2 HERCULE POIROT
Agatha Christie

1 SHERLOCK HOLMES
Arthur Conan Doyle

It may be pushing the envelope just a little, but as these extraordinary characters are universally known (and loved by many) it seems only fair to include them, even though comic books are not strictly books as libraries know them. But hey, who cares? For high drama that saves the world from fates worse than death, bring on the superheroes!

SUPERHEROES

10 THE HULK
They say that if you remember the 1960s you weren't there, but anyone tripping out on LSD would have been best buddies with the Hulk (aka Bruce Banner), a giant green humanoid with personality issues created in 1962.

9 CAPTAIN AMERICA
Weedy Steve Rogers was big in wartime USA, battling the nation's enemies (great punch to Hitler's jaw!), but only after transmogrifying into Captain America. After World War II he retired, but returned powerfully in the Golden Age of Comics (1956–1970).

8 NICK FURY
He was nearing his hundredth birthday and still sorting out the world's problems as a SHIELD agent. But despite taking the Infinity Formula, Colonel Fury wisely decided to hand the superhero baton to his African-American son, Nick Junior.

7 DAREDEVIL
If a blind man survives the killing of two girlfriends by the evil Bullseye, goes to jail, is possessed of the devil and sees the girl he actually marries go raving mad, he deserves superhero status. So let's hear it for Daredevil!

6 WOLVERINE
X-Man James Howlett (pet name Logan) is one of the hard-hitting superheroes spawned in the 1980s. As Wolverine he's a mutant with keen animal senses and the happy ability to regenerate.

He is an authority-hating antihero, so naturally everyone loves him.

5 WONDER WOMAN
Since her debut in 1941, the well-endowed heroine who pursues justice, universal love and sexual equality has become a feminist icon. You may know her as Princess Diana of Themyscira, but this lusty Amazon modestly prefers plain Diana Prince.

4 IRON MAN
Iron Man's magnetic personality suited him for membership of the superhero Avengers team, and billionaire playboy Tony Stark found another career as a steely movie star. Pity about his tailor.

3 SPIDER-MAN
Aracnophobes look away now. Breaking the

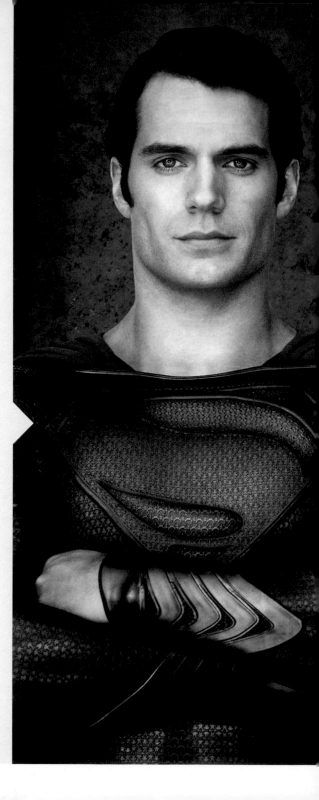

mould, Peter Parker (aka Spider-Man, but don't tell anyone) was the first teenage superhero. His crime-fighting career stalled when his mind was stolen by arch-enemy Doctor Octopus, but it was only a temporary blip.

2 BATMAN
If you go down to Gotham City with evil intent today, you'd better go in disguise – but that may not save you from Batman, who swoops on transgressors in a city that appears amazingly like New York

1 SUPERMAN
Marvel Comics may have cornered the market in average superheroes, but DC Comics can proudly open its stable door to reveal both biggies. And the winner is metamorphic Clark Kent, born 1938, guardian of all that's good.

> "WITH GREAT POWER
> MUST COME GREAT
> RESPONSIBILITY"

**– SPIDER-MAN'S
GUARDIAN, UNCLE BEN**

CHAPTER 2

IMAGINE THAT

As computer games and TV programmes seem to loom ever larger in the lives of today's kids, and an expensive smart phone tops every savvy child's fifth birthday wish list, it's very good to know that stimulating children's books can still fly the flag for good old-fashioned printed words, by capturing and holding the imagination of thoroughly modern 21st-century youngsters.

TOP 10

Many tried and tested children's books have acquired classic status over time, by appealing mightily to generation after generation of young people, and most of them have been in print since they were first published – some a hundred years and more ago. With apologies to those worthy candidates that didn't make the list, here are ten of the very best.

CHILDREN'S CLASSICS

10 *ANNE OF GREEN GABLES*
Canada's classic entry, penned in 1908, tells of orphan Anne Shirley's mistaken allocation to elderly brother-and-sister farmers who wanted a boy, and delights in her home-making adventures when she thrives in the rural environment.

9 *PINOCCHIO*
Italy's classic, published in 1883, created the puppet (longing to be a boy) whose nose extended when he lied. Shame on spoilsport scientists who calculated that he couldn't have told that many lies without his overweight proboscis incapacitating him.

8 *THE SECRET GARDEN*
England's representative is angry, rude and stubborn Mary Lennox (aged 10), who mellows and saves her crippled cousin with the help of the secret garden she unlocks. From self-destruction to redemption!

7 *THE ADVENTURES OF TOM SAWYER*
America's contribution is by former riverboat pilot Samuel Langhorne Clemens (Mark Twain), who turned growing up beside the Mississippi River into an enduring classic of American small-town life – and youthful shenanigans.

6 *TREASURE ISLAND*
Who can forget Blind Pew's arrival at the Admiral Benbow Inn, bearing the dreaded Black Spot? It's the start of a wonderful coming-of-age adventure for Jim Hawkins, brimming with pirates and buried treasure – and the boy does good!

5 *BALLET SHOES*
Nothing works better plot-wise than family adversity reversed by the young ones. This tale of three adoptive sisters doing just that (despite occasional friction) as they act and dance to success is a splendid example of the genre.

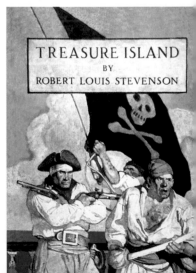

TREASURE ISLAND
BY
ROBERT LOUIS STEVENSON

4 *THE RAILWAY CHILDREN*

It's 1906 and dad's falsely imprisoned for spying. The family downsize to a house beside a country railway that looms large in the lives of the children – Roberta, Peter and Phyllis. They avert a train crash before (surprise!) dad arrives on the 11.54.

3 *SWALLOWS AND AMAZONS*

Children running wild, coping with all sorts of demanding nautical challenges? Shocking! But that's today's hyper-cautious mindset for you – the rival Blackett and Walker kids actually have mighty modern appeal precisely *because* they go it alone.

2 *WINNIE-THE-POOH*

Written by A A Milne for his son Christopher Robin, the adventurous Winnie was named after the lad's stuffed toy, in turn called after a famous bear of that name at London Zoo. Enjoy some timeless, innocent pleasure!

1 *WATERSHIP DOWN*

Runt rabbit Fiver foresees the destruction of his warren. Boss rabbit refuses to listen so Fiver and brother Hazel lead a small party of like-minded bunnies on a dangerous journey to the safety of Watership Down, then have to fight for furry females. Entrancing!

10 *ANNE OF GREEN GABLES*
L M Montgomery

9 *PINOCCHIO*
Carlo Collodi

8 *THE SECRET GARDEN*
Frances Hodgson Burnett

7 *THE ADVENTURES OF TOM SAWYER*
Mark Twain

6 *TREASURE ISLAND*
Robert Louis Stevenson

5 *BALLET SHOES*
Noel Streatfield

4 *THE RAILWAY CHILDREN*
E Nesbit

3 *SWALLOWS AND AMAZONS*
Arthur Ransome

2 *WINNIE-THE-POOH*
A A Milne

1 *WATERSHIP DOWN*
Richard Adams

"DEAD MEN DON'T BITE"

– TREASURE ISLAND

TOP 10

It's sometimes said that children live in a world of their own, and there's certainly something rather touching about the way youngsters step out of their everyday lives and become completely immersed in the infinite variety of fantasy worlds created by imaginative authors. The cleverest writers have the knack of appealing mightily to young escapists, as the chosen ten confirm.

FANTASY **FAVOURITES**

10 *THE BORROWERS*
Meet the little people - no, not the ones you think. It may be fantasy but we're not talking fairies here, but tiny 1950s folk who live unseen in the fabric of an English house, 'borrowing' from the big people to survive.

9 *FIVE CHILDREN AND IT*
'It' is the grumpy Psammead (sand fairy) who grants wishes. But be careful what you wish for, as the five young human stars of this century-old classic discover, after innocent wish-fulfilment goes hilariously wrong.

8 *ARTHUR: THE SEEING STONE*
Medieval life was tough for a knight's second son, who had to fight his own corner to get on. It doesn't help that our hero is left-

handed, but worry you not - young Arthur wins through.

7 *THE IRON MAN*
Clank, clank - here comes the Poet Laureate's metal man, chomping farm machinery for lunch and defending Planet Earth from an intergalactic monster - whilst befriending a wee lad and achieving lasting world peace.

5 *PETER AND WENDY*
He won't grow up (despite being over 100), and flies through the air with the greatest of ease. Peter Pan with pals Wendy, Tinker Bell, Tiger Lily, Captain Hook et al is still happily adventuring in Neverland.

6 *THE GRAVEYARD BOOK*
A toddler survives when his family is slaughtered and is reared by (honestly, it's true!) the ghostly denizens of the local graveyard. All sorts of spectacular supernatural shenanigans follow before it all ends well.

4 *TIMERIDERS*
Moments before they die, three teens are recruited by the mysterious 'Agency'. Sounds unpromising, but it's

actually the start of the out-of-this-world trio's time-travelling adventures as they fix attempts to meddle with history.

3 *THE KNIFE OF NEVER LETTING GO*
This one is seriously weird, featuring a 'New World' where people read each other's minds and a rogue germ is running wild. Teen hero Todd Hewitt is the one trying to make sense of it all – and escape the pursuing horrors.

2 *ARTEMIS FOWL*
This eight-book series features science-fiction fantasy at its best, as young Artemis (eventually) evolves from junior criminal mastermind at odds with the Fairyfolk into a changed man who (sort of) survives a nuclear blast.

1 *THE HOBBIT*
This is the book that launched the amazing fantasy world of Middle-earth. Home-loving Hobbit Bilbo Baggins undertakes a dangerous adventure that climaxes in the Battle of the Five Armies – and that's just the beginning of amazing adventures that (we now know) follow.

10 *THE BORROWERS*
Mary Norton

9 *FIVE CHILDREN AND IT*
E Nesbit

8 *ARTHUR: THE SEEING STONE*
Kevin Crossley-Holland

7 *THE IRON MAN*
Ted Hughes

6 *PETER AND WENDY*
JM Barrie

5 *THE GRAVEYARD BOOK*
Neil Gaiman

4 *TIMERIDERS*
Alex Scarrow

3 *THE KNIFE OF NEVER LETTING GO*
Patrick Ness

2 *ARTEMIS FOWL*
Eoin Colfer

1 *THE HOBBIT*
J R R Tolkien

"YOU ARE WHO YOU CHOOSE TO BE"

– THE IRON MAN

TOP

10

Most kids (whether appreciating it or not) grow up as part of a family, the wonderful unit that nurtures those who need support – young and old alike. Few families are perfect, and that's part of the learning curve. But some are truly dysfunctional, so this list contains tales of the good, the bad . . . and the ugly.

FAMILY STORIES

10 *BUTTERFLY SUMMER* Becky's assumptions about her family change in a wing-beat when she finds an old photo in a box beneath her mother's bed – and it seems new friend Rosa May at the Butterfly Garden may have secrets too.

9 *THE SNAKE-STONE* Authors appreciate the potential of adopted children hankering after knowledge of birth parents. And so, guided only by a small stone and scribbled note, James duly sets off to find his biological mum.

8 *CARRIE'S WAR* Widow Carrie with her three kids visit the past, recalling emotional ups and downs involving the Evans and Gotobed families during her wartime evacuation, 30 years

ago. Don't ask about the mysterious skull.

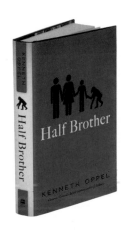

7 *HALF BROTHER* Norwegians can be dark, even if they live in the land of the midnight sun. Vera lives with son Fred, plus her mum, gran and Fred's step-dad – four family generations together. When half-brother Barnum arrives, Fred's life changes for ever.

6 *MY SISTER LIVES ON THE MANTELPIECE* This is one heck of a sad story. A family is ripped asunder after a terrorist attack that kills young Rose (ashes on the mantelpiece), leaving mum, dad, twin sister and younger brother to cope – badly.

5 *MILLIONS* A drama of family relationships masquerading as a thriller. Damian and Anthony have recently lost their mother (as in 'dead'), and have 17 days to spend the vast sum of 'found' money from a train robbery. But guess who wants the cash back?

4 *THE BAD BEGINNING (A SERIES OF UNFORTUNATE EVENTS)* A word of advice to the powers that be – if rich parents die in an arson attack, make sure surviving family members (especially children called Violet, Klaus and Sunny) are not forced to live with the nastiest uncle in the world (called, say, Count Olaf).

3 *THE CURIOUS INCIDENT OF THE DOG IN THE NIGHT-TIME* A mystery novel, but also a gripping *exposé* of family duplicity as 15-year-old hero Christopher discovers his mum isn't dead after all, as dad claims.

2 *THE SUITCASE KID* Nothing is more agonizing to children than family break-up. So when 10-year-old Andrea's parents divorce bitterly, this becomes a coming-to-terms drama as she learns to get along with new families.

1 *PRIVATE PEACEFUL* A saga of brothers growing up in the countryside before World War I, braving a beastly gran and mum who despairs at naughty activities like skinny dipping and a pregnant girlfriend. It turns nasty when two of them go to war.

10 *BUTTERFLY SUMMER*
Anne-Marie Conway

9 *THE SNAKE-STONE*
Berlie Doherty

8 *CARRIE'S WAR*
Nina Bawden

7 *HALF BROTHER*
Kenneth Oppel

6 *MY SISTER LIVES ON THE MANTELPIECE*
Annabel Pitcher

5 *MILLIONS*
Frank Cottrell Boyce

4 *THE BAD BEGINNING (A SERIES OF UNFORTUNATE EVENTS)*
Lemony Snicket

3 *THE CURIOUS INCIDENT OF THE DOG IN THE NIGHT-TIME*
Mark Haddon

2 *THE SUITCASE KID*
Jacqueline Wilson

1 *PRIVATE PEACEFUL*
Michael Morpurgo

"I MUST SURVIVE. I HAVE PROMISES TO KEEP."

– PRIVATE PEACEFUL

TOP 10

By definition, coming of age involves a seething sea of conflicting emotions as innocent children start turning into not-so-innocent young adults (if not immediately in reality, then certainly in their hopes and dreams). And of course it's pursuit of love that causes the most angst in a world, where careless text messages can cause serious grief and pimples are catastrophic.

COMING-OF-AGE DRAMAS

10 *I CAPTURE THE CASTLE*
Scene 1: Impoverished writer lives in castle with daughters Rose and Cassandra. Scene 2: Wealthy American family the Cottons arrive nearby, including eligible sons Simon and Neil. Scene 3 onwards: Who gets to love whom as Cassandra comes of age?

9 *MOCKINGBIRD*
Grim – but isn't that sometimes the way of it? A school shooting devastates Caitlin (her brother a victim). She must find a way to grow through her grief and help herself – and her father – attain closure.

8 *DEAR NOBODY*
Letters from a pregnant, unmarried schoolgirl to her unborn beginning 'Dear Nobody'

– that's clever! It's also the framework for a gritty probe into the effects of unwanted pregnancy on young lovers (and their families). PS: Nobody = baby Amy.

7 *NOUGHTS AND CROSSES*
There may be an agenda here. In an alternative world dark Africans (Crosses) are the masters, while fair Europeans (Noughts) are the slaves. So when Cross Sephy and Nought Callum start falling in love, the explosive game begins.

6 *HOW I LIVE NOW*
World War III erupts and New Yorker Elizabeth ('call me Daisy') departs for the safety of the British countryside, where she falls for Cousin Edmond. But when Britain is dragged

into the war, Daisy will be tested to the limit.

5 *KETCHUP CLOUDS*
This is serious coming-of-age stuff as bubbly Zoe conceals a dark secret – she killed someone she loves. Zoe writes to a death-row prisoner in America as the drama unfolds and suspense builds. So whom did she kill?

4 *LIFE: AN EXPLODED DIAGRAM*
The background may be imminent nuclear holocaust in the 1960s, but this is an awesome coming-of-age

story featuring apparently insurmountable obstacles – class, religion, prudish parents, snobbery. Over to Clem (17) and Francoise (16), then.

3 SOPHIE'S WORLD

Ah, this must be a Scandi coming-of-age story. Teenager Sophie is instructed in philosophy by middle-aged Alberto Knox, but that's only the start of a rather superior thinking girl's progress towards adulthood.

2 THE CATCHER IN THE RYE

How did young Holden Caulfield end up at number two, when he's the agonized star of the world's most famous coming-of-age novel? Well, it's just that American middle-class teenage angst 1950s style is brilliantly observed but a bit *tame*.

1 THE SECRET DIARY OF ADRIAN MOLE AGED 13¾

Adrian's the boy for the number one slot, because never were the emotional ramifications of impending young adulthood more ruthlessly dissected, or humorously recounted.

TOP 10

There's more to life than school, not making the bed and having a bomb-site bedroom. Responsibilities may comprise the realities of everyday life, but they're not that exciting. And excitement is a benign drug that causes youthful craving, whether taken in the form of a hammered games console or, as the adventurous heroes and heroines on this list demonstrate, self-generated.

YOUNG ADVENTURERS

10 THIRTEEN
When you're the thirteenth (and only surviving) 13-year-old on a mad cult leader's hit list, and your liquidation will unleash the spectacular bombing of London, you'd better have your wits about you. Over to you, Adam.

9 THE RUBY IN THE SMOKE
Orphaned and alone, unconventional 16-year-old Sally Lockheart can ride like the wind and shoot straight – the very qualities needed to tackle the opium trade and discover the secret of that smoky gem.

8 GIRL, MISSING
Phew, 'who-are-my-real-parents?' dramas don't come more adventurous than this, as (through dramatic detective work) 14-year-old Laura and friend Jam track down her biological kin on a trip to America.

7 WE DIDN'T MEAN TO GO TO SEA
Resourceful, or what? The Walker children go for a sail on the yacht *Goblin*, but when the skipper goes ashore and fails to return (hit by a bus), the kids perforce undertake a hazardous North Sea voyage.

6 ALONE ON A WIDE WIDE SEA
Featuring the adventurous life and (very tough) times of Arthur Hobhouse. The London orphan is sent to Australia to start a new life, but would have been better off staying put.

5 ROOF TOPPERS
Eccentric Charles Maxim and ward Sophie (once found floating in a cello case after a shipwreck) are fleeing child protection ogres and looking for her mum. When Sophie climbs through the skylight of a Paris hotel the adventure begins . . .

4 JOURNEY TO THE RIVER SEA
The eponymous River Sea is the mighty Amazon and when orphan Brit Clovis ends up in South America, it looms large in her great adventure when she accompanies Finn Taverner in search of a jungle tribe.

3 THE KITE RIDER
Think Ancient China (if you don't know it well, you soon will). Then thrill to the adventures of Haoyou Gou, as he makes a kite to fly the wind in pursuit of his dead father, and perhaps make a career of circus kite-flying.

2 *THE DEVIL AND HIS BOY*
Tom Falconer meets Will Shakespeare in Tudor London while being pursued by killers. He's about to encounter an even bigger fish, as he saves Queen Elizabeth I from assassination and turns out to be her grandson (as history failed to record).

1 *KENSUKE'S KINGDOM*
Michael falls off his parents' yacht in the Pacific and lands on an island, where he is watched over by mysterious Kensuke. The simplicity of Michael's desert-island adventure is coupled with moving human drama.

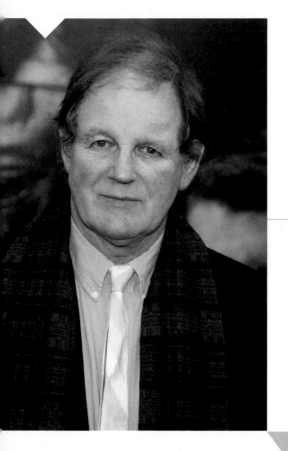

10 *THIRTEEN*
Tom Hoyle

9 *THE RUBY IN THE SMOKE*
Philip Pullman

8 *GIRL, MISSING*
Sophie Mckenzie

7 *WE DIDN'T MEAN TO GO TO SEA*
Arthur Ransome

6 *ALONE ON A WIDE WIDE SEA*
Michael Morpurgo

5 *ROOF TOPPERS*
Katherine Rundell

4 *JOURNEY TO THE RIVER SEA*
Eva Ibbotson

3 *THE KITE RIDER*
Geraldine Mccaughrean

2 *THE DEVIL AND HIS BOY*
Anthony Horowitz

1 *KENSUKE'S KINGDOM*
Michael Morpurgo

"I DISAPPEARED ON THE NIGHT BEFORE MY TWELFTH BIRTHDAY"

– KENSUKE'S KINGDOM

TOP 10

Considering how painfully strait-laced society was for some youngsters in the 19th century (and how miserable it was for the less fortunate), Victorian writers had a happy knack of creating a variety of books that allowed children to escape from the sometimes-depressing constraints of their everyday lives, into exciting worlds that let their imagination run free. Here are ten good'uns.

VICTORIAN **FAVOURITES**

10 *KING SOLOMON'S MINES*

Puffed as 'the most amazing book ever written', this 1885 adventure launched the 'lost world' genre by featuring Allan Quartermain's search for a missing Englishman in unexplored Africa, braving hostile tribes and tribulations before winning through.

9 *THE CHILDREN OF THE NEW FOREST*

Published in 1847, but set in the English Civil War and its aftermath. Four orphaned Royalist children live off the land in the New Forest, dodging Roundheads with the help of a friendly gamekeeper.

8 *WHAT KATY DID*

Tomboy Katy lives beside a lake in Ohio, a feisty 12-year-old who is always getting into scrapes, though dreaming of being beautiful – and loved. A bad accident confines her to bed, but over a long recovery she becomes gentle and kind.

7 *THE PRISONER OF ZENDA*

This regal 1894 adventure sees the king of Ruritania being drugged before his coronation. If he's not there, he loses the throne. But villainous would-be usurper Prince Michael is thwarted when a lookalike (English) cousin steps in.

6 *LITTLE WOMEN*

Dating from 1868–1869, this tale of four sisters (loosely based on the author and her sisters) extols the virtues of work, domestic life and love. It's a coming-of-age saga that tests all four in different ways – and one doesn't survive.

5 *THE ADVENTURES OF HUCKLEBERRY FINN*

Following on from the antics of Tom Sawyer (with Huck's help) this 1884 American classic puts Huck centre stage, as he adventures down the Mississippi River with ex-slave Jim after escaping his drunken father.

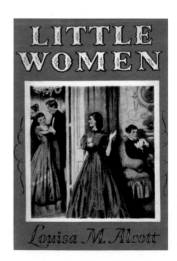

"I HAD ONE WHITE FOOT
AND A PRETTY WHITE
STAR ON MY FOREHEAD"

– BLACK BEAUTY

4 *KIDNAPPED*
Resourceful young David Balfour
is abducted in this 1886 novel, set against
turbulent times in the 18th-century
Scottish Highlands. Betrayed by his Uncle
Ebenezer, David has nail-biting adventures
as he seeks to reclaim his inheritance.

3 *THE TALE OF PETER RABBIT*
Actually, he just missed the old
Queen's death, but author Beatrix Potter
was an enlightened Victorian and Peter
first appeared in 1902. A timeless tale
starring an anthropomorphic family of
bunnies.

2 *BLACK BEAUTY*
One of the best-selling books of all
time, this was its invalid author's only book
and she died soon after publication in 1877.
Black Beauty's harrowing autobiography
was intended to promote kindness to
horses, so his suffering ended with happy
retirement.

1 *THE ADVENTURES OF SHERLOCK
HOLMES*
It might surprise some modern kids that
Sherlock actually appeared in books
before the many film and TV adaptations.
But he did, debuting in these 12 stories
collected together in an 1892 book.

10 *KING SOLOMON'S MINES*
H Rider Haggard

9 *THE CHILDREN OF THE
NEW FOREST*
Captain Frederick Marryat

8 *WHAT KATY DID*
Susan Coolidge

7 *THE PRISONER OF
ZENDA*
Anthony Hope

6 *LITTLE WOMEN*
Louisa May Alcott

5 *THE ADVENTURES OF
HUCKLEBERRY FINN*
Mark Twain

4 *KIDNAPPED*
Robert Louis Stevenson

3 *THE TALE OF PETER
RABBIT*
Beatrix Potter

2 *BLACK BEAUTY*
Anna Sewell

1 *THE ADVENTURES OF
SHERLOCK HOLMES*
Arthur Conan Doyle

TOP 10

If there's one thing guaranteed to appeal to almost all children, it's a good animal story. Youngsters love animals, and love nothing better than a good yarn where an appealing creature is the star. Sometimes they're anthropomorphic, dressing and speaking like humans, while other animal heroes are just, well, interesting animals. But whatever the chosen approach, animal magic never dims.

ANIMAL MAGICIANS

10 *TARKA THE OTTER*
This unsentimental but poetic biography of the eponymous otter published in 1928 has never been out of print. Tarka's life (and eventual death) are full of authentic detail, making for a riveting riverborne read.

9 *THE STORY OF BABAR*
Not long after Tarka hit the bookshops, Babar lumbered in pursuit and this tale of an orphan elephant was an immediate hit. Babar eventually returns to the forest and becomes king of the elephants.

8 *THE BUTTERFLY LION*
Old Millie tells schoolboy Michael about the Butterfly Lion, an albino cub rescued by husband Bertie. The lion was sold to a circus, but Bertie vowed to find it again – and succeeded. But did Michael's meeting really happen?

7 *BORN TO RUN*
The bittersweet story of a greyhound's dramatic journey through life – rescued by a boy, stolen to become a champion, reprieved from death upon retirement and finally finding a home where he can be happy. Heartwarming!

6 *CHARLOTTE'S WEB*
Wilbur the lonely pig is destined for the chop – until Charlotte the spider starts weaving messages into her web that may save him from the bacon factory. Does the plan work? You betcha!

5 *THE ONE HUNDRED AND ONE DALMATIANS*
Cruella de Vil steals Dalmatian pups to be skinned for fur, but they stage a dramatic escape with the help of grown-up Dalmatians and sheepdog Colonel – and get their revenge on the fur thief.

4 *THE HOUSE AT POOH CORNER*
This is Round Two of Winnie-the-Pooh's adventures as he and piglet build a house for Eeyore the donkey, the famous game of Poohsticks is invented – and stripy Tigger bounces into the picture.

3 *THE MIDNIGHT FOX*
City boy Tom is unhappy when his parents dump him on Aunt Millie's farm for two months. He dislikes animals, chickens chase him, lambs stampede and he's really lonely. And then he sees a black fox . . .

2 *THE WIND IN THE WILLOWS*

Water Rat and Mole enjoy life on the river, and try to rein in over-enthusiastic Toad with the help of Badger. But motoring-mad Toad steals a car and goes to jail, while Toad Hall is taken over by weasels, stoats and ferrets from the Wild Wood . . .

1 *THE JUNGLE BOOK*

Kipling's classic fables featured 'man cub' Mowgli and introduced favourite animal characters such as Akela the wolf, Baloo the bear, Shere Khan the tiger and Rikki-Tikki-Tavi the heroic mongoose.

"NEVER HURRY AND NEVER WORRY!"

– CHARLOTTE'S WEB

10 *TARKA THE OTTER*
Henry Williamson

9 *THE STORY OF BABAR*
Jean De Brunhoff

8 *THE BUTTERFLY LION*
Michael Morpurgo

7 *BORN TO RUN*
Michael Morpurgo

6 *CHARLOTTE'S WEB*
E B White

5 *THE ONE HUNDRED AND ONE DALMATIANS*
Dodie Smith

4 *THE HOUSE AT POOH CORNER*
A A Milne

3 *THE MIDNIGHT FOX*
Betsy Byars

2 *THE WIND IN THE WILLOWS*
Kenneth Grahame

1 *THE JUNGLE BOOK*
Rudyard Kipling

TOP 10

It sometimes seems that before Roald Dahl appeared, books for the younger generation were really rather *staid*. It isn't actually true, but things were certainly never the same again after this children's mega-author started doing his 'bad adult' thing back in the 1940s. Described as 'one of the greatest storytellers for children of the 20th century', he died in 1990.

ROALD DAHL BOOKS

10 *DANNY THE CHAMPION OF THE WORLD*
Danny and dad William live in a gypsy caravan, and attract the wrath of landowner Victor Hazell (William is a skilled poacher). Victor's no match for the duo, who kidnap his pheasants and ruin the big shooting party.

9 *THE WITCHES*
Set in Norway (acknowledging Dahl's origins) and Britain, a boy is thrown into the secret world of child-hating witches. Perhaps he'll hatch a plan with his Norwegian gran whereby they turn into mice and fight back . . .

8 *ESIO TROT*
This whimsical love story is illustrated by Quentin Blake, illuminator of so many Dahl books.

Shy Mr Hoppy eventually wins Ms Silver by offering a magic spell that will make her tortoise grow. But all is not as it seems . . .

7 *THE GIRAFFE AND THE PELLY AND ME*
Me is Billy, who dreams of opening a sweet shop. It comes true, but not before alarums and excursions involving Ladder less Window Cleaning Company operatives Pelly (the pelican), Giraffe and Monkey.

6 *THE BFG*
Anticipating the brevity of text messages, BFG equals Big Friendly Giant. He's the only goodie giant, bringer of pleasant dreams, and with help from Sophie (and the Queen of England) he'll defeat those nasty people-eating giants.

5 *FANTASTIC MR FOX*
There's clever Mr Fox (and family) annoying three rather wicked and cruel farmers (Boggis, Bunce and Bean) – so guess who wins when they declare war on the Reynard who raids their farms?

4 *CHARLIE AND THE CHOCOLATE FACTORY*
Charlie Bucket lives in miserable, hungry

circumstances. When he gets to tour the chocolate factory run by mysterious Willy Wonka, along with four really unpleasant kids, things get sticky . . .

3 THE TWITS

The Twits constantly play nasty tricks on each other and abuse their monkeys, the Muggle-Wumps. When Mr Twit tries to trap birds to make pie, Roly-Poly Bird joins forces with the Muggle-Wumps to defeat the horrendous couple.

2 JAMES AND THE GIANT PEACH

Wow – this one is fascinating but seriously surrealistic. James is abused by horrid aunts Spiker and Sponge, until a chance encounter creates a giant peach full of extraordinary characters – and that's just the beginning . . .

1 MATILDA

How to pick one among many worthy of topping the list? In a word, Matilda. Surely Dahl's most iconic – and engaging – character, this five-year-old with magical powers effortlessly outwits stupid parents and the cruel headmistress.

"TWO RIGHTS DON'T EQUAL A LEFT"

– THE BFG

10 DANNY THE CHAMPION OF THE WORLD

9 THE WITCHES

8 ESIO TROT

7 THE GIRAFFE AND THE PELLY AND ME

6 THE BFG

5 FANTASTIC MR FOX

4 CHARLIE AND THE CHOCOLATE FACTORY

3 THE TWITS

2 JAMES AND THE GIANT PEACH

1 MATILDA

There's a golden rule in publishing, for adult and children's books alike, which goes like this – if an author comes up with an idea that will support an ongoing series, the publisher will love him/her to bits . . . all the way to the bank. Of course they're worth every penny, as this succulent selection of 'serials' suggests.

SERIAL **WINNERS**

10 LITTLE HOUSE ON THE PRAIRIE

The third book in the extensive *Little House* series that features semi-autobiographical stories (with the author as main protagonist) about the 19th-century experiences of a typical pioneer family in the American Midwest (though written from the 1930s onwards).

9 THE FAMOUS FIVE

Enid Blyton knew all about profitable series-creation. Her most memorable 'gang' (with apologies to the Secret Seven) was the Famous Five. Julian, Dick, Anne, Georgina (George) and dog Timmy enjoyed 21 bucolic holiday adventures starting in 1942.

8 THE HEROES OF OLYMPUS

Already flushed with the success of previous series, *Percy Jackson & the Olympians*, author Riordan took up the fantasy drama of demigods galore, in a multi-book saga involving Greek and Roman demigods (still among us today).

7 THE CHRONICLES OF NARNIA

Seven books a splendid series make, and this classic collection introduces us to the magical world of Narnia, a fantastical experience for transported children who meet talking animals and mystical beasts, and play key roles in the unfolding drama.

6 BROMELIAD TRILOGY

Also known as *The Nome Trilogy* (as in gnome without the 'g') the master of fantasy introduces us to the little people who live (not without difficulty) among clumping humans as they plot a return to their own world.

5 ALEX RIDER SERIES

The phenomenally successful young spy (fictionally and commercially) well deserves the plethora of books, graphic novels and the other stuff he illuminates with his daring deeds.

4 RUBY REDFORT SERIES

New series from old? That was author/illustrator Lauren Child's inspiration. Her Clarice Bean from the series of that name had a favourite literary character called Ruby Redfort (undercover mystery solver) – who duly went 'series' in her own write/right.

3 THE HUNGER GAMES

First, the *Hunger Games* books. Then, multimedia mayhem swept the world. Easy to see why – that dystopian future where children fight to the death for a hamburger (well, food) is not only page-devouring, but also sensational in motion.

2 HIS DARK MATERIALS

It was touch and go. This stunning trilogy was a genuine contender for top spot, with its eerie coming-of-age drama as Lyra and Will wander through parallel universes where they encounter mythical creatures – and philosophical dilemmas.

1 HARRY POTTER SERIES

What can be added? The amazing series set in and around Hogwarts School of Witchcraft and Wizardry was brought to fruition at café tables – and soon magically transformed its creator from penniless mature student to multimillionairess.

10 LITTLE HOUSE ON THE PRAIRIE
Laura Ingalis Wilder

9 THE FAMOUS FIVE
Enid Blyton

8 THE HEROES OF OLYMPUS
Rick Riordan

7 THE CHRONICLES OF NARNIA
C S Lewis

6 BROMELIAD TRILOGY
Terry Pratchett

5 ALEX RIDER SERIES
Anthony Horowitz

4 RUBY REDFORT SERIES
Lauren Child

3 THE HUNGER GAMES
Suzanne Collins

2 HIS DARK MATERIALS
Philip Pullman

1 HARRY POTTER SERIES
J K Rowling

"YOU'RE NEVER TOO YOUNG TO DIE"

– ALEX RIDER

TOP
10

Time to put pen to paper and create your own top 10 list of children's books...

10

9

8

7

6

5

4

3

2

1

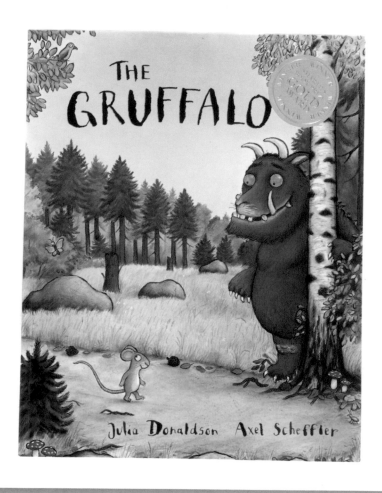

Catch 'em young enough and a child entranced by early reading experiences – whether listening to a bedtime story before drifting into the world of dreams, enjoying the pictures in a well-illustrated book or starting to decipher words – will most probably go on to become a lifelong reader. And that's a gift all parents should give to their offspring.

TALES FOR TINY TOTS

10 *MR MEN/LITTLE MISS SERIES*
Small children of the 1970s and 1980s grew up with these colourful characters with physical attributes (and personalities) based on their names – but which came first, name or character? Still enchanting today.

9 *THE CAT IN THE HAT*
Even older (but still going strong), this superhuman feline (along with Things One and Two) wrecks Sally's house with a gamut of tricks, then magically puts everything to rights before mum returns – an irresistible proposition!

8 *THOMAS THE TANK ENGINE*
Even older (and still puffing happily/unhappily along), Thomas the Tank Engine and loco pals (manufactured in 1946) still give the Fat Controller the run-around, to juvenile cheers.

7 *BLACK DOG*
Parents with little ones frightened of monsters should grab this one. The shaggy canine is scary and the illustrations have an eerie feel that turns the screw, but ultimately the smallest character (yup, called Small) faces down the beast.

6 *MR GUMPY'S OUTING*
This charming picture book has a hero who has never heard of health and safety rules – for Mr Gumpy keeps on loading animals (and two children) onto his boat, which gets heavier and heavier until . . . splash!

ast.
ost?

5 *PADDINGTON BEAR*
  The bear from darkest Peru is welcome in any household with little ones, and has been since 1958, when he arrived bearing a label reading 'Please look after this bear. Thank you.'. Marmalade sandwich, anyone?

4 *THE TIGER WHO CAME TO TEA*
  Simple, and simply delightful. Sophie and mum's tea is interrupted by a tiger who eats and drinks everything, including the tap water, so Sophie can't have her bath - a surefire winner with young readers.

3 WHERE THE WILD THINGS ARE

Carefully arrange 338 words. Add wonderful illustrations. Send a naughty boy in a wolf costume to an island occupied by nasty Wild Things. Let him overcome and play with them before returning home for a hot meal. And you have an enduring winner.

2 THE VERY HUNGRY CATERPILLAR

A biology lesson for little ones, masquerading as a fantastic (literally) children's book dating from 1969. The hungry caterpillar munches through all sorts of goodies (including the book) before emerging as a butterfly.

"PLEASE LOOK AFTER THIS BEAR"

– A BEAR CALLED PADDINGTON

1 THE SNOWMAN

Who needs 338 words, when an extraordinary book for wee ones (older kids too!) can be created in pictures? The snowman comes to life, explores the boy's house and they have an adventure. But when the sun warms the snowman . . .

---

10 MR MEN/LITTLE MISS SERIES
Roger Hargreaves

9 THE CAT IN THE HAT
Dr Seuss

8 THOMAS THE TANK ENGINE
Rev Wilbert Vere Awdry

7 BLACK DOG
Levi Pinfold

6 MR GUMPY'S OUTING
John Burningham

5 PADDINGTON BEAR
Michael Bond

4 THE TIGER WHO CAME TO TEA
Judith Kerr

3 WHERE THE WILD THINGS ARE
Maurice Sendak

2 THE VERY HUNGRY CATERPILLAR
Eric Carle

---

1 THE SNOWMAN
Raymond Briggs

School may be a longed-for (and often unattainable) goal for youngsters in many developing countries, but for those more fortunate education is a fact of life, and not always the happiest one. The best and worst of educational experiences have long fascinated writers ('went there, did that') and the result is a list that contains some really special schooldays stories.

CLASS **TOPPERS**

10 *TOM BROWN'S SCHOOL DAYS*
Schooling doesn't come tougher than this, as the brutal life of boys at an English public school in the 1830s is laid bare in excruciating detail. But (amazingly) young Tom somehow comes through.

9 *MALORY TOWERS SERIES*
Over a century later (but equally distant to today's youngsters) the girls get their turn in this 1940s take on middle-class boarding-school life, as heroine Darrell goes from bolshie first-year to transformed school leaver.

8 *A LITTLE PRINCESS*
A riches-to-rags-to-riches drama published in 1905 that still excites today. Rich girl Sara is treated like a princess at

boarding school – until the money runs out. Then life gets very tough, before all eventually ends rather well.

7 MAGGOT MOON

Beautifully penned by a dyslexic author, this dystopian educational nightmare set in the repressive Motherland stars (dyslexic) Standish, subjected to vicious bullying by classmates – until he escapes into a world of his own.

6 THE BRILLIANT WORLD OF TOM GATES

Tom Gates is the schoolboy from hell we love to love – the grand master of inventive excuses for missing homework, doodler of imaginative dreams, desperately desiring the girl he sits next to.

5 FIRST TERM AT TREBIZON

Echoing the earlier *Malory Towers* format, this is the first of a series that follows trials, tribulations and triumphs of Rebecca Mason as she ascends school years at lively Cornish boarding school Trebizon.

4 THE TURBULENT TERM OF TYKE TILER

The final term for 12-year-old troublemaker Tyke ends badly (Headmaster: 'That child has always appeared to me to be on the brink of wrecking this school, and as far as I can see, has, at last, succeeded.'). The twist's too good to reveal.

3 THERE'S A BOY IN THE GIRLS' BATHROOM

The meanest kid in school tries everything to hide his nicer side. But the story of Bradley's progress from sullen schoolboy to semi-reformed character is a study in positive academic relationships.

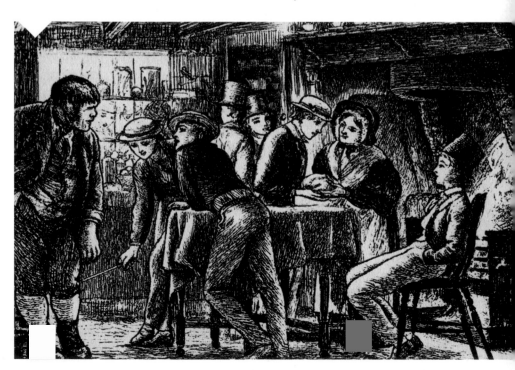

2 *WONDER*
August (Auggie) Pullman has a rare craniofacial deformity and has been home-schooled, but then the 10-year-old goes to school. It isn't an altogether straightforward introduction to American public-school life, but the experience is ultimately uplifting.

1 *BILL'S NEW FROCK*
It may have become a classic children's read that explores gender stereotyping, but it makes number one for the sheer audacity of the plot, as young Bill Simpson wakes up to find he's become a girl, and must attend school in a pink dress.

TOP 10

Every generation of writers produces classic books that ultimately transcend their era, destined to be read again and again as new young readers discover them, and in time introduce them to their own kids. Here are ten that will stand the test of time, featuring many that explore a 21st-century fascination – war in general and Nazi Germany in particular.

MASTERPIECES **IN WAITING**

10 *A MONSTER CALLS*
The idea was Siobhan Dowd's. A boy painfully coming to terms with his mother's terminal cancer is helped by a tale-telling monster who visits by night. Sadly, Dowd died of monstrous cancer before she could write her story.

9 *REMEMBRANCE*
Young people can take tough topics, as this lauded World War I drama confirms. In 1915, teenagers from two Scottish families picnic, but conflict is not as far away as they think. Soon the Great War will change their lives forever.

8 *JOURNEY TO JO'BURG*
The experiences of two young black South African children who undertake a gruelling journey to find and fetch their mother, to help save a sick sibling. It has a steely anti-apartheid edge.

7 *ONCE*
Another tough subject – the story of a boy who leaves the Catholic orphanage (where they don't know he's Jewish, or that he's no orphan) to search for his parents, against the chaos of burning books and an accelerating Holocaust.

6 *WHEN HITLER STOLE PINK RABBIT*
This take on the Jewish experience as the Nazis got really nasty is more hopeful, as it tells the tale of a hunted family successfully fleeing Hitler's Germany (though not without alarms).

5 *THE BOOK THIEF*
Still in Nazi Germany, this one grimly features that ruthless reaper Death – who narrates the story of a girl's relationship with foster parents, neighbours and the young Jewish man who hides in her home.

4 *THE BOY IN THE STRIPED PYJAMAS*
Maintaining the 21st-century fascination of children's authors with Holocaust horrors, this controversial story charts the unlikely friendship of a concentration camp commandant's nine-year-old son with a young Jewish inmate.

3 WAR HORSE

It's wartime again, but this time World War I, where the horrors of the trenches are seen through the eyes of war horse Joey, transported from rural England to the battlefields of France. But will former owner Albert ever get him back?

2 GOODNIGHT MR TOM

World War II this time – but in truth war is just the enabling backdrop to this touching tale of abused evacuee Willie Beech and reclusive Thomas Oakley, as each begins a journey of discovery that will change the other.

1 TOM'S MIDNIGHT GARDEN

This compelling fantasy charts the time-travelling experiences of a lonely lad staying in an urban apartment. He discovers a sunlit Victorian 'midnight garden' when the clock strikes 13, becoming friendly with young Hatty therein. And the brilliant twist is . . .

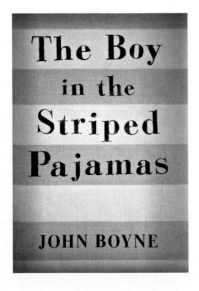

10 A MONSTER CALLS
Patrick Ness

9 REMEMBRANCE
Theresa Breslin

8 JOURNEY TO JO'BURG
Beverley Naidoo

7 ONCE
Morris Gleitzman

6 WHEN HITLER STOLE PINK RABBIT
Judith Kerr

5 THE BOOK THIEF
Markus Zusak

4 THE BOY IN THE STRIPED PYJAMAS
John Boyne

3 WAR HORSE
Michael Morpurgo

2 GOODNIGHT MR TOM
Michelle Magorian

1 TOM'S MIDNIGHT GARDEN
Philippa Pearce

"THEY BURNED ALL YOUR BOOKS"

– WHEN HITLER STOLE PINK RABBIT

TOP
10

There's no happier sound in this world than the spontaneous, uninhibited and infectious laugh of a child. Needless to say, numerous children's authors have made it their mission in life to spread that happiness, by creating books that cause the young ones to smile, and laugh, and forget the mundane realities of life. Here are ten that do just that.

GOOD LAUGHS

10 *BIG NATE: IN THE ZONE*
Kids love cartoons, and Big Nate's trials and tribulations entertain those who chuckle at his regular appearance in over 300 American newspapers. For smilers elsewhere, books are it. Here, Nate can suddenly do no wrong. Really?

9 *GRANNY*
Take a 12-year-old boy confined to the vast family mansion and add a truly repulsive, pathologically mean grandma with evil plans for young Joe Warden. Not funny, the uninitiated might think. Wrong!

8 *JUST WILLIAM*
William Brown crash-landed in belly-laugh territory in 1922, but the eternal 11 year old and his

Outlaws are as funny now as they were then. When scrapes are scraped, the Outlaws are there.

7 *DIARY OF A WIMPY KID*
Gregory Heffley is the wimp in question, beginning on-line life in 2004 and transferring to print in 2007. He's at odds with the neighbourhood in general and his brothers in particular, with hilarious results.

6 *CAPTAIN UNDERPANTS*
Cheap shot! You only have to say 'underpants' to get kids smiling, so accidentally animated superhero Captain Underpants is a guaranteed winner in the humour stakes, even without the contribution of loose cannons George and Harold.

5 *GEEK GIRL*
She's 15, and not at all like the other girls. She's the cool one, but when she's spotted by a model agency and rushed to Moscow for a fashion show problems escalate – including super-geeky stalker Toby.

4 *A BOY CALLED HOPE*
Laugh or cry (or more probably laugh *and* cry) at the happy-sad, messy life of Dan Hope (get it?). We're talking a boy's hopes and dreams after his dad runs off with the fish-and-chip shop lady, as dads do.

3 *THE WORLD OF NORM*
Norm *always* wakes up knowing it's going to be one of those days, and laugh-out-loud adventures follow. We're talking peeing in wardrobes, slipping on

dog sick, eating mouldy pizza - and that's the routine stuff.

2 *RATBURGER*

Zoe's hamster dies, so she adopts a rat. This doesn't go down well at school, but it isn't until Zoe discovers that the blind burger seller is filling his buns with rat meat that things really go haywire.

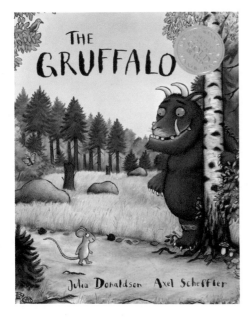

1 *THE GRUFFALO*

A mouse takes a walk in the woods, evading baddies (fox, owl, snake), by threatening them with the imaginary gruffalo. Then he encounters a real gruffalo, who he tricks by claiming to be the most dangerous animal around, proving it as the fox, owl and snake see them together and flee. Smile a minute!

10 *BIG NATE: IN THE ZONE*
Lincoln Peirce

9 *GRANNY*
Anthony Horowitz

8 *JUST WILLIAM*
Richmal Crompton

7 *DIARY OF A WIMPY KID*
Jeff Kinney

6 *CAPTAIN UNDERPANTS*
Dav Pilkey

5 *GEEK GIRL*
Holly Smale

4 *A BOY CALLED HOPE*
Lara Williamson

3 *THE WORLD OF NORM*
Jonathan Meres

2 *RATBURGER*
David Walliams

1 *THE GRUFFALO*
Julia Donaldson

"I NEVER MEANT TO DO IT"

– JUST WILLIAM

TOP **10**

You don't have to be one of those wussie kids with a nightlight to shiver when something goes bump in the night. Parents long ago invented bogeymen with which to threaten children who don't do as they are told, and the tradition persists in some of the creepy creations that haunt book pages. So why do today's kids love these spine-tinglers?

SCARY TALES

10 *THE HOST*
You can call Melanie a head case, because she is – her brain's invaded by alien being Wanderer. Unlike other humans, Melanie refuses to surrender her mind, so together they search for the boy they love.

9 *THE TULIP TOUCH*
Tulip is a compulsive liar, but best friend Natalie is enchanted by her stories. Tulip turns nastier and nastier, and as her games get out of hand Natalie realizes it's too late to save Tulip, and may be too late to save herself.

8 *WITCH CHILD*
Witchcraft was powerful enough in medieval England to see Mary's gran hanged as a witch. When she's rescued by a mysterious woman and starts a new life in the New World, can Mary leave her witchcrafty legacy behind?

7 *HALF BAD*
The Council of White Witches captures or kills black witches, but is Nathan really a black'un? His witch family are notorious, but does that justify imprisonment and torture? Still, he does find romance amidst gory toil and trouble.

6 *HOROWITZ HORROR*
Nine horrendous tales from the master wordsmith, featuring tinglers ranging from killer camera to axe-murderer's bath, being trapped in a lethal computer game to night bus that tours creepy cemeteries. Scary!

5 *THE MIDNIGHT PALACE*
It's 1930s Calcutta. An Englishman saves twin newborns from an unspeakable threat, sacrificing his life in the process. Years later, on Ben and Sheere's sixteenth birthday, the terror returns – and this time escape may be impossible . . .

4 *A STITCH IN TIME*
What's imagined, what's real? Maria can't tell, so which are the invisible barking dog and non-existent squeaking swing? And when she finds a sampler stitched by a girl who died long ago . . .

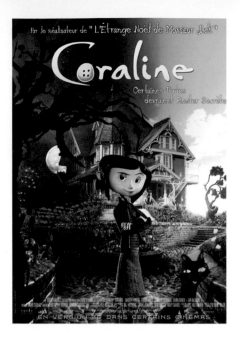

10 THE HOST
Stephenie Meyer

9 THE TULIP TOUCH
Anne Fine

8 WITCH CHILD
Celia Rees

7 HALF BAD
Sally Green

6 HOROWITZ HORROR
Anthony Horowitz

5 THE MIDNIGHT PALACE
Carlos Ruiz Zaphon

4 A STITCH IN TIME
Penelope Lively

3 CORALINE
Neil Gaiman

2 TWELVE MINUTES TO MIDNIGHT
Christopher Edge

1 THE ENEMY
Charlie Higson

3 *CORALINE*
In a parallel world, Coraline's nasty Other Mother hopes to take our heroine to the Other World. When her real parents are imprisoned and she meets the lost souls of three children, Coraline must engage in a deadly battle of wits with her putative parent.

2 *TWELVE MINUTES TO MIDNIGHT*
You're 13 and inherit a newsprint empire when your folks die. You boost magazine circulation by writing macabre tales. You get invited to the notorious Bedlam asylum. You're Penelope Tredwell. You're in deep trouble.

1 *THE ENEMY*
A plague turns adults into zombies, so kids band together to survive the unwelcome attentions of sick grownups. But as cannibalistic adults get cleverer and groups of kids vie for supremacy, things turn *very* nasty.

"THOSE THAT CAN HEAL CAN HARM; THOSE THAT CAN CURE CAN KILL"

– WITCH CHILD

TOP
10

If history teaches us one thing, it's that yesteryear is a fruitful hunting ground for clever authors who choose to use the strange and different lands of times past to good creative advantage. Needless to say, their youthful protagonists (who if real would be long dead) illuminate these historical scenarios in a manner that appeals mightily to thoroughly modern youngsters.

BACKWARD GLANCES

10 *THE DOUBLE LIFE OF CORA PARRY*
Victorian London. Cora (aged 11), rescued from workhouse by benevolent sailor. Becomes homeless and penniless when he dies. Reluctantly embraces crime to survive, allocating the dirty work to imaginary double Carrie. Let drama commence!

9 *SAWBONES*
Ezra MacAdam helps his surgeon boss carve cadavers in 18th-century London. A tongueless corpse is delivered. Cue spies, resurrection men, smuggling, mayhem and murder. And enter rapier-toting conjurer's daughter Loveday Finch.

8 *MY FRIEND THE ENEMY*
It's 1941 and Britain's at war. Peter's dad has gone

to fight, but all that seems far away – until an enemy plane crashes and Peter finds a young German survivor. You don't suppose they might actually be quite alike?

7 *THE EXECUTIONER'S DAUGHTER*
Tudor England. You're the daughter of the executioner, catching the falling heads of unlucky victims and as much confined to the Tower of London as genuine prisoners. Then you find a secret tunnel that leads to freedom . . .

6 *THE CASE OF THE DEADLY DESPERADOES*
A furious frolic in the Old West, as pistol-packing 12-year-old P K Pinkerton joins forces with reporter Sam, Poker Face Joe and photographer's apprentice

Ping to rout the bad guys.

5 *HETTY FEATHER*
Hetty hates leaving kind foster parents for the harsh Foundling Hospital, but is befriended by kitchen maid Ida. After absconding and having exciting adventures Hetty's returned to the Hospital, and finds her mother . . .

4 *WILD BOY*
Gothic horror stalks the seamy streets of 19th-century London. Wild Boy is a hairy sideshow freak, but also a Sherlockian observer. When he's accused of murder, Wild Boy goes on the run with feisty acrobat Clarissa. There's a mystery to unravel!

3 *AT THE SIGN OF THE SUGARED PLUM*
Sensible suggestion – if it's 1665 and the Black Death

is ravaging London (and a fire's due), don't go up to town to see big sis. But kids never listen, so that's precisely what young Hannah does.

2 *STREET CHILD*
Orphan Jim Jarvis manages to escape the brutal harshness of the 1860s workhouse, only to find the dangers lurking on the streets of London are even more frightening. Survival becomes the name of the game!

1 *THE LAST WOLF*
Bonnie Prince Charlie is running from English Redcoats, and so is wee Robbie Mcleod. When he finds and bonds with an orphan wolf cub of the recently killed 'last wolf in Scotland', it heralds an adventure that spans the Atlantic.

10 *THE DOUBLE LIFE OF CORA PARRY*
Angela Mcallister

9 SAWBONES
Catherine Johnson

8 *MY FRIEND THE ENEMY*
Dan Smith

7 *THE EXECUTIONER'S DAUGHTER*
Jane Hardstaff

6 *THE CASE OF THE DEADLY DESPERADOES*
Caroline Lawrence

5 *HETTY FEATHER*
Jacqueline Wilson

4 *WILD BOY*
Rob Lloyd Jones

3 *AT THE SIGN OF THE SUGARED PLUM*
Mary Hooper

2 *STREET CHILD*
Berlie Doherty

1 *THE LAST WOLF*
Michael Morpurgo

"I SCREAMED AND SCREAMED FOR MY MOTHER"

– HETTY FEATHER

TOP 10

Imagination is the name of the game when writing for youngsters – and it's a fairly well tried and tested principle that the wilder the imagined world, the better imaginative kids will like it. Some of today's children's books feature the gritty realities of modern life, but there's none of that to be found in these fanciful flights of fantasy.

FLIGHTS **OF IMAGINATION**

10 *THE FARAWAY TREE* Prolific children's writer Blyton created this innocent enchanted forest without a troll or hobgoblin in sight. Jo, Bessie and Fanny find a magical tree that reaches the sky. And kids love climbing trees . . .

9 *WOLF BROTHER* Go back 6,000 years. Evil swirls, and only 12-year-old Torak and his wolf-cub buddy can vanquish it as they journey through glaciers and dark forests, facing (only slightly) unbelievable dangers along the way.

8 *SKELLIG* The elderly man befriended by 10-year-old Michael turns out to be something that combines human, owl and angel. Whatever, it's more than

coincidence that Michael's baby sis survives a dangerous heart op.!

7 *THE MAZE RUNNER* Fantasy? Surely not. Tom lands in The Glade, surrounded by a maze full of deadly slugs with mechanical arms. When a girl arrives claiming to be 'the last one ever', Tom swings into action . . .

6 *THE FIRE WITHIN* Landlady Liz Pennykettle makes clay dragons (magical, can come to life). Young David Rain moves in with Liz and mischievous 11-year-old daughter Lucy and is given Gadzooks as his personal dragon. Together, they must unlock the 'Fire Within'.

5 *OVER SEA, UNDER STONE* Adventure and fantasy rolled into one doesn't come better than this. Simon, Jane and Barney find a mysterious map while on holiday in Cornwall, and (on behalf of the Light) decipher clues that lead to the Grail (enraging Dark forces).

4 *HOW TO TRAIN YOUR DRAGON* Everyone knows dragons are real (St George slew one), so tales of Hiccup Horrendous Haddock III and his tribe as they try to train dragons in a fantasy Viking world seem almost like a junior documentary..

3 *THE RAVEN BOYS* Blue believes her true love (whoever he is) will die if she kisses him. As

magic eddies everywhere, Blue joins gang-of-four the Raven Boys, led by Gansey, in search of lost king Glendower. But is Gansey her true love?

2 *SKULLDUGGERY PLEASANT*
The undead sorcerer and detective of the title and partner Stephanie (aka Valkyrie Cain) try to prevent Nefarian Serpine destroying the world. Fantasy, horror, humour, mystery and magic – what's not to like?

1 **THE SCHOOL FOR GOOD AND EVIL**
Best friends Sophie and Agatha are about to attend the School for Good and Evil. Beautiful Sophie has dreamed of becoming an enchanted princess, while black-clad Agatha seems destined for, well, the Evil side. Surprisingly, things don't work out that way . . .

10 *THE FARAWAY TREE*
Enid Blyton

9 *WOLF BROTHER*
Michelle Paver

8 *SKELLIG*
David Almond

7 **THE MAZE RUNNER**
James Dashner

6 *THE FIRE WITHIN*
Chris D'lacey

5 *OVER SEA, UNDER STONE*
Susan Cooper

4 *HOW TO TRAIN YOUR DRAGON*
Cressida Cowell

3 *THE RAVEN BOYS*
Maggie Stiefvater

2 *SKULLDUGGERY PLEASANT*
Derek Landy

1 *THE SCHOOL FOR GOOD AND EVIL*
Soman Chainani

"SHOULDER BLADES ARE WHERE YOUR WINGS WERE, WHEN YOU WERE AN ANGEL"

– SKELLIG

TOP 10

Three-quarters of the angst in the world is caused by teenagers coming to terms with hormones (or does it just seem like that at the time?). Boys swagger (and go through agonies of uncertainty inside) while girls play it cool (and go through agonies of uncertainty inside). So little wonder there's abiding interest in teenage love stories . . .

TEENAGE LOVE STORIES

10 *KISSED BY AN ANGEL*
Author Elizabeth Chandler (actually Mary Clair Helldorfer) treats us to the ultimate love story, reaching from beyond the grave as car-crash victim and reborn angel Tristan seeks to protect true love Ivy from a sinister killer.

9 *CHERRY CRUSH*
Chocolate-maker Paddy and daughter Charlotte start a new life, moving in with girlfriend Charlotte and her four daughters. Hint – don't lie to your new family, and don't try to steal your spiteful step-sister's boyfriend (let alone succeed!).

8 *FANGIRL*
Fan fiction hits centre stage, featuring coming-of-age heroine

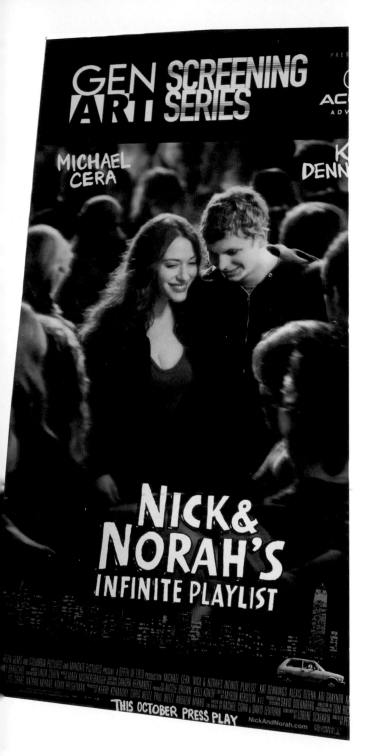

Cath, who watches twin Wren drifting away into the real world, while she writes fan fiction containing passionate emotions she can't experience for herself. Or can she?

7 JUNK
Phew – this really is tough love, as in love can be really tough. Teenage runaways-cum-lovers Gemma and Tar start squatting, and become addicted to heroin. Their downward spiral ends with Tar in prison (rehabilitating) while pregnant Gemma goes home to mum.

6 NICK & NORAH'S INFINITE PLAYLIST
Unlike the lengthy title, this is the shortest, sweetest love story on the list, featuring the eponymous Nick and Norah (both heartbroken) becoming boyfriend and girlfriend for one roller-coaster night as they chase the music.

5 IN BLOOM
No stone remains unturned in the quest for something new – so welcome 'sick-lit' to the list. Awkward young cancer sufferer Francis meets feisty Amber in hospital, and despair is replaced by something worth fighting for.

4 DANCE OF THE DARK HEART

Good battles with evil in the time of King Henry VIII, as tormented Jack Orion feverishly fiddles (he's a violinist) in pursuit of all-consuming love for a lost childhood sweetheart. But will he strike a deal with the devil?

3 FERRYMAN

Train crash. Girl (Dylan) wakes alone in dark tunnel. No sign of other passengers. Boy (Tristan) waiting to guide her through a mysterious wasteland. Stand by for an epic (if paranormal) love story as the ferryman gets cracking.

2 HEART BREAK GIRL

There are two girls in Dante's life – ex-girlfriend Mel and (after she arrives on his doorstep to dump the baby he didn't know about) two-year-old Emma. It's love at first sight, and passion seethes when Mel reappears to reclaim their child.

1 FOREVER

Thirty years on, and still in print, this is the fictional handbook on first love, exploring the joys (and downsides) of teenage sex. Not to mention the inevitable agonies of first heartbreak. A classic.

10 KISSED BY AN ANGEL
Elizabeth Chandler

9 CHERRY CRUSH
Cathy Cassidy

8 FANGIRL
Rainbow Rowell

7 JUNK
Melvin Burgess

6 NICK & NORAH'S INFINITE PLAYLIST
Rachel Cohn & David Levithan

5 IN BLOOM
Matthew Crow

4 DANCE OF THE DARK HEART
Julie Hearn

3 FERRYMAN
Claire Mcfall

2 HEART BREAK GIRL
Malorie Blackman

1 FOREVER
Judy Blume

"YOU CAN'T GO BACK TO HOLDING HANDS"

– FOREVER

TOP
10

Some of the most inspiring children's books feature kids who go it alone without adult help, so it should come as no surprise that young writers are more than capable of knowing what makes good children's literature, and expressing the fruits of their own imagination on the page. Here are ten great books by talented youngsters that prove the point.

YOUNG **AUTHORS**

10 *THE ISOBEL JOURNAL*
Question: How compelling can a stream-of-consciousness scrapbook describing random stuff catching the attention of an 18-year-old girl from somewhere 'where nothing really happens' be? Answer: Utterly.

9 *ERAGON*
Begun by Christopher Paolini when he was 15, it took parents who could self-publish (see, they do have their uses!) before the fantasy world of young Eragon and the dragon egg he found in the mountains hit the big time.

8 *THE HOUSE WITHOUT WINDOWS*
Published in 1927, 12-year-old Barbara Newhall Follet's tale of wee lassie Eepersip was well received, as was

her follow-up two years later. Bizarrely, ten years on she walked out on her marriage with $30 and was never seen again.

7 *THIS AND LAST SEASON'S EXCURSIONS*
The Swiss make great watches, and also produce six-year-old authors. Enter the elderly (compared to Dorothy Straight, below) Christopher Beale with his tales of animal friends, written for his mum in an afternoon.

6 *CONSPIRACY OF CALYPSIA*
What is it about that crisp, clean Swiss mountain air? Young Chris Beale did it aged six, while twins Jyoti and Suresh Guptara drafted their fantasy work aged 11, eventually expanding it into a weighty 2,000-page trilogy.

5 *THE OUTSIDERS*
It's tough if the book's finished when you're 16, but you have to wait two whole years for it to be published. Still, this coming-of-age drama featuring rival groups Greasers and Socs did become a minor 1960s classic.

4 *HOW THE WORLD BEGAN*
No, today's kids *aren't* more precocious than they used to be. Back in 1962, in a mind-blowing role reversal, four-year-old Dorothy Straight wrote/drew this for her gran, boldly tackling the tricky question 'who made the world?'.

3 *ODE ON SOLITUDE*
This is a poem rather than a book, but is included on the grounds that it was written by Alexander Pope

(aged 12) in 1700, creating an incredibly mature reflection on the humdrum benefits of an unremarkable cradle-to-grave bucolic life.

2 *THE DIARY OF A YOUNG GIRL*
The world's most famous youthful diary was found abandoned in the Amsterdam attic where the Jewish Frank family hid until betrayal in 1944. Anne died of typhus in a Nazi concentration camp, leaving the most moving of legacies.

1 *THE YOUNG VISITERS*
Written by nine-year-old Daisy Ashford in 1890, this juvenile gem was not published until 1919 (compete with spelling mistakes, as the title proves). A hilarious tale of late Victorian life, keenly observed with matchmaking eyes from a nursery window.

"I LIE TO MYSELF ALL THE TIME. BUT I NEVER BELIEVE ME."

– THE OUTSIDERS

CHAPTER 3
OUT OF THIS WORLD

Do other worlds exist? Maybe they do, maybe they don't –
but then it hardly matters, because anyone who fancies
exploring the unknown knows that imaginative writers
have created endless parallel universes where all sorts of
weird and wonderful things happen, from ghostly goings-
on to cosmic capers. This list contains some of the more
interesting out-of-this-world scenarios.

TOP 10

Science fiction twinkled to life in the 19th-century, and a new and exciting genre was born. As time has passed, some of the outlandish ideas put forward by Victorian writers have actually turned from science fiction to scientific fact, posing this intriguing question – might any of the extraordinary possibilities proposed in this list actually be just around the corner?

SCI-FI **CLASSICS**

10 *CAT'S CRADLE*
What were people doing on the day the atom bomb dematerialized Hiroshima? Somehow, that question leads inexorably to the bizarre Caribbean island of San Lorenzo, where ruthless discipline is enforced by a giant iron hook.

9 *THE DROWNED WORLD*
Global warming doesn't get worse than this – the world is toast after solar radiation melts ice caps. As the simmering lagoons of post-apocalyptic London are probed by Dr Kerans' scientific team, Strangeman and his pirates arrive . . .

8 *ENDER'S GAME*
Earth is about to be invaded for the third time by (children look away now) the Buggers (alien insectoids, obviously). So can Battle-School trainee Andrew 'Ender' Wiggin (violently) put an end to those nasty Buggers?

7 *FOUNDATION*
The firm bedrock of Asimov's Foundation Series (considered to be amongst the sci-fi master's best work), this original collection of five Galactic Empire stories starts in 0 FE (Foundation Era) and proceeds imaginatively to 135 FE.

6 *THE PLAYER OF GAMES*
Super-gamer Jernau Morat Gurgeh is invited by The Culture's Special Circumstances to

participate in a mysterious journey, travelling to the Empire of Azad in the Small Magellanic Cloud. Once there, a complex game unfolds . . .

5 JOURNEY TO THE CENTRE OF THE EARTH

It's a Victorian blockbuster, as Professor Otto Lidenbrock heads down an Icelandic

volcano, emerging from Italy's Stromboli red-top after adventurous encounters with prehistoric creatures. Not, it turned out, one of the author's better speculations.

4 CHILDHOOD'S END

Enigmatic Overlords stage an invasion of Earth, introducing utopian society at the cost of individual creativity. They're saving humanity from itself, but then children start developing telekinetic powers – and it inevitably ends badly.

3 *NEUROMANCER*
Yup, you're right – there is a cyberpunk genre of science fiction, and this opener to the Sprawl trilogy is a prime example. Disgraced former hacker Henry Dorsett Case hustles a buck in the dystopian underworld of Japan's Chiba City, until he receives an offer he can't refuse.

2 *DUNE*
The world's best-selling sci-fi book features a feudal interstellar society that covets the 'spice' melange, the universe's most precious substance. It's only found on Planet Arrakis, and when young Paul Atreides' noble family is granted stewardship, the trouble begins.

1 ***THE HITCHHIKER'S GUIDE TO THE GALAXY***
Originally a radio comedy, the bizarre adventures of Arthur Dent morphed into books, then a multi-media monolith. Why not? A hilarious electronic guide to the Milky Way should clearly be on everyone's literary sat-nav.

10 *CAT'S CRADLE*
Kurt Vonnegut

9 *THE DROWNED WORLD*
J G Ballard

8 *ENDER'S GAME*
Orson Scott Card

7 *FOUNDATION*
Isaac Asimov

6 *THE PLAYER OF GAMES*
Iain M Banks

5 *JOURNEY TO THE CENTRE OF THE EARTH*
Jules Verne

4 *CHILDHOOD'S END*
Arthur C Clarke

3 *NEUROMANCER*
William Gibson

2 *DUNE*
Frank Herbert

1 *THE HITCHHIKER'S GUIDE TO THE GALAXY*
Douglas Adams

"TIME IS AN ILLUSION. LUNCH DOUBLY SO."

– HITCHHIKER'S GUIDE TO THE GALAXY

What can be said about this amazing author that hasn't already been said a thousand times? Sir Terence David John Pratchett was Britain's best-selling writer of the 1990s and the black-hatted one's prolific output includes over 40 Discworld titles that explode into super-imaginative comic fantasy. It's hard to choose, but with only ten slots available something had to take the pain.

DISCWORLD **DRAMAS**

10 *THUD!*
Opens with the murder of diminutive demagogue Grag Hamcrusher. But is all as it seems, and will ethnic tensions between trolls and dwarfs explode? Over to Ankh-Morpork City Watch's new vampire recruit, Lance-Constable Salacia von Humpeding.

9 *UNSEEN ACADEMICALS*
Soccer satirized? Heresy! But it's chortle time as the Unseen University faculty must play a soccer game under murderous local rules, or be restricted to three meals a day. As a bonus, try sampling one of the Disc's best pies.

8 *GUARDS! GUARDS!*
It's up to the Ankh-Morpork City Watch to spanner the works of secret society the Unique

and Supreme Lodge of the Elucidated Brethren of the Ebon Night, who are about to summon a dragon and install a puppet king.

7 MORT
Enter Death, centre stage. Thinking farm boy Mort gets an apprenticeship with the aforementioned reaper, ushering souls into the next world. But when he falls for the princess he's supposed to help to the other side . . .

6 THE AMAZING MAURICE AND HIS EDUCATED RODENTS
The first Discworld novel for kids, featuring Maurice (a canny cat) who deploys his plague of rats so teenage piper Keith can save town after town – in return for hard cash. Nice little earner.

5 I SHALL WEAR MIDNIGHT
Tiffany Aching's ongoing journey to witchhood is interrupted when she's accused of murdering the local baron. So it's off to Ankh-Morpork to find the heir, despite the evil attentions of the Cunning Man.

4 MAKING MONEY
Moist von Lipwig is jogging along happily when the new chairman of the Royal Bank of Ankh-Morpork (Mr Fusspot, a dog) is bequeathed to him, and the Assassins' Guild will terminate him if he doesn't take over the bank.

3 PYRAMIDS
Prince Teppic (a newly qualified member of the Ankh-Morpork Assassins' Guild) returns home to Ancient Egypt (well, actually Djelibeybi) when his dad dies, only to be greeted by hostile high priest Dios and a dangerous pyramid.

2 NIGHT WATCH
Enter Sir Samuel Vimes, commander of the Ankh-Morpork City Watch.

He's dutifully pursuing master criminal Carcer Dun when he's unfortunately caught in a magical storm that sends him tumbling back in time.

1 THE COLOUR OF MAGIC
What else could top this list, other than the very first Discworld novel, published in 1983 and introducing Sir Terry's unique brand of comedy fantasy (as here personified by trials and tribulations of incompetent wizard Rincewind).

"THERE BE DRAGONS EVERYWHERE"

– THE COLOUR OF MAGIC

Ghost-hunters spend endless time deploying specialist equipment in the hope of confirming the existence of things that go bump in the night, but have yet to come up with anything solid you could nail to a wall. But wait! Who cares about proof? For those who have actually had a spectral encounter, that is the last thing on their minds.

SUPERNATURAL SPINE-TINGLERS

10 *THE HAUNTING OF HILL HOUSE*

Back in 1959 came this eerie encounter with bricks and mortar. When four assorted characters arrive at the evil eponymous pile to investigate the supernatural, it's going to end in terror. But whom will the house claim first?

9 *DARK MATTER*

Spellbinding! It's 1937 and, as war clouds gather, Jack eagerly joins an Arctic expedition. But on the remote island base where they'll overwinter, Jack's companions desert him and he's left alone in 24-hour darkness with . . . something.

8 *THE SUMMONING*

Chloe Saunders wants to be normal but she keeps seeing ghosts, so she ends up in Lyle

House, a home for troubled teenagers. Needless to say, the supposedly safe environment is anything but.

7 *THE LITTLE STRANGER*

Exploration of the changing British class system in the aftermath of World War II – and more. A doctor befriends a landed family with failing fortunes, and realises that nameless evil stalks the corridors of Hundreds Hall.

6 *THE WINTER GHOSTS*

In 1928 war-damaged Freddie Watson has a car crash in the French Pyrenees, finds sanctuary in a small village and meets the beautiful Fabrissa. Together they collide with a tragic, centuries-old mystery.

5 *THE HALLOWEEN TREE*

Trick or treating is always dodgy, considering when it takes place. So when nine lads set out to do the spooky business and one vanishes on a potentially lethal journey, the rest must pursue their pal through time and space.

4 *THE TURN OF THE SCREW*

Ambiguous encounters with the unknown, as a Victorian governess senses supernatural forces at work and becomes convinced that her charges are communicating with ghosts. And so it proves, with tragic consequences.

3 *A CHRISTMAS CAROL*
A ghost story with a happy ending – whoever thought of that? Enter master scribe Charles Dickens, describing life-changing visitations to miserly Ebenezer Scrooge by the ghost of Jacob Marley and the spirits of Christmas past, present and future.

2 *COLLECTED GHOST STORIES*
The acknowledged master of the terrifying tale, M R James was a Victorian academic with an uncanny knack of generating menace from the mundane where everyday objects unleash supernatural creatures bent on fearful retribution.

1 *THE WOMAN IN BLACK*
Gothic ghoulishness unchained, as a spectre's appearance heralds the death of children. When a dark-eyed, pale-faced woman in black appears at a funeral, the man seeking her story little knows that the final chapter will be his own daughter's death.

TOP
10

Some of the best-loved books of all time have featured compelling fantasy worlds, conjured up from some unfathomable place deep in the mind of an author whose imagination rushes in where others fear to tread. Often set against extraordinary backdrops, the appealing/repelling cast of mythical/magical creatures is sometimes – but not always – augmented by mere humans. So join them!

FANTASY WORLDS

10 *A WIZARD OF EARTHSEA*
Young mage Ged is educated by the village witch, then apprenticed to a wizard before joining a school of wizardry (sounds like an idea someone might develop!) before embarking on a voyage of self-discovery. Earthsea's enchanting!

9 *GARDENS OF THE MOON*
This is the opener in the multi-book fantasy epic *Malazan Book of the Fallen*. Magic and power struggles erupt in a world dominated by the Malazan Empire, as the city of Darujhistan is attacked.

8 *AMERICAN GODS*
This plays with the premise that gods exist because people think they do, which doesn't mean

they don't. Join Shadow as he discovers aggressive New Gods rising and tries to persuade Old Gods to repel them. Can it be that simple?

7 *THE PRINCESS BRIDE*
Is it a romance? Is it an adventure? Is it funny? Is it a fairy tale? Is it a wonderful fantasy world? Yes! It's that and more as Buttercup and Westley's love story threads through compelling drama.

5 *THE NIGHT CIRCUS*
The Circus of Dreams (open from sunset to sunrise) features ethereal enigmas like a vertical cloud maze and garden of ice, but there's a dark side as two magicians lock wands in a battle that must end in death.

6 *HOTHOUSE*
When the sun expands and Earth's rotation stops, frenzied plant growth overwhelms humankind, leaving only a tribe of miniature people fighting for survival amidst omnivorous vegetation – as the end of the world looms large.

4 *GORMENGHAST TRILOGY*
If you want to be different, invent a sub-genre. This newbie (back in the 1940s and 1950s) introduced 'fantasy of manners', woven around Titus Groan and Castle Ghormenghast. Think phantasmagorical Regency literature.

3 *ALICE'S ADVENTURES IN WONDERLAND*
Alice follows the White Rabbit down his hole and what follows is delightful,

as Alice changes size and meets a stellar cast of wacky characters, enjoying a mad tea party, crazy croquet and other eccentricities.

2 A GAME OF THRONES

Multimedia mania stemmed from the *A Song of Ice and Fire* series, of which this is the first novel. Here, shenanigans in the Seven Kingdoms surround the Stark family and evil Lannisters ('incest is best').

1 THE LORD OF THE RINGS

This three-volume sequel to *The Hobbit* catapulted hobbits and their allies as they travelled through Middle-earth to the very top of the high fantasy bestseller tree. Set against the War of the Ring, can the gallant band seriously challenge Dark Lord Sauron?

10 A WIZARD OF EARTHSEA
Ursula K Le Guin

9 GARDENS OF THE MOON
Steve Erikson

8 AMERICAN GODS
Neil Gaiman

7 THE PRINCESS BRIDE
William Goldman

6 THE NIGHT CIRCUS
Erin Morgenstern

5 HOTHOUSE
Brian Aldiss

4 GORMENGHAST TRILOGY
Mervyn Peake

3 ALICE'S ADVENTURES IN WONDERLAND
Lewis Carroll

2 A GAME OF THRONES
George R R Martin

1 THE LORD OF THE RINGS
J R R Tolkien

"EVEN FOR MY KIND, PAIN STILL HURTS"

– *AMERICAN GODS*

TOP
10

Obsession with the past (and future possibilities) has long stimulated authorial imagination, leading to an interesting genre of books which not only deal with the past (or speculate about the future), but also feature characters with the ability to go and see for themselves. Time travel fascinates writers and readers alike, so stand by to be teleported . . .

TIME **TRAVELLERS**

10 *THE TIME TRAVELER'S WIFE*
You say traveler, I say traveller – a clue that this existential voyage begins in America, exploring stresses and strains as Henry meets his wife-to-be (aged six) when tripping back from 1991 to 1977.

9 *LIGHTNING*
Oh boy, this one is slippery. Who is the mysterious man who watches over Lara Shane (born in a weird lightning storm), appearing at critical moments in her troubled life to avert disaster? And how do Winston Churchill and Hitler fit in?

8 *THE MAN WHO FOLDED HIMSELF*
Forget origami. Daniel Eakins inherits the Timebelt from Uncle Jim that (you guessed it) lets him time-travel at will. But all his life's a circle; he's Uncle Jim and his son is . . . himself.

7 *THE HOUSE ON THE STRAND*
Dick Young can do what so many would love to achieve – nipping back in time with the help of a powerful experimental drug to observe past events. Hint – be careful what you wish for.

6 *TIMELINE*
When an archaeology professor heads back to the 14th century using quantum technology (the lazy academic approach) he doesn't return, and the rescue party is soon trapped in a dangerous medieval time warp.

5 *THE RESTAURANT AT THE END OF THE UNIVERSE*
What happens to Arthur Dent, Ford Prefect *et al* after they finish hitchhiking the galaxy? Well, they're attacked by a Vogon ship and fail to escape, because the Improbability drive is trying to make a cup of tea.

4 *UP THE LINE*
Sex, humour . . . and time travel. Enter Time Courier Jud Elliot III as he conducts tourists into the

past while grappling with paradoxes of time shifting (like falling in love with your own gran many times removed).

3 *TO SAY NOTHING OF THE DOG*
Mystery, humour and time travel as Oxford academics access the past (strictly for research purposes, meddling with history absolutely forbidden). But things get hairy when one regulation-buster returns with a Victorian cat.

2 *SLAUGHTERHOUSE-FIVE*
Consider the subtitle – *The Children's Crusade: A Duty-Dance with Death* – and conclude that random time traveller Billy Pilgrim's anarchic journeys will be anything but relaxing, as wartime horror mingles with alien abduction.

1 *THE TIME MACHINE*
Dear old H G Wells cannily coined the expression 'time machine', but sadly forgot to patent it. But he did popularize the concept of selective time travel with his imaginative tale of Victorians entering the fourth dimension – time itself.

The zombies arriving at Platform 4 are descendants of animated corpses magically revived by witchcraft in Haitian folklore. Meanwhile, the undead who are actually dead but behaving as if they're alive are also arriving in town. They're all coming to inspire writers – like those represented on this list – who recognise the macabre mayhem promised by such other-worldly creatures.

ZOMBIES & UNDEAD

10 HANDLING THE UNDEAD

It's not a 'how-to' manual, in which case the advice would have been 'with extreme care'. Instead, it's Scandi-style undead horrorsville as Stockholm is rocked by the unexpected reanimation of thousands of deceased citizens.

9 MONSTER ISLAND

Hell's teeth, New York City has been overrun by undead, who are even less polite than the regular inhabitants. When vital AIDS medication must be retrieved by a band of African child soldiers led by former UN employee Dekalb, undead fists fly.

8 UNDER A GRAVEYARD SKY

That airborne zombie plague (it's always a plague) slowly overwhelms civilization, leaving the resourceful Smith family (with a small band of Marines) to create a refuge for survivors as terror ratchets up beneath the ghastly graveyard sky.

7 THE LOVING DEAD

Escape *to* Alcatraz – now that is different. Escapers couldn't survive those lethal currents, so will voracious victims of a zombie plague ravaging (literally) the Bay Area be able to get the good guys who flee to the old island prison?

6 HERBERT WEST – REANIMATOR

Zombies have been around for absolutely ages – well, at least since 1922, when H P Lovecraft served up the recipe for the standing Z horror dish, with its implacably evil ingredients.

5 I AM A LEGEND

Holy Moly! This 1954 horror classic deserves its list slot as another pioneer of the zombie genre, and for popularizing the world-apocalypse-due-to-disease story line. Not to mention the fact that it inspired four or five movies.

4 NIGHT OF THE LIVING TREKKIES

Trekkies? *Star Trek* fans, obviously. But how will these rag-bag fans fare when their nerdy convention is gate-crashed by zombies, released by aliens to plague the world?

3 THE LAST BASTION OF THE LIVING

Save the city if you can – that's the challenge awaiting Vanguard Maria Martinez after she's contacted by the Science War Division. But can the undead hordes of the Inferi Scourge surrounding The Bastion be beaten?

2 *WORLD WAR Z*
Subtitled *An Oral History of the Zombie War*, this apocalyptic horror records personal accounts of experiences during the global war against that fearfully familiar foe, a zombie plague. Life will never be the same again.

1 *DAY BY DAY ARMAGEDDON*
Start an online zombie fan-fiction story, wait for fan mania to erupt, get a conventional publisher – and your diary of deadly disease and walking dead taking over the USA could land you right on top of a zombie and undead Top Ten list.

"GRAB THE BUG-OUT BAG AND ACTIVATE YOUR ZOMBIE PLAN"

– UNDER A GRAVEYARD SKY

In an era where books often feature unbearable people doing unspeakable things, it might be hoped the age of innocence lives on in the form of modern fairy tales. Sadly, it doesn't often turn out that way. As books on this list testify, modern fables deal with contemporary themes where unbearable people do . . . well, see for yourself.

MODERN FABLES

10 WHITE AS SNOW
Snow White, White as Snow – any connection? Oh yes. This is a very dark revisiting of the Grimm fairy tale, replete with rape, violence, a wicked queen and seven dwarves representing the Deadly Sins. Lock up your children!

9 INDIGO
More literary piracy, as Shakespeare's *The Tempest* is reworked into dual imaginative 'reality' jumping from the 17th to 20th century, with an agenda designed to expose and criticize past colonial wrongs. A fable for our times.

8 THE BLUE DIARY
The diary once belonged to a murdered girl, but her killer was never caught – and then a phone call exposes him as a happily married pillar of the community. A cautionary fable about damage done by dark secrets.

7 THE VINEGAR JAR
Despite featuring traditional folk-tale themes within the narrative, this one doesn't have a happy ending, as Rose's failed and failing relationships blur the line between grim reality and make-believe.

6 THE OCEAN AT THE END OF THE LANE
This belter from a master story teller veers between futuristic fable and sheer terror, as dark forces created by the lodger who committed suicide 40 years ago are unleashed.

5 THE BOOK OF LOST THINGS
In a modern take on traditional fairy tales, the Rumpelstiltskin-like Crooked Man becomes both friend and enemy to unhappy 12-year-old David, a boy who crosses over into the fantasy world of his books.

4 THE LAST UNICORN
This tale for today features a mythical creature of yesteryear found in traditional fairy tales – the unicorn. Learning that she's the last of her kind, our heroine embarks on a fantastical and dangerous journey symbolizing the quest for love.

3 FAIRY TALE
Well, are we finally back in traditional fairy-tale land? Er, not exactly. When Eloise is visited by four strange men in darkest Wales, it soon becomes apparent that nothing is

as it seems when humans and slightly scary fairy characters start meeting and mingling.

2 *THE ROBBER BRIDE*
The bride is long-dead Zenia, who once stole men from friends Tony, Charis and Roz. But each gets a different version of Zenia's story as this enigmatic liar's duplicity raises issues of power, friendship and trust between women.

1 *POSSESSION*
The story of two couples told in parallel worlds as two scholars pursue a secret love story between long-dead poets. As in any good fable there's final resolution, when the troubles of the latter have a positive outcome for the former.

"I CANNOT LET YOU BURN ME UP, NOR CAN I RESIST YOU"

– POSSESSION

TOP
10

Who hasn't looked up at a shimmering night sky and wondered what's really out there, whether the universe stretches to infinity, and if there might be intelligent life beyond the final frontier? For sure those pensive star-gazers have included authors of the sort of sci-fi fiction to be found on this list, and their space-flights of fancy know no bounds.

SPACE ODYSSEYS

10 *TAU ZERO*
It's every astronaut's worst nightmare – after a close encounter with a nebula, starship Leonora Christine's ramjet engine keeps accelerating, firing the 50-person crew into a deadly time-dilation zone and divorcing them from humankind.

9 *CONSIDER PHLEBAS*
A space opera introducing the Culture, fighting the Idiran Empire. Mercenary Horza pursues a Culture Mind considered abominable by Idirans. When the Mind takes refuge on a Planet of the Dead everything gets complicated.

8 *LEVIATHAN WAKES*
Ice-miner Jim Holden discovers wrecked spaceship *Scopuli*, and de-ices a mysterious secret the baddies will kill for. When space detective Miller arrives, the duo join forces to crack the mystery.

7 *THE MARTIAN CHRONICLES*
When Planet Earth is on the point of nuclear immolation, humans flee to Mars only to find that aboriginal Martians aren't happy at the arrival of new colonists (think Apaches and Wild West).

6 *OUT OF THE SILENT PLANET*
When Dr Elwin Ransom is drugged and kidnapped he wakes up on a spaceship heading for Planet Malacandra in company with his abductors, who will offer him as a sacrifice to the inhabitants. He escapes, and the adventure begins.

5 *THE RIGHT STUFF*
Is fact stranger than fiction? Actually, no – but this examination of the USA's competitive efforts to beat Russia in the space race is as fascinating as any fiction . . . and more authentic.

4 *ACROSS THE UNIVERSE*
No, not the Beatles track/film of the same name, but the tale of starship Godspeed with its cargo of frozen settlers. When Amy defrosts early, she is in the strange company of crew born over generations, and must solve a murder mystery that could destroy the expedition.

3 *STARSHIP TROOPERS*
Military sci-fi on parade, as Terrans (Earthlings) battle with Arachnids (Bugs). The

intergalactic conflict is seen through the eyes of soldier Juan 'Johnnie' Rico as his exploits in the Mobile Infantry dramatically unfold.

2 THE LITTLE PRINCE

For once, man goes not into space but space comes to man. In one of France's most-translated books, a crashed aviator marooned in the Sahara Desert meets a 'little prince' fallen to earth from asteroid B-612.

1 2001: A SPACE ODYSSEY

Forever associated with the film's haunting theme music (by Richard Strauss), this classic space drama (written after the film's appearance) is so well known that the plot needs no retelling. Suffice to say that the HAL 9000 computer is a *very bad boy.*

"BEHIND EVERY MAN NOW ALIVE STAND THIRTY GHOSTS"

– *2001: A SPACE ODYSSEY*

TOP **10**

Terror, terror on the wall, who is the scariest of them all? Cover your eyes and peek at the list between your fingers to see if this selection of sinister stories fulfils the requirement to shock. For horror is the name of this particular game, and these are the books chosen to set flesh a-crawling, hearts a-jumping and spines a-tingling.

HORROR **SHOWS**

10 *WATCHERS*
A chase story with a difference – Travis Cornell is befriended by Einstein, a genetically engineered dog with supercanine powers. Unfortunately, another terrifying artificial creature known enigmatically as the Outsider is in kill mode. Run for it!

9 *DAEMONIC*
Masterful horror, as recluse Jack Draegerman bribes unfortunates to attend his fortress lair, The Rock, with its labyrinthine interior and (inevitable) lack of exits. Jack's made a deal with something daemonic, something 1950s-horror-movieish, and his 'guests' are lunch.

8 *THE HOWLING*
Rape victim Karyn and husband Roy leave the city for backwoods California, but (ouch!) those woods are full of howling werewolves. Roy dismisses his wife's fears as irrational, and when he's bitten Karyn's alone – as the hungry pack gathers.

7 *ROSEMARY'S BABY*
Move to a spooky apartment building with a history of murder and witchcraft if you must, but never get friendly with elderly eccentric neighbours. Most of all, don't get pregnant – your unborn just might be the Antichrist.

6 *THE AMITYVILLE HORROR*
Subtitled *A True Story*, this terrifying tale of the everyday paranormal is based on the Lutz family's experiences at 113 Ocean Avenue on Long Island, scene of a previous multiple murder. But did the killer really return?

5 *THE RATS*
There's something about rodents (especially rats) that sends shivers up spines. So when giant rats start attacking (and eating) humans, with any who escape with a nip dying a mysterious death, it's worse than horrifying.

4 *DR JEKYLL AND MR HYDE*
This was originally entitled *The Strange Case of Dr Jekyll and Mr Hyde*, for obvious reasons. Strange indeed – metamorphic men may be old hat today, but back in 1886 the schizophrenic duo terrified shocked readers.

3 *AMERICAN GOTHIC*
Art imitates life in this psychological

nightmare, as actual serial killer H H Holmes becomes fictional G G Gregg in this dark depiction of a clinical surgeon who terminates beautiful young women.

2 *THE EXORCIST*

Father Merrin find omens pointing to powerful evil he's battled before. Meanwhile, 12-year-old Regan MacNiel becomes aggressive and disturbed. When demonic possession is suspected, Father Merrin must perform an exorcism, assisted by doubting Father Karras. But will either priest survive a horrifying climax?

1 *DRACULA*

After abandoning lawyer Jonathan Harker to the Brides of Dracula back in Transylvania, the bloodsucking Count visits Britain in pursuit of Harker's girlfriend. It's the start of a deadly game as the toothsome one targets tasty females and the good guys reach for the garlic.

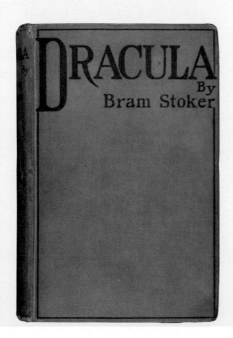

"THE DEVIL DOES A LOT OF COMMERCIALS "

– THE EXORCIST

TOP
10

Time to put pen to paper and create your own top 10 list of spine-tingling horror novels...

10

9

8

7

6

5

4

3

2

1

TOP **10**

Writers seem strangely drawn to the idea of a world gone mad, gleefully imagining what might transpire if many millennia of creating orderly society were swept away by nuclear holocaust, meteor strike or act of God. In truth, the cause is usually but an excuse, as the real agenda is exploring the dystopian aftermath (which usually involves people behaving badly).

DYSTOPIAN **DRAMAS**

10 *EREWHON*
Anagram solvers of the world unite, and visit this mysterious country discovered by the narrator and located . . . where exactly? At first glance the place is an unspoiled Utopia – until the veneer peels off.

9 *THE TRIAL*
How good must it be to inspire an adjective that's a synonym for 'dystopian'? Sadly, Franz didn't live to enjoy the accolade, or even see publication of this truly Kafkaesque book that features a man's trial by remote authority for nameless crimes.

8 *THE DAY OF THE TRIFFIDS*
Bill Masen is hospitalized with bandaged eyes, missing the green meteor shower that blinds nearly everyone else. Happy times for triffids, then, as the mobile plants with deadly stings set about humankind.

7 *FAHRENHEIT 451*
Books conflagrate at this temperature, suggesting the fire-raisers don't live in a tolerant society. No indeed, for this is super-dystopian America and, when fireman Montag starts secretly saving books, he's toast.

6 *BRAVE NEW WORLD*
It's AD 2540, and the world state has got everything under control. Population is limited so there's plenty for all and consumerism is sacrosanct; but idyllic it isn't. Children are hatched and only the chosen few may rule.

5 *1984*
How good must it be to inspire an adjective that's a synonym for 'dystopian', especially when your real name's Eric Blair? The Orwellian state is fiercely authoritarian and life in Airstrip One (Great Britain) oppressive. Only it time-expired.

4 *GULLIVER'S TRAVELS*
It's the package tour to/from hell. This 18th-century satire maroons Lemuel Gulliver among little people (Lilliputians), then big ones who treat

wee Gulliver as a freak on a flying island obsessed with crazy science and among deformed humanoids and noble horses.

3 *LORD OF THE FLIES*
Anyone who thinks kids unchained have the potential for being horrendous should write a book, imagining how they might react if deprived of adult supervision on an uninhabited island. Only it's been done. And this is it. And it's worse than you imagined.

2 *ANIMAL FARM*
If boys behaving like savages are scary, imagine life when animals take over the farm. A satire on Soviet communism featuring the edict 'all animals are equal', but it's not long before Napoleon the pig is more equal than others.

1 *A CLOCKWORK ORANGE*
In dystopian Britain violent teenage culture rules and Beethoven-loving Alex is king. He and his droogs run wild, raping and pillaging. But when society's heavy hand descends on Alex, the methodology is equally disturbing.

"BIG BROTHER IS WATCHING YOU"

– 1984

10 *EREWHON*
Samuel Butler

9 *THE TRIAL*
Franz Kafka

8 *THE DAY OF THE TRIFFIDS*
John Wyndham

7 *FAHRENHEIT 451*
Ray Bradbury

6 *BRAVE NEW WORLD*
Aldous Huxley

5 *1984*
George Orwell

4 *GULLIVER'S TRAVELS*
Jonathan Swift

3 *LORD OF THE FLIES*
William Golding

2 *ANIMAL FARM*
George Orwell

1 *A CLOCKWORK ORANGE*
Anthony Burgess

TOP **10**

Gothic: 'Of or relating to a literary style characterized by gloom, the grotesque and the supernatural' – so now you know. This edgy genre flourished towards the end of the 18th century, burst into flower during the 1800s and is still entertaining those who like their fiction to come on the spooky side. Just don't say you haven't been warned!

GOTHIC **EXTRAVAGANZAS**

10 *THE CASTLE OF OTRANTO*
This marks the Gothic novel's debut. Published in 1764, it launched a genre still with us today. The clever premise involves the 'discovery' of a medieval manuscript describing the life, loves and turbulent times of Manfred (Lord of Castle Otranto) and his family.

9 *THE MYSTERIES OF UDOLPHO*
Round up the soon-up-be-usual suspects – isolated castles, physical terror, psychological trauma, supernatural happenings, a dastardly villain and a put-upon heroine. Published in 1794, this is a template for the perfect Gothic novel.

8 *THE HOUSE OF THE SEVEN GABLES*
Fifty years on came this dark tale of a New England family whose gloomy mansion was cursed in antiquity by an executed man. The supernatural, guilt, retribution and expiation mingle with echoes of witchcraft.

7 *THE OBSERVATIONS*
Escaping her past, Bessie Buckley takes a job in the big house (there's always a sinister house!), working for lovely Arabella. But the mistress has secrets of her own – including an unhealthy obsession with a former maid who died in unexplained circumstances.

6 *GOTHIC TALES*
A series of terrifying tales that represent Victorian high Gothic at its best (or worst, for those of nervous disposition). From chillingly surreal to downright eerie, these supernatural specials really hit the sinister spot.

5 *THE TELL-TALE HEART AND OTHER WRITINGS*
The master of the macabre, mystery, madness and murder is here represented by his collected works. Brace yourself for the horror-filled handbook of Gothic terror.

4 *THE PHANTOM OF THE OPERA*
Yes, there was indeed a book that inspired the films and stage show – a Gothic melodrama where disfigured 'phantom' Erik falls for opera singer Christine, until his jealousy threatens disaster (before final, sad redemption).

3 *NORTHANGER ABBEY*
Jane Austen's first completed book was not

actually published until 1817, after her death. In creating a clever parody of the then-hugely-popular Gothic novel, Austen used many a classic Gothic device of her own.

2 *THE MONK*
Set in Spain, this scandalous sizzler with its convoluted plot is an acknowledged Gothic classic from 1796, full of rather dull goodies and seriously bad baddies, with plenty of rape, incest, secret sex – and that mysterious monk.

1 *THE WOMAN IN WHITE*
This early mystery is a masterpiece, as deception and double-dealing swirl around the heroine, the penniless drawing master who loves her and the evil aristocrat who marries her. It all comes right in the end, but not before dark Gothic secrets must be unravelled.

10 ***THE CASTLE OF OTRANTO***
Horace Walpole

9 ***THE MYSTERIES OF UDOLPHO***
Ann Radcliffe

8 ***THE HOUSE OF THE SEVEN GABLES***
Nathaniel Hawthorne

7 ***THE OBSERVATIONS***
Jane Harris

6 ***GOTHIC TALES***
Elizabeth Gaskell

5 ***THE TELL-TALE HEART AND OTHER WRITINGS***
Edgar Allan Poe

4 ***THE PHANTOM OF THE OPERA***
Gaston Leroux

3 ***NORTHANGER ABBEY***
Jane Austen

2 ***THE MONK***
Matthew Lewis

1 ***THE WOMAN IN WHITE***
Wilkie Collins

"MY BUTTERED TOAST WAITS FOR NOBODY"

– THE WOMAN IN WHITE

TOP 10

The death of the late Gabriel Garcia Marquez served as a reminder that he created the approach to creative writing loosely known as Magical Realism. This cleverly infuses realities of everyday life with a sprinkling of stardust – the magical dimension that elevates the ordinary to the exceptional. So is this list unexpectedly invaded with things too strange to believe?

MAGICAL REALISMS

10 *THE GIRL WHO CHASED THE MOON*
When Emily travels to Mullaby, North Carolina to unravel the secrets of her mother's life, she meets her grandfather for the first time – and inexplicable happenings soon convince her it's no ordinary town.

9 *THE ALCHEMIST*
How many international best-sellers are written in Portuguese? A few, actually (magical reality is a Latin specialty). Here, young Spanish shepherd Santiago travels to Egypt, following a recurring dream telling him there's treasure in those pyramids.

8 *LIFE OF PI*
Indian lad Piscine Molitor 'Pi' Patel from Pondicherry is interested in spirituality and has ample time to ponder the meaning of life when stranded on a lifeboat for 227 days with Bengal tiger Richard Parker (also the name of a tiger hunter).

7 *THE HOUSE OF SPIRITS*
A Latin-American classic in Spanish, weaving the lives and loves of three generations of the Chilean Trueba family into an epic that combines essential elements of magical realism . . . magic, love and inescapable fate.

6 *THE LOVELY BONES*
The harrowing (but compelling) story of a raped and murdered girl watching from on high as friends and family struggle with the concept of 'life goes on', while she tries to come to terms with her fate.

5 *LIKE WATER FOR CHOCOLATE*
Supernatural merges with mundane in this Mexican (yup, Spanish again) domestic drama. Tita longs to marry Pedro, but falls foul of an edict that the youngest daughter must stay home to look after mother.

4 *THE SHADOW OF THE WIND*
The Spanish Connection continues, but this one is from Spain itself. Young Daniel Sempere selects a book from the Secret Cemetery of Forgotten Books. He's fascinated by his choice – but the Devil is too.

3 *BELOVED*
Fleeing and abused slave Sethe is recaptured by her brutal master in the Deep South, but not before killing her 'beloved' two-year-old baby to spare the child captivity. But that's not quite the end of the departed infant . . .

2 *MIDNIGHT'S CHILDREN*
Historical facts merge with historical fiction in this allegory dealing with British India's independence and subsequent partition. Narrator Saleem Sinai is born at the very moment independence takes effect, which imbues him with magical powers.

1 *ONE HUNDRED YEARS OF SOLITUDE*
Back to Spanish, and the book that launched a genre. Seven generations of the Colombian Buendía family first found, then inhabit the city of Macondo, which they are unable to escape as extraordinary events unfold.

TOP 10

It's 21 September 1947. A boy is born. Two years later the father goes out for cigarettes and doesn't return. Along with his adopted brother, the boy is raised by mother Ruth. His given names were Stephen Edwin King, and he went on to become the greatest horror writer the world has known. Here are ten of his best imaginings.

STEPHEN KING SPECIALS

10 *THE STAND*
A book featuring post-apocalyptic fantasy and horror sounds scary. But it's worse than that, as the US military's weaponized influenza strain escapes and decimates the world.

9 *IT*
Pennywise the Dancing Clown enchants kids – and that's the horrific point. For shape-shifting Pennywise is a malign entity that preys on children. As six youngsters become aware of the danger, can they defeat 'the thing'?

8 *THE DEAD ZONE*
After recovering from a five-year coma, high school teacher Johnny finds he has clairvoyant powers, deploying them in a desperate attempt to stop evil ex-Bible salesman Greg Stillson from becoming President – and nuking the world.

7 *MISERY*
Writers beware! If your car crashes on a snowy night don't be rescued by your greatest fan. She may turn out to be a pathological ex-nurse and serial killer bent on destroying your new writing career, before making you revive the deceased Victorian-era romantic heroine she adores.

6 *DOLORES CLAIBORNE*
This monologue unfolds the life of eponymous Dolores, who *didn't* murder her wealthy employer (as police suspect) but *did* murder her abusing husband 30 years ago. The clever, harrowing psychological dissection of a troubled life.

5 *THE GREEN MILE*
This tells of death-row inmate John Coffee, whose healing and empathetic powers impress supervisor Paul Edgecombe. But despite his good works there's no escaping the electric chair for John, as Paul (now aged 104) remembers.

4 *PET SEMATARY*
Oh boy, you'd think people might be wary about interring dead animals (or people) in a burial ground when it became apparent that miraculous reincarnations only led to grief. Not Louis, though, who just keeps on digging.

3 *11/22/63*
The date is one of

America's darkest – the day President Kennedy was assassinated. So if you had the ability to time-travel, wouldn't *you* go back and try to change the course of history? If only life and death were that simple . . .

2 *SALEM'S LOT*
When writer Ben Mears returns to the town where he grew up, he's soon surrounded by homicidal vampires. So he teams up with cross-wielding Mark Petrie, and together they kill the boss vampire – but that's not *nearly* enough.

1 *THE SHINING*
Classic horror, as Jack Torrance takes a caretaker's job at the remote Overlook Hotel with his family. Son Danny has 'the shining' – and this psychic ability lets him see the horrific past. Soon, supernatural forces run riot in the snowbound hotel.

"HUMAN NATURE BABY, GRAB IT AND GROWL"

– *THE SHINING*

TOP **10**

Sometimes it seems that real life – however gritty and dramatic its portrayal may be – just isn't enough to satisfy the cravings of some book readers, perhaps *because* they're seeking brief escape from that self-same actuality. For those would-be escapees, this list contains an assorted selection of tingling tales that feature those out-of-this-world staple ingredients: myth and magic.

MYTHICAL **MASTERPIECES**

10 *THE MASTER AND MARGARITA*

This anti-Soviet satire by a Russian author who died in 1940 only came to light in the 1960s. Meet Satan and his bizarre retinue, along with an extraordinary cast of characters, including Margarita the airborne mistress.

9 *EIRIK THE RED AND OTHER ICELANDIC SAGAS*

Norsemen who colonized Iceland were made of stern stuff, and real or imagined oral tales of adventure in the 10th and 11th centuries were later woven into written stories.

8 *MANUAL OF THE WARRIOR OF LIGHT*

Collected wisdom from many sources is told by the Templar, who faces challenges that reinforce his status as a metaphor for those seeking realization of dreams – and affirmation of life.

7 *THE GOLEM AND THE DJINNI*

The Golem is Chava, a clay creature brought to life, who arrives in New York in 1899. The Djinni (or Jinni, depending on where you live) is Ahmad, an accidently released fire-being. Together, they must make a momentous choice.

6 *JONATHAN STRANGE & MR NORRELL*

Magic regresses to Napoleonic England in the person of the title characters, whose interaction illuminates the division between reason and unreason, Englishness and sundry other magical matters.

5 *RAGNAROCK*

Is it at novel? Is it a true story? Is it magic? Try a taste of all three. A girl evacuated to the countryside in World War II is transformed by a book of Norse myths. But will cruel and greedy gods destroy the world when they die?

4 *THE SILMARILLION*

Tolkien's last work, featuring the creation of 'the world that is', Eä, and acting as a loose prequel to *The Lord of the Rings*. Meet supernatural powers Valar and Maiar, and witness the wars over the Silmarils (three brilliant jewels).

3 *RUNEMARKS*

The old Norse gods linger on, greatly enfeebled, as a newer, more powerful creed – the Order – tries (paradoxically) to magically rid the world of magic. But Maddy has special powers, and the Norsemen won't lie down . . .

2 CLOUD ATLAS
These six stories travel from a 19th-century Pacific island to an apocalyptic future, linked together in a fiendishly clever manner that circuitously returns the reader to the starting point.

1 AESOP'S FABLES
The Greek slave and story-teller's famous fables have somehow travelled from the 5th century BC. So we can still enjoy (and learn from) enchanting fables such as *The Tortoise and the Hare*, *The Goose that Laid the Golden Eggs* and *The Boy who Cried Wolf*.

TOP 10

Many a monster has rampaged through the pages of popular fiction since the days of 19th-century Gothic creatures like the monstrous creation of eccentric scientist Victor Frankenstein, himself the inspired invention of Mary Shelley. The poet's sister certainly knew how to play the monster card to great advantage, and her lead has since been followed by many a skilful dealer.

MIGHTY MONSTERS

10 *THE MISSING LINK* There's a nameless beast lurking in New York's Central Park. When reporter Hudge Stone gets on its trail he becomes involved in a dark drama stretching from African jungles to a secret government scientific study.

9 *KING KONG* This cheeky chappie really is a big strong boy – most people ascend the Empire State Building by elevator, but giant movie monster Kong goes up the hard way. The book was published in advance of the 1933 film for pre-publicity.

8 *BEAST* Before creating a best-seller about a great white shark that terrorizes bathers, why not have a wet run featuring a titanic (it sinks things) squid that has to be bettered by a world-weary hero? It's a question asked and answered by author Benchley.

7 *THE GOLEM* A 1914 tale of the Jewish ghetto in Prague, the monster being the mythical Golem, inextricably woven into the life of Athanasius Pernath, jeweller and art restorer. The Golem represents the ghetto's *zeitgeist*.

6 *PERDIDO STREET STATION* Any book featuring an eccentric scientist called Isaac Dan der Grimnebulin is likely to be weird – but not half as weird as a giant caterpillar that (nourished with hallucinogenic 'dreamshit') turns into a giant subconscious-munching moth. Weird indeed!

5 *THE HAUNTING OF TOBY JUGG* To the author's customary preoccupation with madness and satanic possession may be added a nebulous many-legged monster whose shadowy presence haunts disabled war veteran Jugg.

4 *THE ISLAND OF DR MOREAU* Shipwrecked Edward Prendick finds the doc who owns the island has been trying to turn animals into humans. Unfortunately, all he's managed to engineer are human-animal hybrids that are . . . beastly.

3 *JURASSIC PARK* Scientists may try to clone a woolly mammoth from a deep-

frozen Siberian specimen, raising the uneasy suspicion that those genetically engineered dinosaurs rampaging through Jurassic Park may not be permanently fictional.

2 *ALIEN*
For those preferring to do their shuddering in private, this novelization has all the horror of the celluloid version. Explore derelict spacecraft if you must,

but don't bring back the crewman who gets 'egged'. The shock when an eight-foot alien bursts out of his chest might kill you.

1 **FRANKENSTEIN**
The aforementioned Victor Frankenstein deserves to top the monster list, but not in his own right. No, that honour must go to the grotesque giant Victor created, standing eight feet tall with yellow eyes and taut skin. Despite a mass-murderous spree, this creature loves his maker.

John Duncombe's Edition.

THE MAN AND THE MONSTER!

OR,

THE FATE OF

FRANKENSTEIN;

A PECULIAR ROMANTIC MELO-DRAMATIC

PANTOMIMIC SPECTACLE,

IN TWO ACTS.

Founded principally on Mrs. Shelly's singular Work, entitled,
"FRANKENSTEIN; or, THE MODERN PROMETHEUS;"
and partly on the French Piece,
"Le Magicien et le Monstre."

BY H. M. MILNER.

THE ONLY EDITION CORRECTLY MARKED FROM THE
PROMPTER'S BOOK, WITH THE STAGE BUSINESS, SITUATION
AND DIRECTIONS.

As it is Performed at

The London Theatres.

London:
PRINTED AND PUBLISHED BY JOHN DUNCOMBE,
19, LITTLE QUEEN STREET, HOLBORN.

10 **THE MISSING LINK**
Adam Pfeffer

9 **KING KONG**
Edgar Wallace
& Merian C Cooper

8 **BEAST**
Peter Benchley

7 **THE GOLEM**
Gustav Meyrink

6 **PERDIDO STREET STATION**
China Mieville

5 **THE HAUNTING OF TOBY JUGG**
Dennis Wheatley

4 **THE ISLAND OF DR MOREAU**
H G Wells

3 **JURASSIC PARK**
Michael Crichton

2 **ALIEN**
Alan Dean Foster

1 **FRANKENSTEIN**
Mary Shelley

"PERHAPS EXTINCT ANIMALS SHOULD BE LEFT EXTINCT"

– JURASSIC PARK

TOP 10

Many a toothy tale has been told since London theatre manager and writer Abraham 'Bram' Stoker's reworking of Carpathian Mountain legend created the most famous horror book ever. In 1897, the arrival of Count Dracula from Transylvania laid the foundations for a mighty edifice of books and films featuring vampires – vampires that now come in many shapes and sizes.

VAMPIRE TALES

10 *DARK LOVER*
A New York turf war between vampires and their slayers erupts Earth's last purebred vamp, bloodthirsty killer Wrath, is pursuing slayers who terminated his parents aeons ago. But he must also introduce his half-breed daughter to the sensual world of the undead.

9 *FANGLAND*
If someone's come up with a grand vampire tale, why reinvent the wheel? Actually, reinventing the original *Dracula* story is exactly what's a-tooth here, as Evangeline Harker (sound familiar?) heads for Romania – and gets well-vamped.

8 *DEAD UNTIL DARK*
How refreshing (as it were) – the development of artificial blood has allowed vampires to abandon their naughty bloodsucking ways and come out of the coffin, but that doesn't stop bloody murder and mayhem soaking the Deep South.

7 *HALFWAY TO THE GRAVE*
Half-vamp Catherine Crawfield hunts for her undead dad. But she's captured by vampire bounty hunter Bones and has to turn into a night stalker . . . so when killers appear, the deadly duo are ready.

6 *INTERVIEW WITH THE VAMPIRE*
A touching father-and-adoptive-daughter vampire tale? Well, sort of. Wee Claudia and surrogate dad Louis are both two-century-old vampires, but she's a world-weary woman trapped in a child's body and he's just weary.

5 THE HISTORIAN
A much-praised, eerie tale, spun around 15th-century prince Vlad the Impaler (family name Dracula) and the fictional character he inspired. A modern academic and his daughter go in search of Vlad's tomb – but is Dracula watching?

4 LET THE RIGHT ONE IN
This is Scandi-vampirism, featuring the relationship between 12-year-old Stockholm lad Oskar and ancient vampire child Eli. It soon surrenders to all those Scandinavian obsessions with the darker sides of real life.

3 CARMILLA
This is from the Victorian casebook of occult doctor Hesselius, as (20 years before Bram Stoker got in on the act) female vampire Carmilla (daringly for the time) takes a fancy to a young woman called Laura – catastrophic for the victim's family and friends.

2 TWILIGHT SERIES
Four books best described as vampire-fantasy-romance novels. They feature the love story of teenager Isabella Swan and 104-year-old vampire Edward Cullen. It ends happily, but not before Ed gives Bella a nip to save her life.

1 SUNSHINE
We're in an alternative universe, following Voodoo Wars between humans and the Others (vampires, demons,

werewolves). Abducted by vamps and used as bait for their enemy, Rae 'Sunshine' Seddon happily discovers magical powers that let her run rings round the fanged ones.

"ONE DOESN'T SIMPLY GLUT ONESELF ON BLOOD"

– INTERVIEW WITH THE VAMPIRE

TOP **10**

Once upon a time . . . yes, it's the traditional beginning to many a tall story, and some writers don't need a second invitation before directing their imagination down memory lane, often somewhat further than anyone can actually remember. That being the case, who can be absolutely sure that some of the truly extraordinary events listed didn't once happen?

HISTORY **MAKERS**

10 *THE IMMORTALS OF MELUHA (SHIVA TRILOGY)*
It's 1900 BC. Lord Ram's empire is withering and under attack. But there's hope – when evil stalks the land and all seems lost, a save-the-day hero will emerge. But is rough diamond Shiva the one?.

9 *THE DA VINCI CODE*
The setting and murderous mayhem might be modern, but the sinister grinding wheels were set in motion two millennia ago, when Jesus (allegedly) married Mary Magdalene. Really? Really!

8 *THE WINTER KING*
This is the book that launched the Warlord Chronicles. In Dumnonia, chaos rules (along with High King Uther Pendragon). Heir Mordred is slain, but will Uther's bastard son Arthur wait around for Mordred's pregnant wife to produce a son?

7 *POSEIDON'S CHILDREN*
It's a nasty legacy from the ancient Gods, as an everyday story of seagoing folk turns nasty when empty, bloodstained boats are found drifting. Perhaps the vast remains of that ancient civilization found on the seabed have something to do with it.

6 *BRIDGE OF BIRDS*
Subtitle – *A Novel of an Ancient China That Never Was*. Weaving ancient legends into a fantasy depiction of Imperial China, this was number one book in *The Chronicles of Master Li and Number Ten Ox* series.

5 *LABYRINTH*
Back in 1209, meet Alaïs. Then jump forward to 2005 and meet Alice. Mysteriously, their lives will intertwine as a dramatic

quest for that oh-so-elusive Holy Grail
unfolds. For the sake of tomorrow's
authors, let's hope it's never found.

4 *THE SONG OF ACHILLES*
The Trojan War is the stuff of
(Greek) legend, and this stunningly

imaginative re-rendering features an almighty (get it?) battle between Gods and kings, not to mention an extraordinary love story (think Achilles and Patroclus).

3 *THE METAMORPHOSES*
Are we talking poet Ovid's famous *magnum opus*? We most certainly are, delving back into the Roman psyche to enjoy an epic examination of the history of the world as Ovid knew it, ending with the deification of Julius Caesar.

2 *THE GREEK MYTHS*
Anyone for mythography? Let's take that as a 'yes' and introduce you to a narrator who will lead you through a compendium of Greek myths, though in truth critics have not been kind regarding the author's interpretations.

1 **THE ONCE AND FUTURE KING**
A topper! We're back with Arthurian legend, as a boy turns into the (still historically mysterious) King Arthur, who must reconcile a belief in chivalry with the prevailing reality that might is always right.

10 *THE IMMORTALS OF MELUHA (SHIVA TRILOGY)*
Amish Tripathi

9 *THE DA VINCI CODE*
Dan Brown

8 *THE WINTER KING*
Bernard Cornwell

7 *POSEIDON'S CHILDREN*
Michael West

6 *BRIDGE OF BIRDS*
Barry Hughart

5 *LABYRINTH*
Kate Mosse

4 *THE SONG OF ACHILLES*
Madeline Miller

3 *THE METAMORPHOSES*
Ovid

2 *THE GREEK MYTHS*
Robert Graves

1 *THE ONCE AND FUTURE KING*
T H White

"EVERYONE LOVES A CONSPIRACY"

– THE DA VINCI CODE

What will the world be like in a hundred years, five hundred, a thousand, a millennium or three? It's not possible to say 'ask me again next century' (or whenever), so instead we must depend on the vivid imagination of writers who can create sci-fi scenarios spun around possibilities that just might come to pass (or not!). Scenarios like these?

FORWARD FORAYS

10 *STARTIDE RISING* Terran spaceship Streaker is crewed by seven humans, one uplifted chimp and 150 uplifted dolphins (uplifted = artificially advanced). Advanced they may be, but when 50,000 abandoned spaceships fail to arouse suspicion . . .

9 *BLOOD MUSIC* If you know a renegade biotechnologist called Vergil Ulam, run for it. You should know he's infected (by his own hand) with noocytes (bio computers based on his own lymphocytes) that mean to take over America (and then the world?).

8 *PLANET OF THE APES* Space travellers Jinn and Phyllis find a manuscript detailing adventures of three humans who landed on Betelgeuse (the ninth-brightest star in the night sky). There they found apes in charge of enslaved humanoids. So what will Jinn and Phyllis do about it?

7 *THE CHRYSALIDS* In post-apocalypse Labrador the community follows a simple, rural life, dedicated to preserving 'normality'. People different in any way are killed or banished to the Fringes. So when 10-year-old David finds he's telepathic . . .

6 *REDEMPTION ARK* A classic space opera (romantic, melodramatic adventure set in deep space). The Conjoiners are battling the Dermarchists as the pursuit of 'hell class' weapons aboard the starship *Nostalgia for Infinity* unfolds.

5 *A FIRE UPON THE DEEP* Welcome to the Milky Way and another extraordinary space opera. Think human expedition seeking ancient data archive that promises untold riches, aliens, unpredictable superhuman intelligences, love, betrayal, space battles, genocide and the rest. Then light blue touch paper and retire.

4 *RINGWORLD* A classic, featuring 200-year-old Louis Gridley Wu. Bored, he joins an expedition probing beyond Known Space. They crash on vast, mysterious Ringworld and, after dramatic adventures, escape with the help of a floating police station (as you do).

3 BOOK OF THE NEW SUN

Surprise! There's a Dying Earth subgenre of science fiction, set when the Earth's sun is cooling – and this is an award-winning example. Disgraced torturer Severian is exiled to Thrax . . . and beyond.

2 VULCAN'S HAMMER

In the 1950s pulp fiction went intergalactic and this classic features Planet Earth run by the Unity organization after a catastrophic world war. Enter Vulcan 3, the ambitious artificial intelligence entity. Can it be stopped?

1 THE SIRENS OF TITAN

The richest man in 22nd-century America is really lucky – or is he? Reserve judgement until Malachi Constant has journeyed to Mars ahead of an interplanetary war, gone on to Mercury, returned to Earth (hostile reception) and finished up on Titan.

"TAKE YOUR
STINKING PAWS
OFF ME"

**– PLANET OF THE
APES**

CHAPTER 4

RELATIVITY

The following lists go to the very heart (literally) of the main driving force behind fiction writing since time immemorial — desire to examine relationships between people, and explore the many and varied avenues down which those relationships can lead. It's the broadest of canvasses, with potential that allows those who are artists with words to paint endless fascinating pictures.

TOP

10

There can be no argument about where to start. The canvas may be broad, but it's love that makes the literary world go round. Falling in love, falling out of love, the joys of love, the dark side of love and all the other passionate possibilities have drawn writers like moths to the candles many of the great romantic authors wrote by.

LOVE **STORIES**

10 *BY GRAND CENTRAL STATION I SAT DOWN AND WEPT*
Does the title say it all? More or less, but it's worth adding that this classic of prose poetry is an autobiographical memoir of a passionate 18-year affair with a married man.

9 *SENSE AND SENSIBILITY*
Published anonymously (by 'A Lady'), this was the first Jane Austen novel to get into print, in 1811. It follows Dashwood sisters Elinor and Marianne as they experience reduced circumstances – but also love, romance and heartbreak.

8 *JANE EYRE*
This one was not anonymous, but published under the name Currer Bell in 1847. The soon-to-be-revealed Charlotte Brontë created a landmark love story featuring a brooding hero coupled with a complex heroine who develops before our very eyes.

7 *ONE DAY*
Sometimes, one day never comes. This is the haunting story of a man and woman who remain friends (only) for 20 years, despite secretly harbouring mutual feelings of love. When they finally fuse, tragedy strikes.

6 *THE BELIEVERS*
The lives and loves of a radical New York Jewish family are forensically examined in this family drama. Their experiences painfully confirm that true-life love, romance and relationships are rarely straightforward.

5 *A MIDSUMMER NIGHT'S DREAM*
The glue that holds the Bard's ever-popular comedy together is love – Theseus and Hippolyta are getting married, Hermia won't marry Demetrius (she loves Lysander), Helena loves Demetrius but he doesn't love her and the king of the fairies and his queen are estranged. Then the fun starts.

4 *THE GRADUATE*
Throw two young people who don't think much of each other together. Have them fall in love despite themselves. Let a vengeful mama persuade the heroine to marry another. And you've set the scene for one of the most entertaining (and satisfying) love stories ever written.

3 *A TALE OF TWO CITIES*

One of Dickens's most complex and interesting characters in the person of Sydney Carton confirms that unrequited love can make for a truly memorable romantic hero.

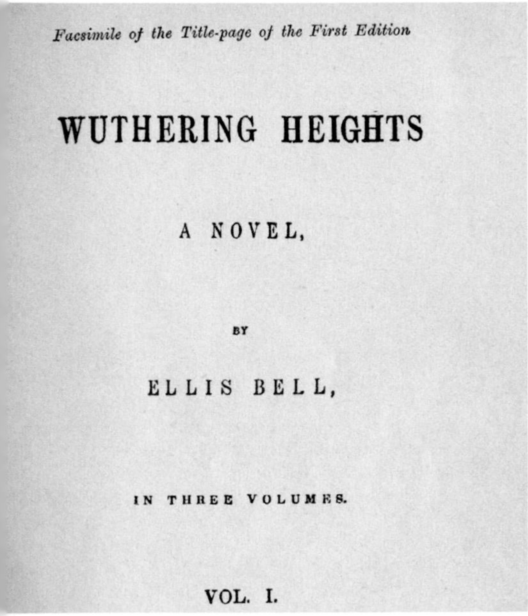

Facsimile of the Title-page of the First Edition

WUTHERING HEIGHTS

A NOVEL,

BY

ELLIS BELL,

IN THREE VOLUMES.

VOL. I.

2 *WUTHERING HEIGHTS*

This time the pseudonym was Ellis Bell, concealing Emily Brontë. She had the sure family touch when it came to drama, creating the darkly romantic Heathcliff, whose love for Catherine (and hers for him) can never be.

1 ***THE HUNCHBACK OF NOTRE DAME***

Love stories don't always end well. This one certainly doesn't – hunchback Quasimodo loves beautiful Gypsy street dancer Esmeralda but she can never be his, and his efforts to save her end in tragedy.

10 ***BY GRAND CENTRAL STATION I SAT DOWN AND WEPT***
Elizabeth Smart

9 ***SENSE AND SENSIBILITY***
Jane Austen

8 ***JANE EYRE***
Charlotte Brontë

7 ***ONE DAY***
David Nicholls

6 ***THE BELIEVERS***
Nicholas Sparks

5 ***A MIDSUMMER NIGHT'S DREAM***
William Shakespeare

4 ***THE GRADUATE***
Charles Webb

3 ***A TALE OF TWO CITIES***
Charles Dickens

2 ***WUTHERING HEIGHTS***
Emily Brontë

---

1 ***THE HUNCHBACK OF NOTRE DAME***
Victor Hugo

There are as many fascinating (and not always dysfunctional) human relationships as there are people in the world, then some, but writers can't help being drawn to those that lead to tears (for the participants and, if done properly, the readers). So let's hear it for a Top Ten that will hopefully produce some serious gushing from those overflowing waterworks.

TEAR JERKERS

10 *ON CHESIL BEACH*
The author says all you need to know in the book's opening sentence 'They were young, educated, and both virgins on this, their wedding night, and they lived in a time when conversation about sexual difficulties was plainly impossible.'

9 *THE ACCCIDENTAL TOURIST*
The death of a son has catastrophic impact on grief-stricken parents in a novel that lays bare the everyday realities of relationships, blurring lines between happiness, sadness and simply carrying on.

8 *DEAR JOHN*
They fall in love one summer. They're parted when he leaves for military service. When he eventually returns she has married another, though still carrying a torch for lost love that can never be rekindled.

7 *THE COLOR PURPLE*
This controversial book deals with the harsh reality of relationships for those who start with less than nothing, chronicling the seriously miserable life of Celie, an abused 14-year-old black girl in the Deep South.

5 *THE GOD OF SMALL THINGS*
This multi-layered story of an Indian family's life and unhappy loves is governed by so-called Love Laws stating 'Who should be loved, and how. And how much.'. Sadly, the rule of law is harsh.

6 *ROOM*
The cruellest sort of 'relationship' as we meet Jack (aged five) and Ma in the close confines of Room, where they are visited by captor Old Nick. An examination of the terrible experiences of women kidnapped and imprisoned for long-term sex.

4 *A THOUSAND SPLENDID SUNS*
The best person to be in Afghan society is not a woman, as we soon discover over half

a century of following the turbulent, interlocking and ultimately tragic stories of Mariam and Laila.

3 *MY SISTER'S KEEPER*
Featuring unrequited love between adults, though the real family drama focuses on Anna, bred as a 'saviour sister' for Kate who suffers from leukaemia. Anna rebels when expected to donate a kidney and it ends up in court.

2 *LOVE STORY*
Not all relationships that end badly are bad. Some of the best tear jerkers involve special love stories brought to an untimely end. And so it is with the funny, romantic and ultimately tragic love of Oliver Barrett IV and Jennifer Cavilleri.

1 *SOPHIE'S CHOICE*
Hobson's Choice is no choice at all. Sophie's Choice is the impossible one that must still be made. Just what that was is not revealed until the end of this searing story of a Holocaust survivor, the man she loves and the man who loves her.

10 *ON CHESIL BEACH*
Ian Mcewan

9 *THE ACCCIDENTAL TOURIST*
Anne Tyler

8 *DEAR JOHN*
Nicholas Sparks

7 *THE COLOR PURPLE*
Alice Walker

6 *THE GOD OF SMALL THINGS*
Arundhati Roy

5 *ROOM*
Emma Donoghue

4 *A THOUSAND SPLENDID SUNS*
Khaled Hosseini

3 *MY SISTER'S KEEPER*
Jodi Picoult

2 *LOVE STORY*
Erich Segal

1 *SOPHIE'S CHOICE*
William Styron

TOP
10

Authors just love messing with minds – first with their own, then with those of the characters they create . . . and finally with those of any readers their imaginative creations ensnare. This collection features ten very different books, but they have one thing in common. They are all gripping psychological dramas, so make ready for a *mêlée* of mind games.

PSYCHODRAMAS

10 *SHUTTER ISLAND*
Boy, this is psychodrama like no other, as two US marshals head for an isolated island hospital for the criminally insane. But is Marshal Edward 'Teddy' Daniels really who he thinks he is?

9 *THE COLLECTOR*
You lack social skills. You collect butterflies. You admire Miranda from afar. You have a windfall and buy a lonely country house. You kidnap Miranda, convinced that you can make her love you, but . . .

8 *ENDURING LOVE*
When a man is killed trying to prevent a child's death, two of the would-be rescuers exchange glances – and for one of them it's the start of a long nightmare, as he's stalked to the point of desperation

by the other. Think de Clerambault's Syndrome.

7 *THE MANCHURIAN CANDIDATE*
Korean War 'hero' Raymond Shaw has been brainwashed to act as a Communist assassin, but one of his fellow captives starts remembering what actually happened in Manchuria. But will he remember enough in time?

6 *GONE GIRL*
Take a marriage that's in deep trouble and present the marital difficulties from both points of view – then make the wife disappear and her husband come under suspicion for her murder. Do you believe one, the other . . . or neither?

5 *THE KILLER INSIDE ME*
A classic mindbender

from 1952. A small-town Texas Deputy Sheriff appears to be nothing more than a small-town Texas Deputy Sheriff, but don't be fooled – he's really a sadistic sociopath and it's not long before bodies start piling up.

4 *REBECCA*
The dark destroyer who dominates this psychological thriller exerts her malign influence from beyond the grave through sinister housekeeper Mrs Danvers, as the naïve 'second Mrs de Winter' suffers mightily by the dead hand of the first.

3 *BEFORE I GO TO SLEEP*
How clever is this one? Imagine waking up every day with no memory of who you are (that's anterograde amnesia for you), and painstakingly

trying to reconstruct a life that may not be quite as it seems.

2 *THE SECRET HISTORY*
The whodunit is abandoned in favour of a whydunit, as the threatening member of a tight group of students is killed by common consent and the reasons for and psychological impact thereof slowly unfold.

1 *THE SILENCE OF THE LAMBS*
Is forensic psychiatrist Dr Hannibal Lektor literature's best/worst-ever baddie? Probably. But his cannibalistic behaviour is (almost) as nothing compared to the fiendish mind games he plays with FBI trainee Clarice Starling.

10 *SHUTTER ISLAND*
Dennis Lehane

9 *THE COLLECTOR*
John Fowles

8 *ENDURING LOVE*
Ian Mcewan

7 *THE MANCHURIAN CANDIDATE*
Richard Condon

6 *GONE GIRL*
Gillian Flynn

5 *THE KILLER INSIDE ME*
Jim Thompson

4 *REBECCA*
Daphne Du Maurier

3 *BEFORE I GO TO SLEEP*
S J Watson

2 *THE SECRET HISTORY*
Donna Tartt

1 *THE SILENCE OF THE LAMBS*
Thomas Harris

"WE'RE NOT MEANT FOR HAPPINESS, YOU AND I"

– REBECCA

TOP 10

The upbeat song in the musical/film of the same name goes 'Oh! what a lovely war', though in truth war is never that. But war has certainly proved to be fertile ground for authors, who have often found inspiration in exploring the impact of the world's seemingly endless armed conflicts on individuals caught up in them. Here are ten such tales.

WARTIME EXPERIENCES

10 *A MONTH IN THE COUNTRY*
This is an 'aftermath' novel, charting the emotions of two World War I veterans when they undertake assignments in and around a country church, trying to recover from remembered horrors.

9 *THE SNOW GOOSE*
A parable of friendship and love. A solitary artist befriends a girl, Fritha, and they nurse a wounded snow goose. The artist is killed after saving many men from Dunkirk beaches, and the goose (embodying his spirit) returns to Fritha.

8 *CAPTAIN CORELLI'S MANDOLIN*
Great love between a fiery Greek girl and a mandolin-playing Italian officer is frustrated by war, as Italian and German occupiers of Cephalonia fall out and Italians are massacred by former allies.

7 *THE HEAT OF THE DAY*
As bombs rain down during the London Blitz, Stella and Robert are lovers. But as time passes a jealous British Intelligence officer who believes Robert is a German spy comes between them in a complex drama of human relationships.

6 *THE GIRL YOU LEFT BEHIND*
It's a time-shifter between World War I and the 21st century, juxtaposing a café behind German lines where Sophie must feed the enemy with London in 2006. The connection? A painting of Sophie by her missing artist husband.

5 *THE ENGLISH PATIENT*
Set against desert war in North Africa, a heartbreaking love story slowly comes to light as a troubled Canadian nurse treats a badly burned mystery man in a bombed-out Italian monastery.

4 *FAIR STOOD THE WIND FOR FRANCE*
In World War II an injured British pilot is sheltered in a French farmhouse and nursed by the farmer's daughter. Yes, they fall in love and, yes, they attempt a dramatic escape from the Germans.

3 *COLD MOUNTAIN*
This time it's the American Civil War and the odyssey of wounded Confederate deserter W P Inman, undertaking the long and perilous journey to Cold Mountain in search of a girl he can't forget.

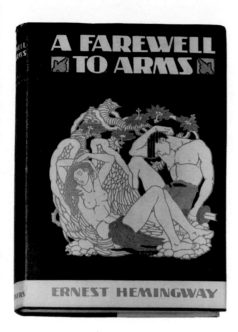

2 *A FAREWELL TO ARMS*
A love story entwined with World War I's turbulent Italian campaign, as wounded American Frederic Henry falls for Catherine Barkley. The course of true love doesn't run smoothly, but run it does – for a while.

1 *BIRDSONG*
In halcyon days when World War I was a distant cloud on the horizon, Stephen Wraysford is sent to France and has a passionate affair with his host's young wife that ends in forced separation. In 1917 the pair meet again, but war has irretrievably damaged them both.

"THERE WAS ONLY VIOLENT DEATH OR LIFE TO CHOOSE BETWEEN"

– BIRDSONG

TOP
10

Time to put pen to paper and create your own top 10 list of novels that have made you cry...

10 _____

9 _____

8 _____

7 _____

6 _____

5 _____

4 _____

3 _____

2 _____

1 _____

TOP 10

Growing old disgracefully is the way to do it, providing you don't mind upsetting just about everyone you come into contact with – and if someone writes about it, that just adds to the general mayhem. Mind you, not all the books on this list feature crusty curmudgeons because there are actually some half-decent senior citizens on parade.

OLD TIMERS

10 LAST ORDERS
Four assorted good old boys (and drinking buddies) set out on a journey from London to scatter the ashes of a fifth in the sea at Margate, fulfilling the last wishes of departed butcher Jack Dodds. Sounds straightforward? If only!

9 *TIME AFTER TIME*
Featuring the comic co-existence of four elderly siblings in Southern Ireland, obsessed with animals and constantly annoying each other. But beneath the apparently light-hearted antics of one-eyed Jasper, April, May and Baby June, a darker reality swirls.

8 *THE EYE OF THE STORM*
Here a powerful matriarch who has finally come to the end of her road manages to control and demean those visiting her death bed, including son Basil and daughter Dorothy.

7 *THE OLD BOYS*
The old boys of their alma mater are now elderly men and the 70-somethings assemble to elect a new president of the Old Boys' Association. But they had fractious rivalries as schoolfellows – and are still at it.

6 *THE TWILIGHT YEARS*
Japanese families care for their own, but that makes life tough when working wife Akiko has to take in her selfish, demanding father-in-law. As he descends into dementia, the old man threatens everything she holds dear.

5 *DOCTOR FAUSTUS*
An ambitious composer makes a pact with the horned one – his soul for 24 years of genius. The result is amazing music, but when the check is finally presented he collapses into madness that consumes his last years.

4 *HAVE THE MEN HAD ENOUGH?*
Touching and funny, this is also a sobering reflection on growing old. Grandma – once the bedrock, always

putting family (especially menfolk) first – needs help as she ages. Do they deliver? Some do, some don't.

3 *ENDING UP*
Devastated by the realities of old age, including physical decay and mental atrophy, the ancient inhabitants of Tuppenny-Hapenny Cottage stay alive by tormenting each other. But when dutiful grandkids arrive for Christmas Day, the festivities implode.

2 *MEMENTO MORI*
Okay, you smug Latin scholars – remind us that the title means 'Remember you must die', which cheerful thought introduces an anonymous phone caller who reminds elderly Dame Lettie Colston and friends of the fact. But who might do such a thing?

1 ***THE DIARIES OF JANE SOMERS***
When a sophisticated woman loses her husband and mother in quick succession, she befriends 90-something Maudie, whose wretched circumstances contrast with her own affluence. It's an unlikely and touching partnership that works well for both.

"BEING OVER SEVENTY IS LIKE BEING ENGAGED IN A WAR"

– MEMENTO MORI

TOP
10

The fairer sex may not always be as saintly as they might be but one thing's for sure – all too often men live up to *their* stereotype by behaving badly. This Top Ten list focuses on some unpleasant literary heroes who have done their (often considerable) bit for the tarnished reputation of the much-maligned male of the species.

BADLY **BEHAVED MEN**

10 *HISTOIRE DE MA VIE* A history of the randy one's life in 12 volumes (he put himself about a bit), this is the autobiography of a womanizer and adventurer whose prowess was such that his name became synonymous with 'great lover'. So who knew he spent years as a librarian?

9 *SILAS MARNER* George Eliot's simple tale of a reclusive weaver's redemption was possible thanks to evil William Dane, who accused his best friend of a theft he himself committed and later married the wrongly disgraced Silas Marner's fiancée.

8 *TAKE A GIRL LIKE YOU* In the prudish 1950s the story of Jenny Bunn's move from gritty North

to sophisticated South was risqué, as her (then laudable) determination to preserve her virginity for the wedding night comes under assault from cruel and caddish Patrick Standish..

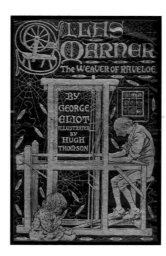

7 *WARLEGGAN* In a grim echo of 21st-century opprobrium, the baddie in this sweeping saga of 18th-century

Cornish life is a banker. George Warleggan steals our dashing hero's girl and comes within a hair's-breadth of ruining him.

6 *UNCLE TOM'S CABIN* This anti-slavery novel needed a simply appalling slave owner, who duly appeared in the vicious form of Simon Legree, who intends to break slave Tom's spirit and Christian beliefs.

5 *TINKER TAILOR SOLDIER SPY* When you're a mole in the British Secret Service, directed by a Russian spy-master who knows the one weakness of dangerous opponent George Smiley, you naturally seduce Smiley's wife to distract him – even though he's a friend and colleague. And that bad-boy traitor is . . .

4 *CLARISSA*
Enter one of the most dastardly dogs in 18th-century fiction – unspeakable Robert Lovelace. After tricking Clarissa into eloping, he stashes her in a brothel and when she refuses his marriage-for-money proposals, rapes her.

3 *THE GINGER MAN*
In post-World-War-II Dublin, American Sebastian Dangerfield is married with a young child, studying law. Sounds a bit dull? Nope – devilishly charming Dangerfield is seriously into drinking, womanizing and general bad-boyism.

2 *RIDERS*
With bulging jodhpurs and a thwack of his riding crop, Rutshire's resident stud (brutish aristocrat Rupert Campbell-Black) cuts a seriously dissolute swathe through the horsey set's fillies. But can he out-gallop good guy Jake?

1 *THE TALENTED MR RIPLEY*
'Identity thief and murderer' would go down well on a bad-boy job application form, and by heck Tom Ripley's good at it. He fools everyone (apart from one he has to kill) before getting away with the unfortunate, deceased Dickie's fortune.

10 *HISTOIRE DE MA VIE*
Giacomo Casanova

9 *SILAS MARNER*
George Eliot

8 *TAKE A GIRL LIKE YOU*
Kingsley Amis

7 *WARLEGGAN*
Winston Graham

6 *UNCLE TOM'S CABIN*
Harriet Beecher Stowe

5 *TINKER TAILOR SOLDIER SPY*
John Le Carre

4 *CLARISSA*
Samuel Richardson

3 *THE GINGER MAN*
J P Donleavy

2 *RIDERS*
Jilly Cooper

1 *THE TALENTED MR RIPLEY*
Patricia Highsmith

"IT WAS NOT WISE TO UNDERESTIMATE ONE'S OPPONENT"

– THE TALENTED MR RIPLEY

TOP 10

Abiding authorial interest in probing human relationships doesn't always have to be an exercise in angst and grief. It's true that people on pages often behave badly, but even so their antics sometimes turn out to be rather entertaining, and (as some of the books on this list confirm) this can often lead to hilarious encounters of the side-splitting kind.

HUMOUROUS HAPPENINGS

10 *THE EXPEDITION OF HUMPHREY CLINKER*
This is an early (published in 1771) example of authorial ingenuity. The lives, loves and thoughts of central characters are examined through their letters, humour residing in very different perceptions of the same events.

9 *VILE BODIES*
The pointed pen of Evelyn Waugh fatally stabs the mores of London society's bright young things between two world wars. Although apparently a traditional romantic comedy, amusement at Adam Fenwick-Symes' vain pursuit of Nina has a satirical edge.

8 *THE LIFE AND LOVES OF A SHE-DEVIL*
Anything featuring an ugly and embittered wife who gains truly spectacular revenge by destroying her unfaithful husband and his fragrant mistress can't possibly be funny, can it? Oh yes it can!

7 *THE WIMBLEDON POISONER*
A man who sets out to poison his wife can have no place on a humorous list. Until, that is, it all goes horribly wrong when neighbours and friends are accidently wiped out – then Inspector Rush closes in.

6 *A FAIRY TALE OF NEW YORK*
You're perennially penniless and arriving in New York (from Ireland) with your late wife's body. It makes sense to take employment at a funeral home to defray interment costs – the start of an engaging journey full of comic pathos.

5 *TALES OF THE CITY*
The city is San Francisco, the humour is sharp and there's extremely funny observation of assorted characters who memorably flounder around in the maelstrom that is America's most 'liberated' of cities.

4 *PORTERHOUSE BLUE*
What exactly is a 'Porterhouse Blue'? Well, it's a fatal stroke engendered by the legendary culinary excesses of Cambridge's Porterhouse College. In a telling satire on university life, the Master's death sparks an entertaining struggle between traditionalists and reformers.

3 *LAKE WOEBEGONE DAYS*
If ever there was a case for an award-winning audio book, this is it. The dry narrative style of author Garrison Keillor adds mightily to his already-hilarious written commentary on Midwestern America.

2 *HIGH FIDELITY*
You're getting on (mid-thirties). You own a record store. Your girlfriend has left you. You revisit former relationships and set out to track down five ex-girlfriends. You're Rob Fleming, hero of one of the funniest record-shop books ever written.

1 *PORTNOY'S COMPLAINT*
One of America's greatest authors arrived with a bang (as it were) in 1969. This comic monologue of a 'lust-ridden, mother-addicted young Jewish bachelor' may be hilarious (then as now) but candid focus on sexuality was controversial at the time.

10 *THE EXPEDITION OF HUMPHREY CLINKER*
Tobias Smollett

9 *VILE BODIES*
Evelyn Waugh

8 *THE LIFE AND LOVES OF A SHE-DEVIL*
Fay Weldon

7 *THE WIMBLEDON POISONER*
Nigel Williams

6 *A FAIRY TALE OF NEW YORK*
J P Donleavy

5 *TALES OF THE CITY*
Armistead Maupin

4 *PORTERHOUSE BLUE*
Tom Sharpe

3 *LAKE WOEBEGONE DAYS*
Garrison Keillor

2 *HIGH FIDELITY*
Nick Hornby

1 *PORTNOY'S COMPLAINT*
Philip Roth

TOP
10

Is it better to have loved and lost than never having loved at all? It's a moot point, but many an author has come up with painful stories of flawed relationships that end in tears, or through unfortunate circumstances beyond the control of participants. So this Top Ten is infused with the sorrow of lost love – however it vanished.

LOST **LOVES**

10 *WASHINGTON SQUARE*

In 1870s New York a father thinks his daughter is plain and dull. When Catherine finds love he assumes the suitor is a fortune hunter and spends years trying to break the engagement, eventually succeeding - losing her in the process.

9 *THE SORROWS OF YOUNG WERTHER*

Johann Wolfgang von Goethe crafted this tragic tale of a young man who takes his own life after accepting that passionate love for a married peasant girl can never be consummated.

8 *AN EQUAL MUSIC*

Violinist Michael never forgot his love for pianist Julia. When they meet again she's married, and they begin an affair.

But in confronting the realities of their lives, lost love found is lost again.

7 THE BRIDGES OF MADISON COUNTY

A lonely married woman has a brief affair with a passing photographer who's recording those Iowan bridges. Their four-day encounter is passionate, colouring the rest of her life.

6 CHÉRI

Fred Peloux (Chéri to his friends) has engaged in a long-term affair with an older woman, Léa. Believing it to be casual, he marries someone else, only to realize that he really loves Léa. But it's too late, and an attempt to rekindle the flame of true love fails.

5 THE WANDERER

In provincial France, 17-year-old Augustin Meaulnes falls madly in love with Yvonne at a party, but doesn't find her again for years. They are finally married, but Augustin soon departs and Yvonne dies in childbirth.

4 THE JEWEL IN THE CROWN

The love of an upper-class Englishwoman and a public-school-educated Indian in 1940s British India was never likely to end happily, and doesn't. She's raped, he's imprisoned, she dies having his child. Ouch!

3 THE END OF THE AFFAIR

London. World War II. Writer begins affair with woman married to dull bureaucrat. Writer wracked by lover's refusal to leave husband. Writer's apartment bombed. Lover breaks off affair, after promising God not to continue seeing him if he lives through bomb-blast.

2 BEFORE SHE MET ME

Sometimes love is not lost, but thrown away. Graham Hendrick escapes a loveless marriage and finds the woman of his dreams, but soon irrational suspicions about her former life precipitate them into a downward spiral.

1 THE REMAINS OF THE DAY
Sometimes, lost love is never found in the first place. Butler Stevens reflects on his long-ago love for housekeeper Miss Kenton, which was mutual. But neither declared their feelings, and the opportunity of a life together was lost forever.

TOP **10**

When all's said and done, there's something awfully reassuring about happy endings, so authors are well aware of the benefits that can accrue from engendering a conclusive feelgood factor. As this Top Ten list lavishly illustrates, readers can experience real pleasure if rewarded with a warm sense of satisfaction after the last page is turned and the book is closed.

HAPPY **ENDINGS**

9 *PS:I LOVE YOU*
Happy and sad can be sides of the same coin. When Holly loses the love of her life to illness, he has planned ahead. Each 'do this' letter he's left (ending 'PS, I Love You') helps her progress towards a (happy) new future.

8 *FOLLOW THE STARS HOME*
When Dianne's husband Tim learns their child will be less than perfect he vanishes, leaving her to cope alone. Tim's brother Alan loyally helps, but she can't accept his love – until a special 12-year-old intervenes.

7 *TRAINSPOTTING*
The chaotic lives of Scottish heroin addicts might seem a somewhat unlikely entrant in the happy-ending stakes, but there is an uplifting message to be found – choose life.

6 *NORTH AND SOUTH*
Cosseted Margaret is uprooted when family circumstances change, and transplanted from gentle South to grim and gritty industrial North. She clashes with the hard-driving Master of Marlborough Mills, and it's not until the very end that undeclared mutual attraction turns to declared love.

5 *OUR MUTUAL FRIEND*
The last novel by the Victorian master is about love and money, not necessarily in that order. After many a Dickensian twist and turn, displaced heir John Harmon gets the girl – and the loot.

10 *LORNA DOONE*
How can this 18th-century drama set on bleak Exmoor have a happy ending? John and Lorna are in love, but ruthless Carver covets Lorna and shoots her on her wedding day. Don't worry – she survives to live happily ever after. He doesn't.

4 *COLD COMFORT FARM*
Orphan Flora Poste heads for remote Cold Comfort farm, where she is reluctantly accepted by distant relatives Aunt Ada Doom and the Starkadders, before proceeding to sort out everyone's festering problems.

3 *THE SHIPPING NEWS*
In New York it begins badly for Quoyle – suicidal parents, wife tries to sell kids to sex trafficker before getting killed with lover. But in Newfoundland it ends well – new job, friendships, girlfriend, LIFE.

2 *PRIDE AND PREJUDICE*
One of the most famous happy endings in history, as Jane and Mr Bingley finally get together, while decent Mr Darcy sorts out disgraced Lydia's elopement and persuades Elizabeth to marry him.

1 *TO KILL A MOCKINGBIRD*
This one finishes atop every list of happy endings, impressive for a novel dealing with rape, murder and racial inequality. But lawyer Atticus Finch remains the best of fathers and the persecutor of kids Scout and Jem comes to a sticky end.

10 *LORNA DOONE*
R D Blackmore

9 *PS:I LOVE YOU*
Cecilia Ahern

8 *FOLLOW THE STARS HOME*
Luanne Rice

7 *TRAINSPOTTING*
Irvine Walsh

6 *NORTH AND SOUTH*
Elizabeth Gaskell

5 *OUR MUTUAL FRIEND*
Charles Dickens

4 *COLD COMFORT FARM*
Stella Gibbons

3 *THE SHIPPING NEWS*
Annie Proulx

2 *PRIDE AND PREJUDICE*
Jane Austen

1 *TO KILL A MOCKINGBIRD*
Harper Lee

"YOU RARELY WIN, BUT SOMETIMES YOU DO"

– TO KILL A MOCKINGBIRD

TOP 10

Happy endings appeal mightily in feelgood-factor terms, but not all authors see it as their duty to send readers on their way with a singing heart. Sadly (a word chosen with care), many writers are less interested in happy outcomes than the darker possibilities provided by flawed human relationships, which often lead to the sort of unhappy endings listed here.

UNHAPPY ENDINGS

10 *ANNA KARENINA* Unhappily married Anna has an affair with dashing Count Vronsky, but their passion is doomed by society's disapproval and growing conviction that Vronsky no longer loves her. She ends it beneath train wheels.

9 *WIDE SARGASSO SEA* Gate-crashing Jane Eyre, this is the story of Antoinette/Bertha, Mr Rochester's first wife – explaining how she became mad (if indeed she did), endured incarceration in the attic of Thornfield Hall and eventually committed suicide.

8 *THE METAMORPHOSIS* Any novel that starts with the hero waking up to find he's a giant bug (which may make him late for work) is bound to end badly, and so it proves. Poor Gregor must permanently inhabit his room, dying there alone and unloved.

7 *THE WOODLANDERS* A classic Hardy knife-twister. Giles loves Grace. Grace loves Giles but marries unworthy Edgar. Edgar deserts her for another, before returning. Grace flees. Unwell Giles provides shelter, thereby dying. Grace returns to miserable marriage. Marty always loves Giles and mourns alone.

6 *THE BLIND ASSASSIN* Iris had an unhappy marriage (and husband Richard raped sister Laura). Laura loved writer Alex, who had an affair with Iris. Laura committed suicide, Iris became estranged from daughter Aimee. Richard committed suicide. Elderly Iris dies alone. No joy there, then.

5 *THE HORSE WHISPERER* Daughter Grace and mum Annie head for Montana after an accident injures Grace and horse Pilgrim. Horse whisperer Tom restores Pilgrim, but he and Annie fall in love. When Grace finds out she rides off, and Tom dies saving Grace and Pilgrim from stampeding mustangs.

4 *THE PICTURE OF DORIAN GRAY* Oscar Wilde's only novel didn't go down well with prudish Victorians, as the once-beautiful hero ends up looking at a picture of his raddled older self in painful reminder of a debauched life.

3 *FOR WHOM THE BELL TOLLS*
During the brutal Spanish Civil War, American Robert Jordan must dynamite a bridge. He falls in love with spirited Maria, blows the bridge and sacrifices himself so that Maria can escape pursuing Fascists.

2 *REVOLUTIONARY ROAD*
Connecticut suburbanites Frank and April Wheeler are energized by the idea of a move to Paris, which collapses when April gets pregnant. When Frank rekindles an old affair she tries to self-abort, dying of blood loss and leaving Frank devastated.

1 *ONE FLEW OVER THE CUCKOO'S NEST*
It's insanely funny when inmates take over the psychiatric ward, devastatingly sad when rambunctious Randle Patrick McMurphy's anarchic campaign of disruption ends with him lobotomized.

10 ANNA KARENINA
Leo Tolstoy

9 WIDE SARGASSO SEA
Jean Rhys

8 THE METAMORPHOSIS
Franz Kafka

7 THE WOODLANDERS
Thomas Hardy

6 THE BLIND ASSASSIN
Margaret Atwood

5 THE HORSE WHISPERER
Nicholas Evans

4 THE PICTURE OF DORIAN GRAY
Oscar Wilde

3 FOR WHOM THE BELL TOLLS
Ernest Hemingway

2 REVOLUTIONARY ROAD
Richard Yates

1 ONE FLEW OVER THE CUCKOO'S NEST
Ken Kesey

"SHE HAS FORGOT 'EE AT LAST, ALTHOUGH FOR HER YOU DIED"

– THE WOODLANDERS

TOP 10

Getting your wires crossed is a neat metaphor for any misunderstanding, but it shouldn't be forgotten that the expression comes from the weird and wonderful world of electricity, where reversed wires can cause a nasty bang, puff of smoke and dead circuit. Will all the wires that get crossed in this list end in disaster? Read on . . .

MISUNDERSTANDINGS

10 *DECEPTION*
A case of 'not understanding', because comprehension of this clever dialogue-only novel only dawns on the reader towards the end, as an American and his married English lady converse before and after making love.

9 *THE MISUNDERSTANDING*
Call misunderstandings the misunderstanding, and write about a scarred war veteran who must work and a bored, beautiful woman who's rich. Have them fall passionately in love, then disassemble the relationship in a welter of mutual misunderstanding. Surely a misunderstanding must!

8 *NO BED FOR BACON*
Turns out that not all misunderstandings are tragic. As Will Shakespeare struggles with Love's Labour Wunne and Francis Bacon covets one of Queen Elizabeth's beds, Viola Compton disguises herself as a boy and catches the Bard's eye . . .

7 *SCOOP*
If your name is William Boot and you write nature notes for the Daily Beast, you might well be mistaken for war correspondent John Courtney Boot and sent off to cover a nasty African war.

6 *THE MIERNIK DOSSIER*
It's 1959. An assorted crowd of expats in Geneva include American spy Paul Christopher. A small group embark on a Cadillac ride from Switzerland to Sudan, each spinning a web of deception to mislead the others.

5 *THE LITTLE FRIEND*
Crossed wires indeed, as young Harriet (obsessed with her brother's death by hanging) trails the baddie she supposes to be the killer around town – while he assumes she's out to get him for altogether different reasons.

4 *A PASSAGE TO INDIA*
An innocent Muslim doctor is accused of sexual assault by an Englishwoman in 1920s British India, when a disorientating cave echo causes her to mistakenly believe she's been attacked.

3 *SPIES*
An elderly man reminisces about a wartime misunderstanding, when as

boys he and a friend erroneously believed the friend's mother was a German spy, following her in an attempt to find the truth – which turned out to be far from their fevered imaginings.

2 *THE GO-BETWEEN*

One summer, poor boy Leo stays with upper-class school friend Marcus. He innocently becomes a go-between for lovers Marian (sister to Marcus) and tenant farmer Ted. Naïve Leo entirely fails to understand the nature of their relationship and potentially tragic consequences of his involvement.

1 *ATONEMENT*

In 1935, 13-year-old Briony witnesses a sexual moment between older sister Cecelia and housekeeper's son Robbie, which she misinterprets as assault. Later, she sees them making love and assumes it's rape. Unfortunately her misunderstandings have dire consequences.

"YOU FLEW TOO NEAR THE SUN AND YOU WERE SCORCHED"

– THE GO-BETWEEN

10 DECEPTION
Philip Roth

9 THE MISUNDERSTANDING
Irene Nemirovsky

8 NO BED FOR BACON
Caryl Brahms And S J Simon

7 SCOOP
Evelyn Waugh

6 THE MIERNIK DOSSIER
Charles McCarry

5 THE LITTLE FRIEND
Donna Tartt

4 A PASSAGE TO INDIA
E M Forster

3 SPIES
Michael Frayn

2 THE GO-BETWEEN
L P Hartley

1 ATONEMENT
Ian McEwan

Obviously, life was much more romantic way back when than it is now, to judge from the enthusiasm with which writers have looked to historical settings when crafting their romantic tales. Of course the past wasn't really that romantic (quite the contrary for most people), but the whole point is to transport readers from the tangible present into another world.

HISTORICAL **ROMANCES**

10 *WAVERLEY*
Considered the first historical novel, this 1814 winner charts the dramatic experiences of Edward Waverley during the Jacobite rebellion, switching from the Hannoverian side to fight for Bonnie Prince Charlie at the Battle of Prestonpans.

9 *MAID OF BUTTERMERE*
The maid was beautiful shepherdess Mary Robinson. In 1802 she bigamously married con-man John Hatfield ('Colonel Hope') who claimed to be the brother of an earl – and was later hanged. This novel embroiders their fascinating story.

8 *THE DRESSMAKER*
The history stretches back to World War II. Naïve, 17-year-old Liverpudlian Rita lives with two aunts,

dressmaker Nellie and worldly-wise Marge. When Rita starts seeing an American, dreams of becoming a GI bride end badly.

7 *THE SEALED LETTER*
Based on a Victorian scandal, this is a tale of forbidden love, secrets and betrayal. Emily hasn't seen old friend Helen for years, and when they meet again reluctantly helps the unhappy wife have an affair. But renewed friendship soon unravels in spectacular fashion.

6 *THE KING'S GENERAL*
Set in the English Civil War, this West Country drama follows the fortunes of Richard and Honor, lovers who never married. After Parliamentarians take Cornwall, Royalist Richard is wounded during a revolt, tended by Honor – and betrayed.

5 *WINTER IN MADRID*
An unusual historical setting – Madrid in 1940, after the Spanish Civil War. This spy-drama-cum-lost-love story is interesting in its own right, but also for

its detailed description of harsh life in postbellum Madrid.

4 *THE BLUE FLOWER*
An almost eerily compelling evocation of the past, as young Fritz (later German philosopher and romantic poet Novalis) stuns his family in 1794 by declaring love for, and intention to marry, 12-year-old Sophie.

3 *THE PILLARS OF THE EARTH*
Building a medieval minster was a massive

undertaking – and this sweeping novel featuring the building of Kingsbridge Cathedral in the 12th century (and dramatic lives and loves surrounding the enterprise) is almost as ambitious.

2 *GIRL WITH A PEARL EARRING*
What happens when an author hangs an enigmatic Old Master copy on her wall for years? She inevitably crafts a compelling fiction starring the Dutch painter (Vermeer) and his young sitter, The Girl with a Pearl Earring.

1 *MUSIC AND SILENCE*
If you want to write an unexpected historical romance, choose the court of Christian IV of Denmark in 1629-1630 and explore the (true-life) ending of Christian's second marriage and start of his third, then add a fictional love affair to froth the mix.

10 *WAVERLEY*
Walter Scott

9 *MAID OF BUTTERMERE*
Melvyn Bragg

8 *THE DRESSMAKER*
Beryl Bainbridge

7 *THE SEALED LETTER*
Emma Donoghue

6 *THE KING'S GENERAL*
Daphne Du Maurier

5 *WINTER IN MADRID*
C J Sansom

4 *THE BLUE FLOWER*
Penelope Fitzgerald

3 *THE PILLARS OF THE EARTH*
Ken Follett

2 *GIRL WITH A PEARL EARRING*
Tracy Chevalier

1 *MUSIC AND SILENCE*
Rose Tremain

"BE SORRY THAT YOU MADE ME SO HAPPY"

– THE PILLARS OF THE EARTH

TOP
10

There's something about families that brings out the best in people – and sadly in some instances the worst in people. The family is a unit that underpins societies the world over, but where once the demands of survival cemented families together, books on this list suggest that the modern world sometimes offers plenty of opportunity for familial friction and fragmentation.

FAMILY **DRAMAS**

10 *A HOUSE AND ITS HEAD*

A gender struggle within a Victorian family? Surely not. But then again, when despotic Duncan Edgeworth (constantly sparring with wife Ellen and two growing daughters) hastily marries a younger woman after being widowed, her wilful ways set in train a series of searing events.

9 *THE FORSYTE SAGA*

This series deals with the nouveaux-riche Forsytes, as Soames Forsyte attempts to confirm the family's status by acquiring possessions, including reluctant wife Irene (eventually making the point by raping her). With their relationship at its heart, the saga rumbles on over two generations.

8 *THE BROTHERS KARAMAZOV*

Featuring the author's recurring themes of guilt and salvation, the troubled story of the Karamazov brothers after patriarch Fyodor is murdered dwells darkly on themes of faith and morality.

7 *A HOUSE FOR MR BISWAS*

A tale of the two families of Mohun Biswas - his own as he grows up in Trinidad, and the one he joins (rather against his will) by marrying Shama Tulsi. He doesn't thrive in the new household, and strives for independence from the traditional Hindu family.

6 *THE POISONWOOD BIBLE*

This cautionary tale of an American missionary family in the Belgian Congo deals with Nathan Price's stubborn attempts to baptize uncooperative villagers, while four daughters gradually come to understand and appreciate the local culture.

5 *MY FAMILY AND OTHER ANIMALS*

This is an enchanting memoir of the eccentric English Durrell family, living in glorious freedom on the Greek island of Corfu in the 1930s. Gerald entertainingly describes local fauna, including brother Lawrence.

4 *THE SON*
A stirring American family saga ranging from 19th-century Comanche attacks to 20th-century oil booms, charting the rise and rise of a Texas family as they strive for land, influence and power.

3 *A THOUSAND ACRES*
With apologies to Shakespeare, whose King Lear provides the father-and-three-daughters plot framework, this family drama revolves around an Iowa farm. When one daughter refuses her share, secrets start to emerge.

2 *THE GATHERING*
Uncomfortable truths hover when a mother and eight siblings gather in Dublin for the wake of brother Liam Hegarty, an alcoholic suicide victim. Narrated by 39-year-old Veronica, who probes the family's past to try and make sense of his death.

1 *THE MAN WHO LOVED CHILDREN*
Unsparing analysis of a dysfunctional Australian family in 1940 Sydney. Dad provides well but mum is selfish, snobbish and a poor household manager, spoiling everything. Transplanted to America for a 1960s revival.

10 *A HOUSE AND ITS HEAD*
Ivy Compton-burnett

9 *THE FORSYTE SAGA*
John Galsworthy

8 *THE BROTHERS KARAMAZOV*
Fyodor Dostoevsky

7 *A HOUSE FOR MR BISWAS*
V S Naipaul

6 *THE POISONWOOD BIBLE*
Barbara Kingsolver

5 *MY FAMILY AND OTHER ANIMALS*
Gerald Durrell

4 *THE SON*
Philip Mayer

3 *A THOUSAND ACRES*
Jane Smiley

2 *THE GATHERING*
Anne Enwright

1 *THE MAN WHO LOVED CHILDREN*
Christina Stead

TOP 10

Some memorable relationships in literature do not involve lovers, but friends. In exceptional cases, friendship can go far beyond the conventional and assume a central role in the lives of those involved, as this list confirms. But it would be wrong to assume that great friendships are always benign, as sometimes the passions stirred can actually prove to be destructive.

FRIENDS

10 *EMBERS*
It's 1942, and an elderly Hungarian general is dining with an old friend from military academy who had vanished from his life for 41 years. A brilliant examination of the nature of friendship, and changing values.

9 *FEMALE FRIENDS*
Evacuated from wartime London, three girls become friends – a friendship that survives turbulent marriages, shared lovers and demanding children in this witty, sharp, compassionate novel.

8 *THE FOLDED LEAF*
In 1920s Chicago an unlikely friendship forms between awkward Lymie Peters (who gets good grades) and star athlete Spud Latham (who doesn't). They're best buddies, but as adolescence turns to young adulthood Lymie lusts after Sally Forbes, but she loves Spud and the friendship sunders.

7 *THE SEA OF FERTILITY*
A Japanese epic stretching from 1912 to 1975. Law student Shigekuni Honda becomes a respected judge, dealing with reincarnations of schoolfriend Kiyoaki Matsugae in an attempt to defy their karma.

6 *HOLES*
Don't get confused by back stories involving 19th-century Texas and Latvia, instead focus on the unlikely but powerful friendship of ill-matched duo Stanley Yelnats and Zoro at delinquent camp, as they're forced to dig holes in search of long-buried outlaw treasure.

5 *THE KITE RUNNER*
Momentous events unfold in Afghanistan as the monarchy collapses, Soviets invade and the Taliban triumph. Amir and his friend Hassan engage in innocent kite flying, but friendship founders on a terrible act of betrayal by Amir.

4 *THE GOLDFINCH*
A complex tale of Theo Decker's troubled adolescence and young adulthood, shot through with an on-off-on close relationship with Boris. It begins with shoplifting and dope smoking in Las Vegas and culminates in a dramatic shoot-out in Amsterdam.

3 OF MICE AND MEN

Greater love hath no man . . . During America's Great Depression migrant workers George Milton and Lennie Small dream of owning land. But things get out of hand when they find ranch work, and in the end George shoots gentle giant Lennie to save him from a lynch mob.

2 TALKING IT OVER

Nerdy Stuart and flamboyant Oliver have been best friends since school, despite being so different. But when best man Oliver falls in love with Stuart's bride Gillian at the wedding, things can never again be the same.

1 THE GOLDEN NOTEBOOK

Disturbed Anna Wulf's notebooks are opened, revealing the story of a special friendship. Remarkable conversations between Anna and Molly reveal that they've stood by each other through all the vicissitudes life has thrown at them.

"WE LOOKED AT EACH OTHER AND JUST LAUGHED"

– *THE GOLDFINCH*

TOP 10

Girls behaving badly? Heaven forbid – but that thought hasn't stopped a generation of authors (mostly of the female persuasion) chronicling the lives, loves, trials and tribulations of young women coming to terms with the fact that (with occasional ignoble exceptions) those of the female persuasion are expected to stand firmly on their own two feet, because equality (almost) rules.

CHICK LIT

10 *MR MAYBE* Heart versus head? It's a classic chick-lit dilemma as big-spending 27-year-old Libby Mason has to decide between penniless but tasty Nick and boring but fabulously rich Ed. She's always intended to marry money, but now . . .

9 *THE NANNY DIARIES* The shock-horror story of a university student who takes a nannying job with a wealthy Manhattan family (X). As the Xs marriage comes under strain Nanny gets far more deeply involved with family life than a mere employee ever should.

8 *HEAD OVER HEELS* Single mum Jessie never revealed the identity of son Oliver, but then big daddy moves in next door with glam wife. He's interested in getting closer to Jessie, who can't see a happy ending. But is her assumption right?

7 *YOUNG WIVES' TALES* Lucy steals Rose's husband but domestic responsibilities drag. Rose makes the best of lonely single motherhood. Connie's successfully juggling marriage, kids and work. As the three grapple with modern life, surprises await.

6 *SEX AND THE CITY* The chick-lit true-life manual, as New York newspaper columnist Candace Bushnell charts a hilarious (and poignant) course through the city's clubs, bars, trendy eateries and parties as the ambassador for 30-something women in search of the glamorous life – and love.

5 *SOMETHING BLUE* Darcy Rhone is beautiful, in love with Rex and secure in a lifelong friendship with Rachel. But when Rex calls off the wedding Darcy experiences the ultimate betrayal. She flees to London, only to discover that she isn't as irresistible as she assumes.

4 *WATERMELON* Sweet-natured 29-year-old Claire has it all – adorable husband James, good job, great pad. Her first baby's a bonus, until James tells her in the recovery room that he's leaving. Back in Dublin, her quirky family helps her heal and start over.

3 *CHRISTMAS AT ROSIE HOPKINS' SWEET SHOP*

Rosie's eagerly anticipating Christmas in the country village of Lipton. Her boyfriend is flying from Australia to join the family celebrations. But when tragedy strikes, Rosie's world shatters.

2 *THE SECRET DREAMWORLD OF A SHOPAHOLIC*

Becky Bloomwood is the chick-lit heroine par excellence, overspending wildly as she cuts a swathe through trendy London shops, even as she crosses swords with rich and eligible men.

1 *BRIDGET JONES' DIARY*

The diary that started a chick-lit avalanche, as 30-something Bridget (supported throughout by loyal friends) reveals painful angst about her weight, over-indulgence in cigarettes and booze, job worries – and most of all love life.

10 *MR MAYBE*
Jane Green

9 *THE NANNY DIARIES A NOVEL*
Nicola Kraus

8 *HEAD OVER HEELS*
Jill Mansell

7 *YOUNG WIVES' TALES*
Adele Parks

6 *SEX AND THE CITY*
Candace Bushnell

5 *SOMETHING BLUE*
Emily Griffin

4 *WATERMELON*
Marian Keyes

3 *CHRISTMAS AT ROSIE HOPKINS' SWEET SHOP*
Jenny Colgan

2 *THE SECRET DREAMWORLD OF A SHOPAHOLIC*
Sophie Kinsella

1 *BRIDGET JONES' DIARY*
Helen Fielding

"WHY DOES NOTHING EVER WORK OUT?"

– BRIDGET JONES' DIARY

TOP 10

What is it about old folk (those aged, say, 30 or more) that can seem so tiresome to bright young things (those aged, say, 20 or less) – and *vice versa*? And why do parents sometimes find their children intolerable, and kids insist that their parents are unbearable? It's all part of those fascinating generation games, which are not always destructive.

GENERATION GAMES

10 *OLD GORIOT*
In post-Napoleonic Paris Father Goriot lives in penury, having generously supported two married daughters. He has interesting encounters with residents of his boarding house but both daughters disappoint. And when he suffers a stroke and dies, after raging at his daughters' disrespect, neither attends the funeral.

9 *UNLESS*
Narrator Reta Winters is a 44-year-old writer, wondering what reasons led daughter Norah to drop out of university and take to the streets with a sign on her chest reading GOODNESS. A tricky parental problem indeed.

8 *WISE CHILDREN*
On the birthday of twins Dora and Nora Chance (aged 75), and natural father Melchior Hazard (aged 100), Dora reflects on his rejection, her 'official' father Peregrine Hazard (incest there?), guardian Grandma Chance and life in a theatrical family.

7 *HIDEOUS KINKY*
Autobiographical, or what? By Esther Freud (daughter of painter Lucien, grand-daughter of Sigmund), this is the story of a mother who settles in a cheap Marrakesh hotel (funded by artist dad in London). But the daughters rebel.

6 *BONJOUR TRISTESSE*
Spending the summer with libertine father Raymond on the Riviera, 17-year-old Cécile enjoys the lifestyle and likes the latest mistress. But when Raymond announces he's marrying sophisticated Anne, Cécile must battle for his affections.

5 *MY SON, MY SON*
The story of two successful men - dramatist William Essex and Irish friend Dermot O'Riordan – and their respective sons, also friends. But as fathers learn the hard way, sons sometimes don't turn out as they hope.

4 *THE JOY LUCK CLUB*
In 1949, four Chinese women have recently arrived in San Francisco. United in loss but willing to hope, they form the Joy Luck Club. It's the start of a wonderful examination of the sometimes painful connection between mothers and daughters.

3 *ORANGES ARE NOT THE ONLY FRUIT*
Adopted Jeanette is brought up within the super-strict Pentecostal community as one of 'God's chosen', with a future in missionary work. But then, aged 16, she rebels, leaving it all for the girl she loves.

2 *WE NEED TO TALK ABOUT KEVIN*
There's been a school massacre – and your son's Kevin's the killer. A tough place to be for Eva Khatchadourian as she reflects on the disaster, analysing their cold, adversarial relationship and his turbulent younger years.

1 *FATHER AND SON*
This evocation of childhood in a stern Plymouth Brethren home in Victorian England charts the journey of poet Edmund Gosse as he rejects his father's fundamentalism and a harsh religious upbringing.

"A BOY IS A DANGEROUS ANIMAL"

– *WE NEED TO TALK ABOUT KEVIN*

TOP 10

It seems life can sometimes be stranger than fiction – or if not *actually* more bizarre than the wildest imaginings of creative writers, then utterly fascinating in its own right when revealed by people (famous or otherwise) who feel the need to record their own autobiographical stories for posterity, and do so as entertainingly as the ten on this list.

AUTOBIOGRAPHIES

10 *LIFE*
If you're a Rolling Stone you don't write a book for the money, but a $7.3 million advance was useful pocket money. Read all about guitarist Richard's roots, musical influences, turbulent relationship with Mick Jagger, drug taking, women – we might be talking rock 'n' roll.

9 *EXPERIENCE*
Written by himself (unlike Life) this memoir by Martin Amis was stimulated by the death of father Kingsley, providing almost voyeuristic insight into the son's take on fascinating family, friends, big-name acquaintances and beautiful women loved and left.

8 *THE MOON'S A BALLOON*
Actor David Niven's retelling of his early life is one of the most entertaining biographies every written, charting tongue-in-cheek progress through humiliating school days, wartime army service and early Hollywood success.

7 *LONG WALK TO FREEDOM*
Written by one of the most iconic heroes of the modern world, this initially depressing (but ultimately inspiring) autobiography charts Nelson Mandela's early life, resistance to apartheid, long prison sojourn (a commuted death sentence) and triumph as South Africa's first black President.

6 *GOODBYE TO ALL THAT*
'That' was an England changed forever by World War I, a cataclysm Robert Graves saw at first hand before being gravely wounded. Just 34 when he wrote this, he was still haunted by nightmares from the trenches.

5 *I KNOW WHY THE CAGED BIRD SINGS*
A significant autobiography by an important civil rights campaigner, the late Maya Angelou. Describing formative years, she records the change from victim of racism to resilient young woman who resisted prejudice.

4 *THE DIVING BELL AND THE BUTTERFLY*
Moving insight into the paralysis of French journalist Jean-Dominique Bauby. His life is chronicled as a prelude to the stroke that left him with locked-in syndrome, able to move only his head and one eye,

which he blinked to choose the words he composed. He died days after publication.

3 *ORANGES ARE NOT THE ONLY FRUIT*
Adopted Jeanette is brought up within the super-strict Pentecostal community as one of 'God's chosen', with a future in missionary work. But then, aged 16, she rebels, leaving it all for the girl she loves.

2 *THE DIARIES OF SAMUEL PEPYS*
Member of Parliament and naval administrator, the decade-long diary kept by Samuel Pepys provided intensely personal insight into his own life and valuable commentary on major events in Restoration England. Not published until the 19th century.

1 **WILD SWANS**
An ambitious biography (and autobiography) featuring three generations of Chinese women – grandmother, mother and daughter – spread over a century. The grandmother moved from noble concubine to wife. The mother was a member of Mao's Red Army in revolutionary times. Daughter Jung Chang joined the infamous Red Guards, before becoming disillusioned and leaving for England.

"MARRIAGE WAS A TRANSACTION, NOT A MATTER OF FEELINGS"

– WILD SWANS

TOP

10

You know how it is – you don't get on with the parent-in-law (or boss, or noisy neighbour, or stern teacher, or indeed anyone else with the capacity to annoy). As writers have gleefully proved, there are countless permutations when it comes to folk falling out with each other, or simply struggling to co-exist. Here are but ten tasty examples.

DIFFICULT **RELATIONSHIPS**

10 *VALLEY OF THE DOLLS*

A sometimes harrowing review of the experiences of three women in post-World-War-II America. Jennifer falls for soon-to-become-insane singer Tony, Anne has a long on-off-on relationship with unfaithful Lyon and Hollywood star Neely suffers two failed marriages – but her really bad relationship is with pills and booze.

9 *THE READER*

A 15-year-old German boy has a confusing clandestine relationship with an older woman, but years later when he sees her in the dock Michael realizes that Hannah had been concealing dark wartime secrets.

8 *COUPLES*

The contraceptive pill promised sexual liberation, but this 1960s drama following the affairs of ten young married couples in New England suggests that their self-absorbed sexual relationships and games answered nothing.

7 *HOTEL DU LAC*

Edith retires to the hotel in emotional disarray after an unsatisfactory affair and failed marriage. But she starts to find herself, and when Mr Neville asks for her hand she is able to reject the charming womanizer – and avoid another disastrous relationship.

6 *THE HEART IS A LONELY HUNTER*

Published in 1940, this debut novel examines the troubled relationship between two deaf mutes, ending when Antonopoulous is confined to a mental asylum. This leaves John Singer alone, observing the difficulties of four acquaintances.

5 *THE NIGHT WATCH*

Back to the World War II era again, and the tangled relationships of three lesbians, one straight woman and a gay man. As the timeline scrolls backwards to 1941, it becomes apparent how difficult some of those relationships have been.

4 THE PROGRESS OF LOVE
A divorced woman learns her mother has died and reflects back on the summer when she was 12 – starting to deconstruct her parents' apparently stable relationship in an attempt to understand grudges that outweighed love.

3 A SPELL OF WINTER
In the early 20th century brother Rob and sister Catherine have been abandoned to the care of servants. The children only have each other, and the relationship eventually becomes incestuous. But there may be hope . . .

2 THE GROUP
Banned in Australia, this story of eight American women graduating in 1933 sensationally describes their lives, loves, relationships and the difficulties they face – usually caused by men.

1 THE MASTER
This observation of the life of writer Henry James concerns dysfunctional engagement with himself after choosing seclusion, rejecting a close relationship with his family and adored sister, not to mention the fellow writer he'd once been *very* close to.

10 VALLEY OF THE DOLLS
Jacqueline Susann

9 THE READER
Bernhard Schlink

8 COUPLES
John Updike

7 HOTEL DU LAC
Anita Brookner

6 THE HEART IS A LONELY HUNTER
Carson McCullers

5 THE NIGHT WATCH
Sarah Waters

4 THE PROGRESS OF LOVE
Alice Munro

3 A SPELL OF WINTER
Helen Dunmore

2 THE GROUP
Mary McCarthy

1 THE MASTER
Colm Tóibín

"IDEAS WERE SACRED, SECOND ONLY TO GOOD MANNERS"

– THE MASTER

CHAPTER 5

WORLD OF BOOKS

Books come in all shapes and sizes, innumerable languages and assorted genres, aimed at as many readers as there are people who read. But the prestige enjoyed by books is based on awareness that fiction can explore and illuminate the human condition, providing perception-changing insights. Or then again books can simply be great entertainment! Read on, Macduff . . .

TOP **10**

Dramatic change in the past century provided rich soil that nurtured the imagination of authors everywhere, who produced innumerable offerings on every theme under the sun. This book can only cover a fraction of that creative explosion, and this list can contain no more than ten such novels. But each and every one of them is an undisputed 20th-century classic.

20TH-CENTURY **CLASSICS**

10 *THE MAGUS*
This postmodern metafiction published in 1965 features a young Brit teaching English on a Greek island, becoming enmeshed in the psychological net of a master manipulator whose illusions become ever more sinister.

9 *THE ALEXANDRIA QUARTET*
A tetralogy published between 1957 and 1960, the first three books explore the same series of events and relationships in Alexandria before and during World War II, seen through three different sets of eyes. The fourth book relates subsequent developments.

8 *THE PRIME OF MISS JEAN BRODIE*
In 1930s Edinburgh progressive teacher Jean Brodie selects six bright students, who are treated to wide-ranging insights. But she's in a love triangle and one of the six (never revealed) will betray Miss Brodie and destroy her career.

7 *SONS AND LOVERS*
A semi-autobiographical masterpiece published in 1913. Paul Morel detests his violent father but loves his mother. He has sexual relationships with two young women but returns to his mother before she dies, leaving him alone in the world.

6 *BRIDESHEAD REVISITED*
An examination of the relationship between Charles Ryder and the aristocratic Marchmain family, especially dissolute son Sebastian. But on another level this deals with Catholicism and its impact on the characters.

5 *THE GOOD SOLDIER*
Set just before World War I, this enigmatic novel describes collapsing relationships, the death of three characters and madness of another. But how reliable is narrator John Dowell's rambling recollection?

4 *THE REGENERATION TRILOGY*
It's World War I again, as three 1990s novels blend fact and fiction in a searing indictment of war's shattering impact on participants, even as they remain individuals who form relationships with others.

3 *A BEND IN THE RIVER*
A young man of Indian extraction leaves his family's successful trading business on the African coast and heads for the interior, where he establishes his own shop amidst the chaos and violent change that accompanied the colonial era's messy ending.

2 *THE SEA, THE SEA*
Playwright Charles Arrowby retires to a secluded seaside house to write his memoirs. When he encounters a lover from his youth for the first time in decades he becomes obsessed with rekindling the relationship, entirely unaware of his own egotism and selfishness.

1 *THE BLIND OWL*
This haunting Persian masterwork was published in 1937 and features a narrator who has lost love and drifts into a frenzy as he makes murderous confessions to an owl-shaped shadow on the wall in a surrealistic orgy of despair about the human condition.

10 **THE MAGUS**
John Fowles

9 **THE ALEXANDRIA QUARTET**
Lawrence Durrell

8 **THE PRIME OF MISS JEAN BRODIE**
Muriel Spark

7 **SONS AND LOVERS**
D H Lawrence

6 **BRIDESHEAD REVISITED**
Evelyn Waugh

5 **THE GOOD SOLDIER**
Ford Madox Ford

4 **THE REGENERATION TRILOGY**
Pat Barker

3 **A BEND IN THE RIVER**
V S Naipaul

2 **THE SEA, THE SEA**
Iris Murdoch

1 **THE BLIND OWL**
Sadegh Hedayat

"THE FINGER OF DEATH POINTS AT US"

– THE BLIND OWL

TOP
10

The 21st century has seen no diminution in the outpourings of talented creative writers, while the increasing complexity of the modern world has ensured that the range and scope of subject matter they are able to choose from has never been greater. The books on this Top Ten list have been chosen to represent a fascinating cross-section of contemporary classics.

CONTEMPORARY CLASSICS

10 *THE ROAD HOME* Leaving behind a dead wife and young daughter, Lev abandons Eastern Europe in hope of a better life in England. But London is a place full of weird Britishness, which Lev must engage with if his future is to blossom.

9 *LIFE AFTER LIFE* Ursula Todd is born on a cold night in 1910, but dies. On a cold night in 1910 Ursula Todd is born, lustily alive. That dual life is unusual, as she repeatedly dies in this hugely inventive, amusing and poignant tale.

8 *WHITE TEETH* An epic handbook for multicultural London. Wartime buddies Archie Jones (dull, married to a beautiful Jamaican half his age) and Samad

Iqbal (devoutly Muslim, married to feisty Alsana as arranged) enjoy an unlikely friendship in this riotous tale of engaging families.

7 *THE SENSE OF AN ENDING* Home alone and retired, Tony Webster recalls 1960s schooldays when his gang of four were inseparable – until life parted them. Tony's reflections are interrupted when a bequest from his university

girlfriend's mother arrives, making him re-evaluate everything.

5 *THE ROAD* A father undertakes a terrible post-apocalyptic journey through a blasted landscape with his son, trying to protect the boy from cannibals and other dangers. They're the good guys, but the father still dies.

6 *IF NOBODY SPEAKS OF REMARKABLE THINGS* A breathtaking evocation of city life, as the everyday activities of a Northern street are disrupted by a terrible event. It makes no headlines, but those who witness it will be changed forever.

4 *AND THE MOUNTAINS ECHOED* Published in 2013 but set in

1952. Abdullah and adored sister Pari live a harsh life in remote Afghanistan. Then the siblings journey with their father to Kabul, little knowing he plans to sell Pari to a childless couple.

3 *SWEET TOOTH*
This 2012 novel takes an 'I was there' authorial look back at 1970s social upheaval, as Serena Frome graduates from Cambridge and is recruited by MI5. She must infiltrate the left-leaning intelligentsia, but falls for her target.

2 *NEVER LET ME GO*
Published in 2010, this acclaimed novel is narrated by 31-year-old Kathy, who looks back to her education at an apparently idyllic yet weirdly distorted English public school. But what fate darkly awaited its students in the wider world?

1 *WOLF HALL*
Historical drama of the highest order, this award-winning 2009 novel fictionalizes the rapid rise to power of Thomas Cromwell amidst the machinations and intrigue of Henry VIII's court.

10 ***THE ROAD HOME***
Rose Tremain

9 ***LIFE AFTER LIFE***
Kate Atkinson

8 ***WHITE TEETH***
Zadie Smith

7 ***THE SENSE OF AN ENDING***
Julian Barnes

6 ***THE ROAD***
Cormac McCarthy

5 ***IF NOBODY SPEAKS OF REMARKABLE THINGS***
Jon McGregor

4 ***AND THE MOUNTAINS ECHOED***
Khaled Hosseini

3 ***SWEET TOOTH***
Ian McEwan

2 ***NEVER LET ME GO***
Kazuo Ishiguro

1 ***WOLF HALL***
Hilary Mantel

"WE CAN'T STAY TOGETHER FOREVER"

– NEVER LET ME GO

TOP
10

Life proceeds apace, as e-books and the many media devices via which they can be perused ensure that the choice of writing available to readers has never been greater. But this list has been chosen as a reminder that perspectives and insights of earlier generations should not be forgotten, for they are the firm foundations upon which today's classics are built.

HISTORIC MASTERPIECES

10 THE ILIAD

With copious references to Greek legends, this Ancient Greek epic poem tells of the decade-long siege of Troy in the Trojan War, starring quarrelling warriors Achilles and King Agamemnon.

9 JUDE THE OBSCURE

Old Thomas could turn that screw, so don't expect a happy ending for ambitious stonemason Jude. He's tricked into marrying Arabella, who deserts him. He falls for Sue, who marries another. When they do get together, it ends in juvenile murder and suicide. Jude dies alone.

8 HEART OF DARKNESS

A novella mirroring Conrad's experiences as a riverboat skipper in Africa. A trip on the Congo River ends badly as natives revolt, but the gripping narrative is an excuse to examine the morality of colonialism.

7 GREAT EXPECTATIONS

Nothing unlucky about the 13th Dickens novel, for it's one of his best, containing everything he held dear – poverty and wealth, love and rejection, the triumph of good over evil.

6 MIDDLEMARCH

The multiple plots involve assorted inhabitants of this provincial town, serving as a vehicle for the author's serious commentary on issues such as political reform, the status of women, nature of marriage, hypocrisy and idealism.

5 TOM JONES

This jaunt through mid-18th-century life includes themes such as villainy and repentance, virtue and hypocrisy . . . but the heart of the matter is good-but-flawed Tom Jones's redemption through the love of Sophie Weston.

4 VANITY FAIR

The title borrows the endless fair at Vanity from The Pilgrim's Progress, symbolizing sinful attachment to worldly things – perfect for a satire on early 19th-century British life. The plot is driven by the fortunes of contrasting

THE

HISTORY

OF

TOM JONES,

A

FOUNDLING.

In SIX VOLUMES.

By HENRY FIELDING, Eſq;

—— *Mores hominum multorum vidit.* ——

---

female characters Amelia (gentle but impoverished) and Becky Sharp (ruthless social climber).

3 *PERSUASION*
Jane Austen's swansong, satirizing the inanities of life in Bath (which Jane herself suffered). Along with the title theme of persuasion, the Royal Navy looms large in Anne Elliot's long separation from, and final reconciliation with, Captain Frederick Wentworth.

2 *WAR AND PEACE*
A monolith of world literature, this sweeping 1869 epic is set against Napoleon's invasion of Russia, exploring its impact on society through the medium of five noble families, cleverly blurring the line between meticulous historical fact and fiction.

1 *CRIME AND PUNISHMENT*
Is murder permissible in the pursuit of higher goals? That's the question impoverished Rodion Raskilnikov tortures himself with as he contemplates killing elderly female pawnbroker Ivanovna. The book is taken up with the angst-ridden aftermath of his axe-murders (for another is killed too).

10 *THE ILIAD*
Homer

9 *JUDE THE OBSCURE*
Thomas Hardy

8 *HEART OF DARKNESS*
Joseph Conrad

7 *GREAT EXPECTATIONS*
Charles Dickens

6 *MIDDLEMARCH*
George Eliot

5 *TOM JONES*
Henry Fielding

4 *VANITY FAIR*
William Makepeace Thackeray

3 *PERSUASION*
Jane Austen

2 *WAR AND PEACE*
Leo Tolstoy

1 *CRIME AND PUNISHMENT*
Fyodor Dostoyevsky

"MAN IS A VILE CREATURE!"

– CRIME AND PUNISHMENT

TOP
10

Strangely – considering the percentage of TV entertainment time taken up by sit-coms, comedy and comedians – the world of books is not over-endowed with humour. Of course there are many amusing books, such as the chosen ten on this list. But authors tend to take themselves seriously and write accordingly, so the ones who can raise a laugh are *very* special.

COMIC CUTS

10 *ALL CREATURES GREAT AND SMALL*
Written by country vet James Wight, who worked in Thirsk, this hilarious take on rural life might be summarized by that good old Yorkshire expression 'there's nowt as queer as folk' (and their animals!).

9 *MOAB IS MY WASHPOT*
Intellectual funny man Stephen Fry didn't disappoint with this 1997 autobiography charting his early life, which is both amusing and ferociously candid.

8 *TOP GEAR – THE ALTERNATIVE HIGHWAY CODE*
Sensational TV viewing figures suggest that the antics of boys behaving badly in cars (and other chariots) smashes into the humour zone, and this

anarchic motoring manual proves it.

7 LET'S PRETEND THIS NEVER HAPPENED

Any book that includes a chapter entitled And Then I Snuck a Dead Cuban Alligator on an Airplane is likely to have the fun factor, and ain't that the truth when it comes to the crack-you-up life of Jenny Lawson, The Bloggess.

6 THE UNCOMMON READER

Wry humorist Alan Bennett offered an imaginative tale of Queen Elizabeth II getting hooked on books after a meeting in a mobile library. It provides a reading list fit for a monarch – and a right regal laugh.

5 THE GIRL WHO SAVED THE KING OF SWEDEN

While we're on the royalty rumble, spare a thought (and continuous laughs) for Soweto-born Nombeko Mayeki. Her luck changed for the better when she was run over, but now she's on the run with the fate of the world (and the King of Sweden) resting on her broad shoulders.

4 ME TALK PRETTY ONE DAY

This uproariously funny memoir follows a tough encounter of the non-comprehending type after two Americans stormed ashore in Normandy – without a word of French to help.

3 HOW TO BE A WOMAN

Come rant with her! Best-selling author Caitlin Moran (a woman) puts a smile on the face of all those thorny questions that bedevil the life of stressed females of the (supposedly sophisticated Western) kind. Brazilians? Botox? Babies? Men?

2 I FEEL BAD ABOUT MY NECK

Academy-award-winning screenwriter and director Nora Ephron looks at real life (hers) with mirth-making results. What's not to laugh about in throwaway lines like 'never marry a man you wouldn't want to be divorced from'?

1 *NOTES FROM A SMALL ISLAND*
The grand master of amusing observation of the world and the sometimes bizarre people who populate it wrote this delightfully funny farewell tribute to Britain, before returning to his native America. But wait, there's a happy ending – he's back!

TOP 10

The USA may have been a latecomer to the writers' ball, but in true American get-up-and-go style its authors proved to be very quick on their feet, and the almost ferocious energy, drive and confidence that propelled the young nation to the top of the international dance card also elevated it to number one status as the world's literary leader.

AMERICAN GREATS

10 *HERZOG*
His life in ruins, Moses E Herzog (recently abandoned by manipulative second wife) mentally writes letters that are never sent, to people living and dead. But when his traumatic life threatens to stabilize he letter-writes no more.

9 *BLOOD MERIDIAN*
Initially unnoticed, this unsettling tale of 'the kid' and his interaction with the murderous, scalp-hunting Glanton Gang in mid-19th-century Tex-Mex borderlands, featuring epic baddie Judge Holden, is now tagged 'McCarthy's Masterpiece'.

8 *THE NEW YORK TRILOGY*
This 1980s classic (originally three books) purports to be detective fiction – but that's like saying Moby Dick is a fishing story. This trio reads like fast-paced thrillers, but it's not long before enigmatic hidden depths are glimpsed.

7 *WHAT WE TALK ABOUT WHEN WE TALK ABOUT LOVE*
With a title like that, who needs a book? Seriously folks, this collection is included to show American mastery of that most challenging of literary forms, the short story.

6 *THE CORRECTIONS*
A modern(ish) classic featuring a dysfunctional Midwestern family. The children have gone east to escape and prosper (not altogether successfully), while tyrannical patriarch Alfred Lambert gets Parkinson's disease, cranking up the pressure on long-suffering wife Enid. Then they gather for a family Christmas . . .

5 *THE AGE OF INNOCENCE*
This 1921 Pulitzer prizewinner (by the first woman to win the fiction title) is a cautionary tale of upper-class New York life in the 1870s, commenting on the contrast between rigidly proper conventions and hidden machinations.

4 *RABBIT, RUN*
Awesome American angst, as 28-year-old former high-school basketball star Harry 'Rabbit' Angstrom goes on the run from his unsatisfactory life, only to find that he swiftly creates an additional set of problems.

3 *THE GRAPES OF WRATH*
A Great Depression 'bible', with the Joad family representing thousands of displaced 'Okies' and 'Arkies' who loaded everything they had onto an old pickup truck and headed west in search of a better life.

2 *THE GREAT GATSBY*
Troubled author Fitzgerald was always broke, which perhaps contributed to his portrayal of iconic Jazz-Age American, Jay Gatsby. Mysterious millionaire Gatsby's obsession with Daisy Buchanan preaches a cautionary tale about the American Dream. The greatest US novel? Quite possibly!

1 *THE OLD MAN AND THE SEA*
A memorable fable inspired by Hemingway's love of big game fishing, this story of an epic struggle between an unlucky Spanish-Cuban fisherman nd a giant marlin revived and cemented the author's reputation – and contributed significantly to his winning the Nobel prize.

10 *HERZOG*
Saul Bellow

9 *BLOOD MERIDIAN*
Cormac McCarthy

8 *THE NEW YORK TRILOGY*
Paul Auster

7 *WHAT WE TALK ABOUT WHEN WE TALK ABOUT LOVE*
Raymond Carver

6 *THE CORRECTIONS*
Jonathan Franzen

5 *THE AGE OF INNOCENCE*
Edith Wharton

4 *RABBIT, RUN*
John Updike

3 *THE GRAPES OF WRATH*
John Steinbeck

2 *THE GREAT GATSBY*
F Scott Fitzgerald

1 *THE OLD MAN AND THE SEA*
Ernest Hemingway

"A MAN CAN BE DESTROYED BUT NOT DEFEATED"

– THE OLD MAN AND THE SEA

TOP 10

European literature goes back for millennia, into the dim and distant dawning of modern civilization as we know it. But (even without considering great Brits, included elsewhere) this list shows European writers have never been content to rest on their Greek and Roman laurels, but instead have constantly striven to advance creative use of the written word, with notable success.

EUROPEAN GIANTS

10 *THE MAGICIAN OF LUBLIN*
Written by a Polish Jew who escaped to America as the Nazi threat loomed, the protagonist is Yasha Mazur – con man, mystic and stage magician. Personal problems threaten his career, then he gets one last chance . . .

9 *PERFUME*
No need to get sniffy about this one – it's an acknowledged German masterpiece with an extraordinary plot. A perfume apprentice in 18th-century France stalks and murders virgins in search of the perfect scent. And that's just the start of it!

8 *THE TIN DRUM*
Another German special, taking a painful backward look at the Nazi era when 1959 Germany was trying to forget. The medium of the message is drum-toting grocer's son Oskar, who shatters glass with a scream.

7 *SIDDHARTHA*
Also originating from Germany but set in ancient India, this 1922 novel follows a young Brahmin's journey of self-discovery as he renounces worldly possessions and takes to the road in search of enlightenment.

6 *DEATH IN VENICE*
Based on the author's own experiences and emotions during a 1911 visit to Venice, this novella features a writer travelling to the romantic city in search of inspiration, suffering catastrophic inner passion after observing and obsessing about a beautiful youth.

5 *CANDIDE*
This lauded French satire was published in 1759. A novella with a fantastical, unpredictable and fast-moving plot follows young Candide's unfortunate fall from an idyllic paradise, and subsequent disillusionment

as he experiences awful hardships of the real world.

4 *THE UNBEARABLE LIGHTNESS OF BEING*
A 1982 Czech postmodern novel set in 1968 during and immediately after the brief flowering of the Prague Spring, before the Russian tanks rolled in. Featuring two men, two women and a dog (perm any two from five).

3 *THE LEOPARD*
This lauded tale of a 19th-century Sicilian nobleman struggling to reconcile old and new values amidst revolution and civil war is now considered an Italian masterwork. But it was only published (posthumously) after several rejections.

2 *SOLDIERS OF SALAMIS*
As the Spanish Civil War draws to a close, 50 Nationalist prisoners are slated for execution. Writer Rafael Sanchez Mazas escapes into the forest, only to be confronted by a militiaman who – instead of shooting him – turns and walks away. Why?

1 *LES MISÉRABLES*
One of the greatest 19th-century novels became one of the 20th century's greatest musicals. The main theme of each is the same – ex-convict Jean Valjean's valiant struggle for redemption against the turbulent background of post-Napoleonic France.

10 **THE MAGICIAN OF LUBLIN**
Isaac Bashevis Singer

9 **PERFUME**
Patrick Süskind

8 **THE TIN DRUM**
Günther Grass

7 **SIDDHARTHA**
Hermann Hesse

6 **DEATH IN VENICE**
Thomas Mann

5 **CANDIDE**
Voltaire

4 **THE UNBEARABLE LIGHTNESS OF BEING**
Milan Kundera

3 **THE LEOPARD**
Giuseppe Tomasi Di Lampedusa

2 **SOLDIERS OF SALAMIS**
Javier Cercas

1 **LES MISÉRABLES**
Victor Hugo

"SOLITUDE GIVES BIRTH TO THE ORIGINAL IN US"

– DEATH IN VENICE

TOP 10

For a mega-island with an arid heart – populated by apocryphal Outbackers in bush hats with dancing corks, sun-bronzed young gods and goddesses disporting in the blue waters of Bondi Beach and countless backyard barbecue chefs – Australia has produced a surprisingly large contingent of distinguished writers, with a little help from neighbouring New Zealand. This list amply confirms their creditable credentials.

AWESOME ANTIPODEANS

10 *AN IMAGINARY LIFE* When the paternalistic treatment of Australia's aboriginal inhabitants was becoming an issue, this allegorical story describes exiled Roman poet Ovid's bond with a wild child brought up by wolves, before capturing him from nature to educate him.

9 *BLINDSIGHT* New Zealand author Maurice Gee crafted this tale of old woman Alice Ferry, who sees her long-lost brother on the street, starting a flashback to childhood. She's hiding secrets – then someone claiming to be her brother's grandson turns up.

8 *THE BONE PEOPLE* Another New Zealand entry. It puts together and lays bare three disparate characters – solitary part-Maori artist Kerewin, the mute boy Simon who arrives in a storm and his volcanic Maori foster-father Joe.

7 *THE SLAP* At a Melbourne barbecue, a man slaps a boy who has been misbehaving, uncorrected by his parents. It's an action with serious ramifications, as subsequently escalating events are seen through the eyes of different participants.

6 *THE GREAT FIRE* The conflagration of World War II is over, but the shadow of Hiroshima lingers on. A young woman living in Japan tends her dying brother, and falls in love with a brave former soldier trying to make sense of his life.

5 *ONCE WERE WARRIORS* This depicts the travails of a slum-dwelling Maori family, highlighting the problem of domestic violence and Maori alienation in a gritty tale of a sensitive mother, brutal father and six ill-educated children.

4 *A TOWN LIKE ALICE* English heiress Jean Paget met Aussie Joe Harman when both were prisoners of the Japanese. She assumed he died, but on discovering he's alive goes to find him in the Outback. Together, they invest her money to create a thriving community – a town like Alice (Springs).

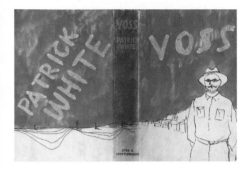

3 *VOSS*
Inspired by Ludwig Leichhardt's ill-fated 19th-century expedition into the Australian interior. German explorer Voss sets out to cross Australia, after meeting orphan Laura who has just arrived in New South Wales. It doesn't end well.

2 *OSCAR AND LUCINDA*
Gamblers Oscar Hopkins (an Anglican priest) and Lucinda Leplastrier (glass-factory heiress) meet on the boat to Australia. She bets him that he can't transport a glass church to remote Bellingen. It proves to be a life-changer.

1 *PICNIC AT HANGING ROCK*
Spooky. In 1900, a natural formation makes trouble when schoolgirls and a teacher from a picnic party vanish while climbing Hanging Rock. Those who survive have no memory of what happened, contributing to an enigmatic mystery that is never explained.

10 *AN IMAGINARY LIFE*
David Malouf

9 *BLINDSIGHT*
Maurice Gee

8 *THE BONE PEOPLE*
Keri Hulme

7 *THE SLAP*
Christos Tsiolkas

6 *THE GREAT FIRE*
Shirley Hazzard

5 *ONCE WERE WARRIORS*
Alan Duff

4 *A TOWN LIKE ALICE*
Nevil Shute

3 *VOSS*
Patrick White

2 *OSCAR AND LUCINDA*
Peter Carey

1 *PICNIC AT HANGING ROCK*
Joan Lindsay

"HUMAN RELATIONSHIPS ARE VAST AS DESERTS"

– VOSS

TOP 10

The Victorians called it 'The Dark Continent', as the last great land mass to hide its secrets. But Africa succumbed to rapacious colonizers, who soon carved up the spoils. The colonial era was brief, but its legacy often catastrophic – yet that very turmoil has produced authors who speak for the emerging continent, as it reaches erratically for a better future.

AFRICAN MUST-READS

10 *THE PALM-WINE DRINKARD*
This 1952 novel is a seminal work of Nigerian and African literature. With echoes of magical realism, a man 'drinken' on palm wine visits Deads' Town, entering a ghostly world of supernatural beings.

9 *CUTTING FOR STONE*
A story of medicine and miracles, love and betrayal moves between Ethiopia and New York. Twin boys born of the secret union between a British surgeon and a beautiful Indian nun make their own medical history.

8 *THE BEAUTIFUL THINGS THAT HEAVEN BEARS*
Ethiopian immigrant Sepha Stephanos – torn between roots and new identity – runs a store in Washington DC. As gentrification of his run-down neighbourhood begins, he's locked into resistance to change.

7 *WE NEED NEW NAMES*
Living in Paradise, a Zimbabwean shanty that is anything but, Darling and her friends make mischief and have fun, also playing the country game – if you could choose one, which would it be? But winning isn't quite as anticipated.

6 *PURPLE HIBISCUS*
In postcolonial Nigeria 15-year-old Kambili Achike belongs to a wealthy family. Unfortunately, there's no hiding from a violent father and the family unit disintegrates around her in this coming-of-age drama that ends on a hopeful note.

5 *CRY, THE BELOVED COUNTRY*
Published in 1948, this South African saga features two men – one black and one white – who must come to terms with losing sons. Black priest Stephen Kumalo heads for Jo'burg to sort out family problems, but they're beyond solving.

4 *THE FAMISHED ROAD*
Spirit-child Azaro lives in an African slum, and the young abiku is

harassed by siblings who want him to return to the spirit world. But for love of his labourer father and hawker mother he stubbornly refuses, as real life unfolds around him.

3 JULY'S PEOPLE

A violent ending to South African apartheid, imagined before the evil system actually ended peacefully. But the story of a liberal white family saved from revolution by their black servant remains an intelligent examination of the relationship between races.

J. M. Coetzee

2 DISGRACE

Cape-Town academic David Lurie loses everything. Twice-divorced and disgraced, he heads for his daughter's farm to seek refuge. Rural rhythms soothe, but the violence endemic in post-apartheid South Africa soon shatters the tranquillity.

1 THINGS FALL APART

A 1958 Nigerian classic, the archetypal African novel now studied in schools all over the continent. Set in the nine villages of fictional Umuofia, wrestling champion and local leader Okonkwo describes the life, times and customs of his people.

10 THE PALM-WINE DRINKARD
Amos Tutuola

9 CUTTING FOR STONE
Abraham Verghese

8 THE BEAUTIFUL THINGS THAT HEAVEN BEARS
Dinaw Mengestu

7 WE NEED NEW NAMES
Noviolet Bulawayo

6 PURPLE HIBISCUS
Chimamanda Ngozi Adichie

5 CRY, THE BELOVED COUNTRY
Alan Paton

4 THE FAMISHED ROAD
Ben Okri

3 JULY'S PEOPLE
Nadine Gordimer

2 DISGRACE
J M Coetzee

1 THINGS FALL APART
Chinua Achebe

"GROW WHEREVER LIFE PUTS YOU DOWN"

– THE FAMISHED ROAD

TOP **10**

Before e-books could stash a thousand titles in a postcard-sized library, the proverbial 'holiday read' was an important contributor to the bottom line of publishers. The airport trade may have slowed nowadays, but happily some traditionally minded holidaymakers who still like turning real pages exist, in sufficient numbers to ensure a profitable future for titles like these.

HOLIDAY **READS**

10 *CHESTNUT STREET*
An imagined street in Dublin is peopled by a wonderful panoply of characters, created by an author renowned for perception and humour. Over to Bucket Maguire, Madame Magic and the rest of the hugely entertaining cast.

9 *NEVER GO BACK*
Author Lee Child hit the jackpot with ex-military cop Jack Reacher, as the one-man crime-cracker stormed his way across America (and to massive book sales). This is unputdownable, as were the previous 17 in the series.

8 *THE COLLECTORS*
There's nothing like a good thriller to absorb idle beach time, and this is very like a good thriller. When the body-count escalates in Washington, crypt-keeper Oliver Stone and the Camel Club swing into action.

7 *POWER PLAY*
Here's one for the kids (and sneaky parental peeks after bedtime). Another Graphic Guide Adventure educates even as it entertains, featuring kids unravelling a murder mystery that may derail the well-intentioned Summit of World Leaders.

6 *MISTRESS*
Master thrill-smith James Patterson comes up with a sexy journey through a world of danger and deceit, obsession and paranoia, as the unrequited love of Ben's life is slain – and he starts to uncover the secrets of Diana's double life.

5 *THE SOLDIER'S WIFE*
The actuality of those touching family reunions on the airfield tarmac is probed by an author noted for superior domestic psychodrama. The returning hero can't wait to see his adored wife and kids, but the army's a demanding mistress.

4 *BE CAREFUL WHAT YOU WISH FOR*
The Clifton Chronicles entertainingly continue the unstoppable yarn-spinning career of the prince of popular potboilers. The warring Clifton and Barrington families hit the 1960s with all guns blazing (metaphorically speaking).

3 *CONFESSIONS OF A WILD CHILD*
A Jackie Collins sizzler should be high on any luggage list, and this is the

usual over-the-top, sexy, trashy treat the world has come to know and love. Here we follow the path of Lucky Santangelo from wild child to powerful empress.

2 *TELL NO ONE*
There's life after Myron Bolitar, but in this case Harlan Coben's alternative hero David Beck is haunted by death. Eight years ago he was knocked out and his wife was kidnapped and murdered. But (as usual) all is not as it seemed.

1 *LEAVING TIME*
A good holiday read doesn't have to be lightweight, and this heavyweight American author has created another mini-masterpiece. Jenna Metcalf unravels the mystery of her mother's decade-old disappearance with the help of unlikely allies.

"PART OF BEING A PARENT WAS BEING ON CALL AT ALL TIMES"

– POWER PLAY

Funded by a fortune left by Scandinavian inventor and armaments manufacturer Alfred Nobel, the ultimate accolade for any writer is the Nobel Prize for Literature. This prestigious award recognizes an author's contribution to world literature, as represented by their body of work. However, for the purposes of this Top Ten list a single representative title has been selected.

NOBEL **PRIZEWINNERS**

10 *JULY'S PEOPLE*
The South African political activist was recognized in 1991 as a woman 'who through her magnificent epic writing has – in the words of Alfred Nobel – been of very great benefit to humanity'. The book imagines a bloody revolution against apartheid.

9 *BUDDENBROOKS*
The 1929 laureate is renowned for analyzing the German and European soul, giving insight into the psychology of artists and intellectuals. The epic *Buddenbrooks* records the decline of a North German merchant family over four generations.

8 *CANCER WARD*
The Russian dissident was honoured in 1970 for resistance to Soviet totalitarianism and exposing the horror of the Gulag camps. In Cancer Ward he explored the guilt of those involved in Stalin's Great Purge.

7 *THE GLASS BEAD GAME*
Reconciliation, anyone? The 1946 prize went to anti-Nazi German writer Hesse. In *The Glass Bead Game* he probes favourite themes – the quest for self-knowledge, truth and spirituality.

6 *THE SOUND AND THE FURY*
Mississippian Faulkner achieved fame after winning the 1949 prize for nuanced descriptions of life in the South, notably fictional Yoknapatawpha County. This book charts the terminal decline of the formerly influential Compson family.

5 *MY NAME IS RED*
This Turkish writer scooped the country's first-ever Nobel prize in 2006. He's Turkey's best-selling author, despite an academic career in the USA. *My Name is Red* blends philosophical puzzles with romance and mystery in 16th-century Istanbul.

4 *HUMBOLDT'S GIFT*
Canadian-born Bellow worked in America. The 1976 laureate is regarded as one of the 20th century's most influential authors. Humboldt's Gift deals with the relationship between power and art in a materialistic USA.

3 *CRABWALK*
Danzig-born Grass arrived in West Germany in 1945. His first novel, The Tin Drum, was a major foundation of European magical realism. The 1999 laureate's Crabwalk combines fact and fiction whilst considering how the past can affect the present.

2 *DEAR LIFE*
Writing in English, the Canadian Munro won in 2013 for her mastery of the short story (Dear Life is a 2012 collection of them). Often set in Ontario's Huron County, her stories explore the complexities of human nature.

1 *THE GOOD TERRORIST*
True Brit Doris Lessing died in 2013, after winning her Nobel prize in 2007 (its oldest recipient) as grand mistress of the female experience. Her *The Good Terrorist* features well-meaning squatter Alice, drawn into organizing violent acts.

10 NADINE GORDIMER
July's People

9 THOMAS MANN
Buddenbrooks

8 ALEKSANDR SOLZHENITSYN
Cancer Ward

7 HERMANN HESSE
The Glass Bead Game

6 WILLIAM FAULKNER
The Sound And The Fury

5 ORHAN PAMUK
My Name Is Red

4 SAUL BELLOW
Humboldt's Gift

3 GÜNTER GRASS
Crabwalk

2 ALICE MUNRO
Dear Life

1 DORIS LESSING
The Good Terrorist

"ACCEPT EVERYTHING AND TRAGEDY DISAPPEARS"

– THE GOOD TERRORIST

TOP
10

We're talking epic journeys, and on this list fact and fiction can mingle together harmoniously. Some of the best writing ever committed to paper records the travels (and frequent tribulations) of those whose curiosity about the world we live in is insatiable. But fiction writers, too, are stimulated by the possibilities of going 'on the road', often with extraordinary results.

ROAD **RUNNERS**

10 *IN PATAGONIA*
Announcing his intentions to an employer with terse telegram 'Have gone to Patagonia', Chatwin wove a masterful tapestry of historical fact and anecdote about his South American adventure, though some suggest the work contains embroidered truth.

9 *A SHORT WALK IN THE HINDU KUSH*
A classic travel book from 1958, lauded for its whimsical Englishness, amusing narrative, historical insight into Nuristan and comical engagement with an ancient book of grammar. Needless to say, the 'short' walk was anything but.

8 *THE RINGS OF SATURN*
Straight faces, please, at the book's subtitle in the original German - Eine Englische Wallfahrt (as we all know, 'an English pilgrimage'). This erudite 1995 novel ostensibly centres on a walking tour in Suffolk, but there's more to it than that.

7 *FEAR AND LOATHING IN LAS VEGAS*
The subtitle A Savage Journey to the Heart of the American Dream says it all about a seminal road trip, as Raoul Duke (Hunter S Thompson himself) and attorney Dr Gonzo head for Las Vegas in a drug-induced haze.

6 *THE BEACH*
If there is such a thing as 'backpacker lit', this is it. A young backpacker searches for a legendary beach unsullied by tourism, there to join fellow free spirits. But be careful what you wish for . . .

5 *THE LOST CONTINENT*
You must be looking hard if you travel 13,978 miles trying to find it - it in this case being small-town America. Typical of author Bill Bryson's work, this blacktop-ramble is a humorously observed commentary on backwoods Americana.

4 *A TIME OF GIFTS*

Recalling the first part of an 18-year-old's epic journey across Europe from Holland to Constantinople (on foot) in 1933–1934. Written many years later, it combines youthful excitement at a great adventure with mature insight.

3 *ON THE ROAD*

Published in 1957, this is the Beat movement handbook, a *roman à clef* road trip featuring many of the key 'Beat' players by any other name, including the author himself as narrator Sal Paradise. Think poetry, jazz and drugs.

2 *THE WORST JOURNEY IN THE WORLD*

A memoir of a three-man expedition to collect three emperor penguin eggs during the 1911 Antarctic winter. The men returned to base camp exhausted and near death – two subsequently died with Scott, returning from the South Pole.

1 *THE CANTERBURY TALES*

Definitely the daddy of all road runners, though progress was undoubtedly sedate on this 14th-century pilgrimage from London to Canterbury, giving those larger-than-life characters ample time to tell their terrific tales.

"I WAS FILLED WITH PROFOUND MISGIVING"

– A SHORT WALK IN THE HINDU KUSH

TOP 10

A *roman à clef* work might best be described as 'faction' – a novel with a key (as the dull English-speakers would put it) is one where real-life episodes and/or people appear, though (sometimes thinly) disguised with a veneer of fiction. But just how easy is it to sort out the real from the imagined in this Top Ten selection?

ROMAN À CLEF

10 *THE BELL JAR* Who might heroine Esther Greenwood in a 1963 book by Victoria Lucas really be? All becomes clear when the author is revealed as poet Sylvia Plath, drawing on experience of the descent into clinical depression. She committed suicide shortly after publication.

9 *THE GHOST* This thriller features a British Prime Minister having much in common with Tony Blair (and a wife who is not dissimilar to wife Cherie). It's gripping fiction elevated by the imagined connection with reality.

8 *THE UNTOUCHABLE* This borrows from British espionage blunders, identifiably featuring runaway Soviet spy Guy Burgess and narrated by a homosexual art historian mirroring Anthony Blunt – the notorious 'Third Man' who wasn't unmasked for decades.

7 *POSTCARDS FROM THE EDGE* Read all about film actress Suzanne Vale as she reassembles her life after a drug overdose. She survives rehab, works again and starts dating, but can she ever trust herself? And the author is . . . actress Carrie Fisher.

6 *THE DEVIL WEARS PRADA* If you're assistant to demanding Vogue editor-in-chief Anna Wintour, working life may seem horrendous. But as an author having a dig at Manhattan's elite, it provides more than enough best-seller material to guarantee fame and fortune.

5 *THE MOON AND SIXPENCE* No hint of self-revelation here, as the author borrows from an altogether different life story – that of Frenchman Paul Gaugin – to provide a framework for his tale of a middle-aged stockbroker who abandons work and family to become an artist.

4 *THE CARPETBAGGERS* This swashbuckling saga of American robber barony starring Jonas Cord seems uncannily like a retelling of the life and times of Howard Hughes, and might the fictional Rina Marlowe be Hughes' squeeze Jean Harlow?

3 *POINT COUNTER POINT*
This complex 1928 novel is notable for the number of real people who feature, thinly disguised (including author Huxley, who appears as Philip Quarles). Notables include painter Augustus John and D H Lawrence.

2 *TENDER IS THE NIGHT*
The author's last novel, into which he poured himself, schizophrenic wife Zelda, her lover Edouard Jozan, his own lover Lois Moran, ambivalent feelings for parents, alcoholism, psychiatry and feelings of professional failure.

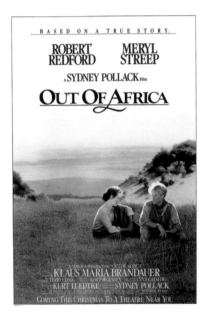

1 *OUT OF AFRICA*
This should have been called *My Life* by Baroness Karen von Blixen-Finecke (aka Karen Blixen). It is a vivid portrait of a spirited woman who threw herself body and soul into the somewhat decadent 'Happy Valley' life in colonial Kenya after World War I.

10 *THE BELL JAR*
Sylvia Plath

9 *THE GHOST*
Robert Harris

8 *THE UNTOUCHABLE*
John Banville

7 *POSTCARDS FROM THE EDGE*
Carrie Fisher

6 *THE DEVIL WEARS PRADA*
Lauren Weisberger

5 *THE MOON AND SIXPENCE*
W Somerset Maugham

4 *THE CARPETBAGGERS*
Harold Robbins

3 *POINT COUNTER POINT*
Aldous Huxley

2 *TENDER IS THE NIGHT*
F Scott Fitzgerald

1 *OUT OF AFRICA*
Isak Dinesen

TOP
10

Time to put pen to paper and create your own top 10 list of travel writers...

10 _____

9 _____

8 _____

7 _____

6 _____

5 _____

4 _____

3 _____

2 _____

1 _____

TOP 10

Some memorable relationships in literature do not involve lovers, but friends. In exceptional cases, friendship can go far beyond the conventional and assume a central role in the lives of those involved, as this list confirms. But it would be wrong to assume that great friendships are always benign, as sometimes the passions stirred can actually prove to be destructive.

EROTIC NOVELS

10 *LACE*
Described by one newspaper as 'a feminist tract disguised as a bonkbuster', this is an explicit erotic novel packed with spicy sexual ingredients, but also the story of an enduring friendship between four women ('Which one of you bitches is my mother?').

9 *SCRUPLES*
A transformation novel, as plump and unloved Wilhelmina goes to Paris and returns to America (no longer a virgin) as slim, chic Billy. In New York, guided by new roommate Jessica, she embarks on a frenetic voyage of sexual discovery.

8 *LES LIAISONS DANGEREUSES*
An 18th-century tale of two French aristocrats who humiliate and degrade others through seduction. Vicomte de Valmont and ex-lover the Marquise de Merteuil vie to corrupt innocents sexually, happily boasting about their manipulative abilities.

7 *THE STORY OF O*
Published under a *nom de plume* in 1954, this is Parisian tale about a beautiful photographer who is subjected to a demeaning regime of female submission (in homage to the Marquis de Sade).

6 *EMMANUELLE*
On the dubious premise that love and sex must be disassociated, young French expat Emmanuelle (after joining the mile-high club twice en route) experiences all sorts of sexual freedom with both sexes in Bangkok (where else?).

5 *LADY CHATTERLEY'S LOVER*
This raunchy tale of gamekeeper and upper-class lady was too erotic (explicit sex, naughty words) for the prim British establishment, being banned from (Italian) publication in 1928 until a sensational 1960 trial legalized it.

4 *TROPIC OF CANCER*
Published in 1934 in Paris (and promptly banned in the USA), this has been denounced as 'notorious for its candid sexuality' and praised for helping to establish free expression in literature. Sexual encounters are said to be related to the author's experiences.

3 *FANNY HILL*
An early entry into the canon of erotica, as the eponymous heroine (in a romp officially titled *Memoirs of a Woman of Pleasure*) enjoys a prolonged orgy of explicit sex. Denounced as pornography in 1749 for 'corrupting the King's subjects'.

2 *LOLITA*
Dealing with an ultimate no-no subject of our times, this downbeat tale features an obsessed older man who grooms his 12-year-old step-daughter. Of interest to the modern defence lawyer, because Lolita herself is ambivalently portrayed as a manipulative instigator.

1 **FIFTY SHADES OF GREY**
As publishing phenomena go, this trilogy is phenomenal – engorging from hopeful internet-self-published to awesome international heights as quickly as one can crack a whip or meet a multimillionaire with . . . oops, censored.

10 **LACE**
Shirley Conran

9 **SCRUPLES**
Judith Krantz

8 **LES LIAISONS DANGEREUSES**
Pierre Choderlos De Lacios

7 **THE STORY OF O**
Pauline Réage (Anne Desclos)

6 **EMMANUELLE**
Emmanuelle Arsan

5 **LADY CHATTERLEY'S LOVER**
D H Lawrence

4 **TROPIC OF CANCER**
Henry Miller

3 **FANNY HILL**
John Cleland

2 **LOLITA**
Vladimir Nabokov

1 **FIFTY SHADES OF GREY TRILOGY**
E L James

"I'D LIKE TO BITE THAT LIP"

– FIFTY SHADES OF GREY

TOP
10

The definition is a bit stuffy; a fictional story created in comic-strip format and presented as a book'. But that sounds formal, while the graphic novel is a fluid entity that is always evolving and thus – as the entries on this list confirm – proving that there's plenty of innovative new growth to be found on the novel tree.

GRAPHIC NOVELS

10 *THE NAO OF BROWN* The heroine is a delightful half-Japanese shop worker who falls in love with Nobodaddy, a father figure who looks like a character from one of the *Ichi* comics she adores. Sugar-sweet? Er no, because Nao harbours dark desires to harm other people.

9 *GHOST WORLD* This cult classic features high-school graduates Enid Coleslaw and Rebecca Doppelmeyer as they mooch about town, cynically observing people, criticizing popular culture and speculating about the future (which will see them drifting apart).

8 *BUILDING STORIES* Innovation is the name of the game, remember? This extraordinary boxed set published in 2012 consists of 14 printed works Ð newspapers, books, flip books and broadsheets. The central character (along with a Chicago brownstone) is a nameless one-legged woman.

7 *AKIRA* This Japanese manga series set in post-apocalyptic Tokio deals with power, corruption and social isolation. This serialization is a dramatic evocation of turmoil, and the six-volume set was one of the first complete manga works translated into English.

6 *THE INCAL* A sci-fi series written in French and set in Jodoverse, the author's fictional universe. Private Investigator John DiFool is the (somewhat flawed) hero, getting by with the help of 'concrete seagull' Deepo, even as intergalactic bounty hunter The Metabaron closes in for the kill.

5 *JIMMY CORRIGAN THE SMARTEST KID ON EARTH* Who is the smartest kid on earth? Why, that would be Jimmy Corrigan, even though he's a rather cheerless and meek middle-aged man. But that's in real life. In his imagination, he can escape to childhood – though not always with satisfactory results.

4 *THE DARK KNIGHT RETURNS* Batmen swooped back in 1986, when 55-year-old Bruce Wayne gallantly unfurled his creaking wings and returned from retirement to battle with the Gotham City Police (and US government, why not?).

3 *LOCAS* Who says graphic can't be thoughtful literature? Locas is the brilliantly depicted story of bi-sexual Mexican-American Maggie as the anarchic 1980s Southern California rock scene cranks up – a coming-of-age drama with disturbing undertones of racial tension.

2 *PERSEPOLIS*
The graphic take on the autobiography, as Iranian Marjane Satrapi depicts her dramatic growing-up years during the Islamic Revolution that began with the overthrow of the Shah. Originally published in French, now much translated.

1 **MAUS**
A scarily creative graphic novel with serious intent, as American cartoonist Art Spiegel interviews his father about Holocaust survival, visually substituting animals for races (Polish Jews = mice; other Poles = pigs; Germans = cats). The first 'graphic' Pulitzer prizes winner.

"NINE HOURS LATER, WORLD WAR III BEGAN"

– AKIRA

TOP
10

There are plenty of ways of skinning a cat (assuming you're so minded) and the allegory is one of the sharpest tools in the authorial flensing kit. This technique whereby literary characters or events symbolize or represent concepts and ideas is popular because it enables writers to deal with complex matters in a manner that makes them easier to comprehend.

ALLEGORIES

10 *DOCTOR FAUSTUS*
We all know what this one's about, but it's one of the earlier renditions (published in 1604) of that ominous German tale of the man who sells his soul to the devil. Might doomed Doc Faustus be a stand-in for everyman?

9 *THE DIVINE COMEDY*
This epic poem from the early 14th century is considered to be the apex of Italian literature, presenting an imaginative allegorical vision of the afterlife and encapsulating Christianity's medieval world view.

8 *HAROUN AND THE SEA STORIES*
With one bound we leap forward nearly 700 years, to this 1990 children's book dedicated to the author's son. But magical tales are allegories of problems afflicting mankind in general and modern India in particular.

7 *THE SCARLET LETTER*
Back to the 19th century for the publication of a book set even further back, in the 1640s. This romantic historical novel woven around a woman's shaming in Puritan society is also an allegorical commentary on the fall from grace.

6 *THE PLAGUE*
A French toughie, as La Peste sweeps through the Algerian city of Oran. This existential classic is an examination of the human condition, but also an allegory of French resistance to Nazi occupation in World War II.

5 *JONATHAN LIVINGSTON SEAGULL*
Of course this 1970s cult classic can be read as the biography of an imaginary seagull, but most people appreciate that it's an

allegorical fable cleverly expressing universal ideas regarding human potential.

4 *THE PILGRIM'S PROGRESS*
Back in 1678, master-criminal John Bunyan (twice jailed for holding religious services outside the governance of the established Church of England) published the world's greatest Christian allegory, depicting everyman's journey from this world to Heaven.

3 *INVISIBLE MAN*
This is told by an invisible narrator who isn't really invisible, but considers himself so because he is black in 1950s America. His story begins in the 1920s and serves as an allegory for the racist treatment of African Americans.

2 *THE NAME OF THE ROSE*
This is not only a complex murder mystery set and solved in a medieval

Italian abbey (with thanks to Sherlock Holmes), but also an allegory of the search for the meaning of life.

1 THE BIBLE

The greatest allegory of them all? The world's most-read book has to top a list, and this is the chosen one. Some believe the various versions are factual, but most accept that it's a sacred guide showing the human race how to behave well. If only.

10 DOCTOR FAUSTUS
Christopher Marlowe

9 THE DIVINE COMEDY
Dante

8 HAROUN AND THE SEA STORIES
Salman Rushdie

7 THE SCARLET LETTER
Nathaniel Hawthorne

6 THE PLAGUE
Albert Camus

5 JONATHAN LIVINGSTON SEAGULL
Richard Bach

4 THE PILGRIM'S PROGRESS
John Bunyan

3 INVISIBLE MAN
Ralph Ellison

2 THE NAME OF THE ROSE
Umberto Eco

1 THE BIBLE

"THE GULL SEES FARTHEST WHO FLIES HIGHEST"

– JONATHAN LIVINGSTON SEAGULL

TOP
10

Mostly, aspiring authors can't wait to see their name on a book jacket for the first time, and when it happens that's surely the best day of their authorial life. But every so often a special book comes along that – for reasons that are sometimes very apparent and sometimes not so obvious – is written by the enigmatic 'Anon'.

ANONYMOUS **OFFERINGS**

10 *O: A PRESIDENTIAL NOVEL*
No wonder the author kept stumm – it's observe-and-tell insight into the manipulative genius of spin gurus running a Presidential election campaign. No prizes for guessing who 'O' might be.

9 *EVELINA*
Originally 'anon' but no longer so (author Fanny Burney was 'outed' by a jealous rival), this 18th-century story of a genteel young woman's entry into society had a sharp satirical edge that explains Fanny's desire for anonymity.

8 *GO ASK ALICE*
The 'authentic' diary of an anonymous teenage girl describing descent into drug addiction was a 1971 sensation, but suspicion soon pointed to the book's 'editor', Beatrice Sparks, as the imaginative author.

7 *THE EPIC OF GILGAMESH*
Unavoidably anonymous, as authorship of this epic from ancient Mesopotamia is lost in misty time (as in 2000 BC). One of the earliest surviving literary works.

6 *PRIMARY COLORS*
Another US Presidential campaign-trail 'factional' whistle blast, illuminating the first Clinton run in 1992. Initially anonymous, nay-sayers suggested to conceal the author's possible lack of true inside knowledge. He turned out to be savvy columnist Joe Klein.

5 *THE SONG OF ROLAND*
French literature's oldest survivor, quilled by a long-forgotten hand. This heroic poem composed in the 11th century describes events surrounding the Battle of Roncevaux in 778, during Charlemagne's reign

4 *SIR GAWAIN AND THE GREEN KNIGHT*
A 14th-century Arthurian tale by who-knows-who, as the mysterious Green Knight (is he the Green Man, is he Christ?) grants Sir Gawain one axe-blow for a return strike in a year and a day. Gawain beheads him, but knows he's in trouble when the green one picks up his head.

3 *LUCY IN THE SKY*
From first swig to last breath, this legacy diary charts the fall and fall of a 16-year-old girl from Santa Monica as alcohol drowns her. Is it

the true tragedy of Anon, or another slick marketing ploy?

2 *BEOWULF*
Again the 'anon' label is down to the passage of time, for this epic by an anonymous poet was written somewhere between the 8th and 11th centuries. An important work of Anglo-Saxon literature, recording a mixture of history and myth.

1 ***ONE THOUSAND AND ONE NIGHTS***
Cuckolded Persian king decides women can't be trusted. He takes virgin brides, executing each one next morning to avoid repetition. But the Vizier's daughter tells him an unfinished story – an ongoing ploy that allows her to survive for 1,001 nights (at least). Who thought up those stirring stories? Nobody knows.

"OPEN SESAME!"

– ONE THOUSAND
AND ONE NIGHTS

TOP
10

Where would movie moguls be without books? And where would lucky authors be without casually remarking 'You may have heard that my latest has been optioned by Hollywood' to anyone who'll listen? Yup, the relationship between authors and the silver screen (and latterly TV as a consolation prize) has always been symbiotic, as this impressive list of dual incarnations confirms.

BOOKS TO FILMS

10 *EMPIRE OF THE SUN* Serious novels can engender seriously absorbing films. This story of juvenile wartime privation was transformed by theatre and cinema royalty – writer Tom Stoppard and director Steven Spielberg – into a film that won multiple Academy Awards.

9 *SCHINDLER'S ARK* A harrowing but uplifting book (Schindler's List in the USA) – made for a harrowing but uplifting film. It's that man Spielberg again, co-producing the World War II drama about the Nazi party member who saved thousands of Jews.

8 *THE GUNS OF NAVARONE* Representing all thriller writers whose work underpinned action movies, this World War II adventure charts a daring attack on threatening German guns. Complete with author MacLean's signature traitor-in-the-camp.

7 *DO ANDROIDS DREAM OF ELECTRIC SHEEP?* It's a long title for a 1968 sci-fi novel that inspired a film with an altogether sharper tag – Blade Runner, featuring bounty hunter Rick Deckard's search for rogue androids.

6 *FORREST GUMP* A man of low IQ, Forrest Gump is nonetheless full of homely wisdom. He bumbles through life and American history (even getting the girl at one point), enjoying totally improbable adventures. The film won Academy Awards and made megabucks . . . but took liberties with the novel.

5 *DR ZHIVAGO* Haunting Lara's Theme introduced the 1965 film starring Omar Sharif and Julie Christie, a glossy (and hugely successful) reworking of Boris Pasternak's 1957 novel – a sweeping, epic romance set against the turbulent history of early 20th-century Russia.

4 *THE GODFATHER* One book doth three mighty films make. With a little help from author Mario Puzo, his original 1969 novel *The Godfather* was memorably extended into the best Mafia movie franchise ever. The first and second films won multiple Oscars.

3 *DREAMCATCHER*
A Stephen King sci-fi shocker written in 2001 after his near-fatal car accident. A movie soon followed – for which Hollywood producer could possibly resist worm-like aliens with razor-sharp teeth that snack on humans?

2 *PSYCHO*
Anyone of a certain age will shudder at the sight of a black-and-white female form viewed indistinctly through a shower curtain, for they know what is about to happen – suddenly and shockingly. Robert Bloch's 1959 chiller turned into one of suspense-master Alfred Hitchcock's most memorable films.

1 *GONE WITH THE WIND*
The author's one-book wonder just has to be Number One. The 1936 Pulitzer prizewinning novel is America's second-most-popular read (after the Bible), and this sweeping Southern romantic drama became a record-smashing box-office blockbuster.

10 *EMPIRE OF THE SUN*
J G Ballard

9 *SCHINDLER'S ARK*
Thomas Keneally

8 *THE GUNS OF NAVARONE*
Alaistair Maclean

7 *DO ANDROIDS DREAM OF ELECTRIC SHEEP?*
Philip K Dick

6 *FORREST GUMP*
Winston Groom

5 *DR ZHIVAGO*
Boris Pasternak

4 *THE GODFATHER*
Mario Puzo

3 *DREAMCATCHER*
Stephen King

2 *PSYCHO*
Robert Bloch

---

1 *GONE WITH THE WIND*
Margaret Mitchell

TOP
10

The bullied schoolboy has long known that laughter can be a potent weapon when turned on the tormentor, and writers with an agenda have been quick to appreciate that a sure-fire way of giving the object of their wrath a resounding poke is by using satire – whereby the more widely readers smile, the deeper the injury to their target.

SATIRICAL **SPECIALS**

10 *THE HISTORY MAN*
Cruel campus satire as the Kirks stumble from the Swinging Sixties – sex, drug-taking, personal freedom and radical leftism – into the 1970s. By then gender equality is creaking, radical sociology lecturer Howard Kirk is playing manipulative campus politics, and his exhausted wife is having affairs.

9 *A CONNECTICUT YANKEE IN KING ARTHUR'S COURT*
Humorist Mark Twain wrote this satirical comedy about a man transported back to the court of King Arthur as a double-barrelled blast at contemporary society and the romanticized fascination with times past beloved by some 19th-century novelists.

8 *THE SCREWTAPE LETTERS*
A Demon Screwtape writes to Junior-Tempter Wormwood, who must secure damnation of 'the Patient'. This 1942 book satirizes Christian apologetics, who aim to provide rational justification for their faith.

7 *FIGHT CLUB*
An edgy construct that doesn't use humour – quite the reverse – but still manages a satirical sideswipe at corporate America as the mano-a-mano fist-fighting club goes nationwide and the narrator's fragile psyche crumbles.

6 *AMERICAN PSYCHO*
The target is rapacious late-1980s Wall Street; fat-cat banker Patrick Bateman is the weapon, calmly narrating mundane details of his everyday life (and murderous night forays). His killing spree soon gets out of hand – or does it?

5 LOOK WHO'S BACK

This one shocked Germany by offering a hilarious 'heil' to a nationally taboo subject. Adolf Hitler wakes up in 2011 Berlin and doesn't like what he sees. It's not long before his rants go viral via TV and YouTube – and people start paying attention. The Führer's back!

4 NAKED LUNCH

A chaotic late-1950s collection of bizarre incidents and events involving junkie William Lee (using assorted aliases) as he journeys from the USA to Mexico, on to Tangier and into a dreamlike Interzone. The alternative take on American life.

3 CHANGING PLACES

Comic consequences ensue when an academic from Rummidge (England) undertakes a half-year exchange (of lives and wives) with another from Plotinus (California). Underlying the humour there's serious commentary on academe and academics.

2 WELCOME TO THE MONKEY HOUSE

An extensive 1968-published collection of varied but intertwined short stories, shot through with Kurt Vonnegut's edgy satire as he takes aim at society in general and human nature in particular.

1 THE BONFIRE OF THE VANITIES

This tale of greed, recklessness, legal machinations, self-serving investigative journalism and betrayal serves up a satirical slice of New York City in the 1980s, when Wall Street was king and to hell with everything – and everyone – else.

"BULLSHIT REIGNS"

– THE BONFIRE OF THE VANITIES

CHAPTER 6
PAGE TURNERS

The happy notion of the book as uncomplicated entertainment package is a well-established proposition, and this is the theatre where assorted page-turners offer escape to an exciting world that has something for everyone. And while many titles chosen for inclusion on the following lists harbour no ambition to explain the meaning of life, they can be very well written indeed.

TOP 10

There's something compulsive about a chase, although the outcome is rarely in doubt as you don't find many titles that proceed along the lines of 'we chased him/her/it for the whole book but lost them on the penultimate page'. So, although the destination may not always be obvious, you'll definitely get there in the end – after invariably enjoying an exciting journey.

CHASE **THRILLS**

10 *THE GREATEST MOVIE CAR CHASES OF ALL TIME*
Sadly, books don't do car chases that often or very well, so here's a rapid tyre-smoker to serve as a reminder of what word-bound chaseholics are missing.

9 *THE PELICAN BRIEF*
Sharp-as-a-tack law student Darby Shaw connects murders of two Supreme Court judges to future interests of ruthless oil tycoon Victor Mattiece. Her cleverness is soon on the run, narrowly escaping death – but revenge is sweet as Darby becomes the baddie's nemesis.

8 *ROGUE MALE*
A classic 1939 gallop. British sportsman stalks European dictator (guess who that might be). Will he shoot? We never find out. He's caught and tortured, before escaping and becoming the target of a deadly manhunt.

7 *A MATTER OF HONOUR*
When you accidentally come by a document that allows Russia to claim Alaska back from the USA, there's only one course of action that honour permits – run like hell before the KGB catches you, the CIA kills you or friends betray you.

6 *THE HUNTER*
This crime caper sees double-crossed Parker escaping jail and pursuing the dirty rat who left him for dead, bloodily working his way up 'The Outfit' in search of money due. But will he himself be terminated before he reaches the top?

5 *FIRST BLOOD*
Memo to swaggering small-town sheriffs everywhere – be very careful *not* to bully passers-by before checking that their name *isn't* John Rambo, or you'll soon be involved in a wilderness chase that ends badly – for you.

4 *THE GETAWAY*
This super-violent, pulpy crime caper sees paroled bank robber Doc McCoy pull off one final job before retiring. But there's double-crossing afoot and Doc and wife/moll Carol decamp speedily towards Mexico, hotly pursued by sadistic former partner-in-crime Rudy.

3 *THE EYE OF THE NEEDLE*
A World War II ripping yarn, as German spy Henry Faber discovers D-Day target is Normandy and flees towards U-boat rendezvous with war-winning/losing info, chased by ex-copper Bloggs and the entire British security apparatus.

2 *THE HUNT FOR RED OCTOBER*
Techno-chasing *par excellence*, as Soviet super-submarine Red October (commanded by strangely disillusioned Captain Ramius) flees from pursuing hunter-killer subs with cunning CIA help (orchestrated by impossibly brilliant Jack Ryan).

1 *THE DAY OF THE JACKAL*
The most perfectly crafted chase thriller ever, notable for maintaining gripping tension even though the reader knows the meticulous and unstoppable assassin can't possibly complete his mission to kill French President Charles de Gaulle. But there's a twist . . .

"WILL YOU ASSASSINATE DE GAULLE?"

– THE DAY OF THE JACKAL

10 THE GREATEST MOVIE CAR CHASES OF ALL TIME
Jesse Crosse

9 THE PELICAN BRIEF
John Grisham

8 ROGUE MALE
Geoffrey Household

7 A MATTER OF HONOUR
Jeffrey Archer

6 THE HUNTER
Donald E Westlake

5 FIRST BLOOD
David Morrell

4 THE GETAWAY
Jim Thompson

3 THE EYE OF THE NEEDLE
Ken Follett

2 THE HUNT FOR RED OCTOBER
Tom Clancy

1 THE DAY OF THE JACKAL
Frederick Forsyth

TOP 10

War tends to get those authorial juices pumping fast – especially if the author in question was actually there. Hearteningly, exciting fictional page-turners that feature bullet-proof war heroes are counterbalanced by those more sombre books that highlight the futility of it all (usually crafted by the aforementioned writers who actually experienced the horrors of war for themselves). This list contains both.

WAR **STORIES**

10 *FORGOTTEN VOICES OF THE GREAT WAR*
By way of sober pause for thought before we get started, consider this moving, unputdownable collection of interviews with people who lived through the Great War (to end all wars).

9 *WHERE EAGLES DARE*
He saw Royal Navy action, but author MacLean's war stories are larger than real life. This one features a gallant Allied band penetrating an impenetrable German *schloss* amidst a welter of double- and triple-cross action.

8 *ALL QUIET ON THE WESTERN FRONT*
World War I soldiers are killed, or survive after experiencing excruciating physical and mental angst, with consequent difficulties in subsequent civilian life. This ironically titled novel is by a German vet - yup, 'twas the same for soldiers on both sides.

7 *THE THIN RED LINE*
It's personal (the author fought through the World War II campaign described), it's about emotional horrors, it's gruesome, it involves killing by hand, disinterring corpses for fun and stealing gold teeth, it's war.

5 *SHARPE'S TIGER*
Indestructible (rescued for mission behind enemy lines after suffering only 200 of scheduled 2,000 lashes for attacking sadistic sarge Hakeswill) Richard Sharpe's Indian back story is revealed in this subcontinental sword-swisher.

6 *BOMBER*
It was fiction (date - 31 June 1943), but this account of an RAF raid gone wrong is a

meticulously accurate description of the mechanics. All sides of the story revealed as Lancaster bombers mistakenly destroy German market town.

4 *THE KEY TO REBECCA*
The central character is based on a real German spy, but is infinitely more intelligent, determined and ruthless than the man himself. Authentic action from World War II's North Africa campaign. Dramatic narrative that cleverly blends facts with fantastic fiction.

3 *THE EAGLE HAS LANDED*
Disguised Germans commandos infiltrate Norfolk to kidnap Winston Churchill. They actually end up kidnapping a village, though to be fair they also get the main man (almost).

2 *THE NAKED AND THE DEAD*
Author Norman Mailer saw army service (as a cook). All you really need to know about this seminal Pacific-set war novel comes from the writer's own mouth; 'When it came to taking care of myself, I had little to offer next to the practical sense of an illiterate sharecropper.'

1 *CATCH-22*
Catch it if you can - this is conflict cult daddy number one, as surrealistic humour shoots down nonsensical justifications offered to men who must put their lives on the line time after time in wartime, while all they naïvely want to do is survive.

10 *FORGOTTEN VOICES OF THE GREAT WAR*
Max Arthur

9 *WHERE EAGLES DARE*
Alistair Maclean

8 *ALL QUIET ON THE WESTERN FRONT*
Erich Maria Remarque

7 *THE THIN RED LINE*
James Jones

6 *SHARPE'S TIGER*
Bernard Cornwell

5 *BOMBER*
Len Deighton

4 *THE KEY TO REBECCA*
Ken Follett

3 *THE EAGLE HAS LANDED*
Jack Higgins

2 *THE NAKED AND THE DEAD*
Norman Mailer

1 *CATCH-22*
Joseph Heller

"THAT'S SOME CATCH, THAT CATCH-22"

– CATCH-22

TOP 10

The eternal sea has exercised siren influence over many an author, some spending their entire professional careers writing about nothing else. From this dedicated perspective they have created compelling lives on the ocean wave that are sometimes happy, sometimes sad – but invariably rollicking. So say hello to nautical adventurers who bestride the pages of sea sagas chosen for this list.

NAUTICAL ADVENTURES

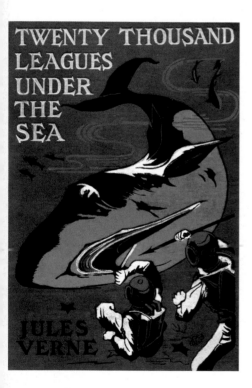

10 *TWENTY THOUSAND LEAGUES UNDER THE SEA*
Phew – it turns out the leagues in question are horizontal rather than vertical in this prescient 19th-century tale of anti-social Captain Nemo and his sub *Nautilus*, mistaken by US Navy pursuers for a sinister sea monster.

9 *CAPTAIN BLOOD*
Come swash a buckle with a sharp-witted Irish doctor who's sold into slavery, before escaping to become infamous buccaneer Captain Blood, scourge of the Caribees.

8 *MR MIDSHIPMAN HORNBLOWER*
A logical starting point, in a prequel describing the first steps on shaky sea legs of one Horatio Hornblower, destined to become the fictional Royal Navy's answer to another Horatio (as in Nelson).

7 *LORD JIM*
With the rest of the crew, Jim abandoned passengers aboard a sinking ship. But they were saved and he spends the rest of his life trying to atone for that moment of cowardice, when he lost the chance of becoming a hero.

6 *THE CRUEL SEA*
A definitively detailed description of naval warfare in the unforgiving North Atlantic, as outnumbered convoy escort vessels battle U-boat packs from early disasters to ultimate victory – by an author who was there.

5 *POSEIDON'S ARROW*
If ever a dashing hero reflects the author's personal wish list then water-walking, classic-car-and-vintage-plane-collecting Dirk Pitt is he – except author Cussler usually makes a cameo personal appearance in the books anyway. Here, Dirk defeats a dastardly baddie bent on trousering the world's rare minerals.

4 *THE PERFECT STORM*
Truth may have been scarier than fiction in this based-on-fact creative drama of fishing boat Andrea Gail of Gloucester, Massachusetts, lost at sea during the mega-storm of 1991.

3 *MASTER AND COMMANDER*
This one launched the enduring Napoleonic naval careers of Jack Aubrey and philosophical surgeon Stephen Maturin, as they sail into battle aboard the brig Sophie. Note – the film of the same name has a different plot.

2 *JAWS*
Snap! That's the sound everyone fears as a deadly denizen of the deep terrorizes a New England seaside community. But all may be well (or not) as grizzled shark-hunter Quint takes to the blood-stained briny in search of that homicidal great white shark.

1 *MOBY-DICK*
If there's one thing deadlier than a great white shark, it's a great white whale. As avenging 'grand, ungodly, godlike' Captain Ahab of Pequod could have testified had he (or more than one of his crew, who told the terrible tale) lived, hell hath no fury like an irritated sperm whale.

10 **TWENTY THOUSAND LEAGUES UNDER THE SEA**
Jules Verne

9 **CAPTAIN BLOOD**
Rafael Sabatini

8 **MR MIDSHIPMAN HORNBLOWER**
C S Forester

7 **LORD JIM**
Joseph Conrad

6 **THE CRUEL SEA**
Nicholas Monserrat

5 **POSEIDON'S ARROW**
Clive Cussler

4 **THE PERFECT STORM**
Sebastian Junger

3 **MASTER AND COMMANDER**
Patrick O'Brian

2 **JAWS**
Peter Benchley

1 **MOBY-DICK**
Herman Melville

"FOR HATE'S SAKE I SPIT MY LAST BREATH AT THEE"

– MOBY DICK

TOP
10

Sometimes, it seems that authors just aren't imaginative enough and must perforce turn to life as it's actually lived (and sometimes extinguished) for their inspiration. But wait. Perhaps that is an unfair accusation, for many of the books chosen for this Top Ten list feature crimes that are as interesting – and bloody – as any that stain fictional pages.

TRUE CRIMES

10 *BLOOD AND MONEY*
Bleak exploration of sensational true-life crimes in Texas. Glam daughter of oil millionaire slain. Plastic-surgeon husband accused of murder, but freed after mistrial. Husband killed, supposedly by robber. Robber killed by cop, supposedly resisting arrest. Pick the truth out of that!

9 *HELTER SKELTER*
The insider's guide to notorious 1960s murders of actress Sharon Tate and others by bearded patriarch Charles Manson and the dysfunctional 'Family'. Written by his trial prosecutor, with a little help.

8 *THE ONION FIELD*
Cop author Wambaugh's writing career progressed to fiction after he started with this close-to-home true-lifer. The field in question saw the murder of one of two LAPD officers kidnapped by petty hoods after a car-stop.

7 *THE MONSTER OF FLORENCE*
It's a mystery still, but this analysis of *Il Mostro*'s deadly deeds does deliver a good suspect. The Monster killed 16 people, mainly couples, between 1968 and 1985. Several suspects were charged, none convicted.

6 *THE EXECUTIONER'S SONG*
Meticulous analysis of events leading up to two murders, the subsequent trial and execution of ex-con Gary Gilmore in 1977. Famously the first man executed in the USA after a 10-year *moratorium*, he *wanted* to die (by firing squad).

5 *THE STRANGER BESIDE ME*
Creative writer investigates 1970s murders, little suspecting a charming, friendly fellow she knows well will turn out to be the killer. Necrophiliac mass murderer, rapist and kidnapper Ted Bundy (executed 1989) it was. Anyway, she wrote it all down.

4 *COLUMBINE*
A cautionary tale for our times. Two popular American students shot up their school in 1999 and killed unlucky 13 people – after leaving more than enough clues regarding their disturbed minds and shocking but still preventable intentions. Nobody bothered to take notice.

3 *THE SUSPICIONS OF MR WHICHER*
A true-life Victorian murder mystery as gripping as any fiction. Young Francis Kent is found almost decapitated in a privy and Scotland Yard 'tec Whicher investigates. Did he get it right? Probably.

2 *ALL THE PRESIDENT'S MEN*
Not a body in sight except, metaphorically, that of disgraced President Nixon. A gripping record of top-level political shenanigans, written by the *Washington Post*'s Watergate investigators. PS: Deep Throat was FBI man Mark Felt.

1 **IN COLD BLOOD**
Still the true-crimer they all want to beat. This 1966 bloodbuster examines, in the round, the 1959 murders of Kansas farmer Herbert Clutter, his wife and two of four children. Parolees Dick Hickok and Perry Smith were executed for the killings

10 **BLOOD AND MONEY**
Thomas Thompson

9 **HELTER SKELTER**
Vincent Bugliosi & Curt Gentry

8 **THE ONION FIELD**
Joseph Wambaugh

7 **THE MONSTER OF FLORENCE**
Mario Spezi & Douglas Preston

6 **THE EXECUTIONER'S SONG**
Norman Mailer

5 **THE STRANGER BESIDE ME**
Ann Rule

4 **COLUMBINE**
Dave Cullen

3 **THE SUSPICIONS OF MR WHICHER**
Kate Summerscale

2 **ALL THE PRESIDENT'S MEN**

Carl Bernstein & Bob Woodward

1 **IN COLD BLOOD**
Truman Capote

TOP 10

What is it about Scandinavia that produces the expanding band of authors who have developed the distinctive approach to crime writing known as Nordic *Noir*? These downbeat Scandi-thrillers tend to share an unadorned writing style and create a dark mood steeped in moral complexity, which sounds a tad depressing. But somehow it has proved to be a globe-conquering formula.

SCANDI-CRIME **BOOKS**

10 *THE PRINCESS OF BURUNDI*
Christmas is coming. It's a snowy night. A young father fails to show for supper. Soon, a killer is terrorizing a Swedish town. Enter (pregnant) Inspector Ann Lindell. But who needs maternity leave when a dangerous game's afoot?

9 *THE BOY IN THE SUITCASE*
No cop she, but a determined Danish Red Cross nurse. You may presume that when an estranged friend leaves Nina Borg a locker key and she finds a drugged three-year-old suitcased therein, it's the end of her desire for the quiet life.

8 *THE ICE PRINCESS*
Small-town Sweden. Her parents have passed away and writer Erica Falck returns. Childhood friend found frozen solid in bath. Erica asked to investigate by grieving parents. Joins forces with detective Patrick Hedström. Town's dark secrets no longer safe.

7 *THE KEEPER OF LOST CAUSES*
If you're a top Copenhagen cop who failed to draw as colleagues died in a bullet hail, don't expect promotion. Then get promoted to head up (one-man) Department Q, the cold (it's Scandinavia) case squad.

6 *THE HYPNOTIST*
Inspector Joona Linna (typical male Scandi-cop with issues) wants to unlock the mind of the only witness to a triple homicide, a grievously wounded boy. Hypnotist Erik Bark had sworn never to do such a thing again, but breaks his promise. Cue terrifying events.

5 *MISS SMILLA'S FEELING FOR SNOW*
A Danish Scandi with serious social undertones, as half-Inuit Smilla suspects the single set of child's footprints across a snowy apartment building roof don't prove suicide – and so it proves.

4 *THE SNOWMAN*
Snowmen don't kill people in Norway (or anywhere else) do they? Probably not, but Harry Hole (please say 'Hool') soon realizes that a series of murders have one thing in common - a watching snowman.

3 *SIDETRACKED*
Bet that the sweltering Swedish summer

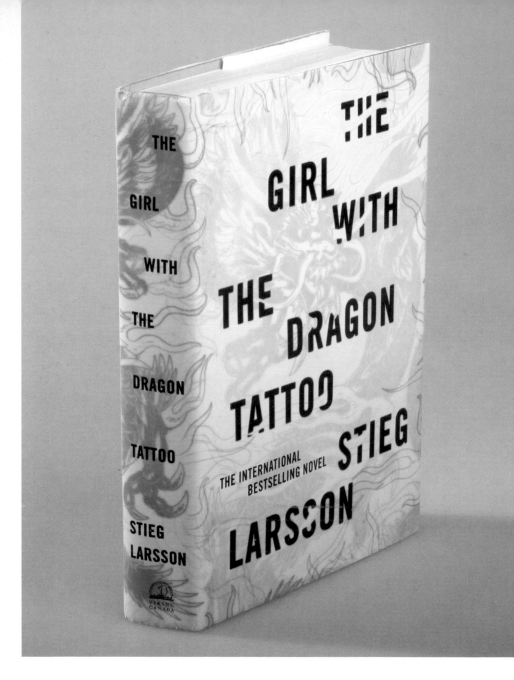

of 1994 didn't pass without incident in Ystad. You win. An axe maniac is scalping the town's successful senior citizens, and a young female immigrant is bent on self-immolation. Now bet that morose Kurt Wallender will sort it. You win.

2 *ROSEANNA*
Meet detective Martin Beck of the Swedish national police. The meticulously solved murder (of an American tourist) is less important than this series first from writing duo Sjöwall and Wahlöö (in 1965) that really set the Scandi-wagon rolling.

1 *THE GIRL WITH THE DRAGON TATTOO*
Ultimate Nordic *Noir*, as writer/publisher Mikael Blomkvist probes a long-buried family secret – an investigation soon involving multi-talented, dragon-tattooed, troubled-but-brilliant hacker Lisbeth Salander.

10 *THE PRINCESS OF BURUNDI*
Kjell Eriksson

9 *THE BOY IN THE SUITCASE*
Lene Kaaberbol

8 *THE ICE PRINCESS*
Camilla Lackberg

7 *THE KEEPER OF LOST CAUSES*
Jussi Odler-olsen

6 *THE HYPNOTIST*
Lars Kepler

5 *MISS SMILLA'S FEELING FOR SNOW*
Peter Hoeg

4 *THE SNOWMAN*
Jo Nesbo

3 *SIDETRACKED*
Henning Mankell

2 *ROSEANNA*
Maj Sjowall-wahloo

1 *THE GIRL WITH THE DRAGON TATTOO*
Stieg Larsson

"AS A GIRL SHE WAS LEGAL PREY"

– THE GIRL WITH THE DRAGON TATTOO

TOP
10

Some pages just don't seem to stop turning – ever. There's something about these eternally young titles that catches the imagination of generation after generation of readers, who take real pleasure in unearthing a gem that will catch and hold their attention to the last page. Here are just ten of the never-out-of-printers that have aged like fine literary wine.

ENDURING FAVOURITES

10 *THE LOST WORLD*
If you get an idea for a dinosaur book called, say, *Jurassic Park*, be aware that Professor Challenger discovered living dinosaurs in South America a century ago, along with pterodactyls and ape men. So there!

9 *THE RED BADGE OF COURAGE*
A realistic masterpiece featuring Private Henry Fleming, who flees a battlefield in the American Civil War, only to return in search of that painful 'red badge of courage' (wound).

8 *THE SCARLET PIMPERNEL*
Aristocratic heads are falling like rain after visiting *Madame la Guillotine*. Enter foppish Englishman Percy Blakeney, who in true pre-superhero style morphs into the steely Scarlet Pimpernel – fearless foiler of fervent French revolutionaries.

7 *THE THREE MUSKETEERS*
Strange title, as everyone knows there were four: Athos, Porthos, Aramis and d'Artagnan. Or perhaps the fiery young Gascon didn't actually become a Musketeer until the end of a sweeping adventure full of treachery, murder and sword play.

6 *ROB ROY*
Surprisingly, this real Highland outlaw isn't the hero of a romantic saga bearing his name, although he does keep supporting Frank Osbaldistone's efforts to restore the family fortunes and win the fair dame.

5 *BEAU GESTE*
If you're a traditional upper-class Englishman, there's only one decent thing to do after confessing (falsely) to stealing a priceless jewel – join the French Foreign Legion. It's a decision that will stretch that stiff upper lip to the limit.

4 *AROUND THE WORLD IN 80 DAYS*
Can it be done? Well yes, quite easily – now. But in 1873 when Phileas Fogg and valet Passepartout gave it a go for a £20,000 bet, it wasn't so easy. Trains, boats, elephants

and wind sledges helped (no balloons in the book), but it'll be tight.

3 THE LAST OF THE MOHICANS
This is *the* novel about pre-Revolutionary America, set in 1757 during the French and Indian War and loosely based on real events. But Hawkeye, Chingachgook, Uncas and the evil Magua are memorable fictions.

2 THE THIRTY-NINE STEPS
A superb spy thriller, as Richard Hannay runs from the law – and pursuing German agents – on the eve of World War I. After being chased over half of Scotland, our resourceful hero thwarts the plot to steal Britain's military secrets.

1 THE WAR OF THE WORLDS
The blueprint for countless mankind v extraterrestrial bouts in years to come, this 1898 Martian invasion special scared the hell out of readers, then American radio audiences in the 1930 Orson Welles' adaptation.

10 THE LOST WORLD
Arthur Conan Doyle

9 THE RED BADGE OF COURAGE
Stephen Crane

8 THE SCARLET PIMPERNEL
Baroness Emma Orczy

7 THE THREE MUSKETEERS
Alexander Dumas

6 ROB ROY
Walter Scott

5 BEAU GESTE
P C Wren

4 AROUND THE WORLD IN 80 DAYS
Jules Verne

3 THE LAST OF THE MOHICANS
James Fennimore Cooper

2 THE THIRTY-NINE STEPS
John Buchan

1 THE WAR OF THE WORLDS
H G Wells

"ALL FOR ONE AND ONE FOR ALL"

– THE THREE MUSKETEERS

TOP 10

Welcome to the lucrative (for authors) and satisfying (for readers) world of the complex and/or damaged detective (possessing troubling flaw, quirky character trait or bearing painfully debilitating mental cross). And of course once a tortured 'tec makes the popular grade, numerous repeat performances (and TV or movie stardom) can beckon. Here are ten books featuring detectives who made it big.

COMPLEX DETECTIVES

10 *TRENT'S LAST CASE* Gentleman sleuth Philip Trent was supposed to have but one outing – in this 1913 send-up where he does a Sherlock-like job on the evidence before reaching erroneous conclusions and (shock, horror!) falling in love with the *femme fatale*. But he returned.

9 *THE REMORSEFUL DAY* Melancholy, opera-loving, crossword-buff, ale-swilling, bachelor Inspector (we at last find out it's Endeavour) Morse, with ever-stolid Sergeant Lewis's help, tries to hose another killer off Oxford's blood-stained streets. Then he dies after featuring in 13 books. Unlucky.

8 *WHISKEY SOUR* Inspector Jacqueline 'Jack' Daniels in a book with *that* title? Actually, yes – appropriately introducing the Chicago PD 'tec with a chaotic personal life, as she aims to halt murderous mutilations perped by The Gingerbread Man.

7 *RATKING* A name like Aurelio Zen should indicate calmness, but doesn't. The complex Italian copes with conflicting demands (girlfriend, aged mother, pressured job, office politics) by escaping into his current case. This, his debut, sees him sorting a sensitive kidnapping.

6 *DEAD LIKE YOU* Inspector Roy Grace's wife vanished long ago (that's *his* cross to bear), but this very believable Brighton cop still goes efficiently about his business, here pursuing elusive rapist and murderer the Shoe Man.

5 *THE TROUBLED MAN* With one lumber, Kurt Wallender lurches from Scandi-Crime to Complex Detective. Fair enough, he's over-qualified in both departments. The angst-ridden Swede's (allegedly) last case is a biggie – a massive spy scandal.

4 *BLACK AND BLUE* Inspector John Rebus is Edinburgh's answer to Scandi Noir – he's *the* titan of Tartan Noir. Personally shambolic Rebus can still crime-crack, here tackling infamous killer Bible John while under internal investigation (led by an old enemy) and external press scrutiny.

3 *ORIGINAL SIN*

Steadily promoted, poetry-penning Scotland Yard heavy hitter Adam Dalgleish (now a stratospheric Commander) is an intensely private, cerebral sleuth. Here he probes dark doings at The Peveril Press, proving that publishing can be perilous.

2 *THE DROWNING POOL*

Wham, bam - world-weary Philip Marlowe clone Lew Archer's in town, plagued by former failures and doing his cool Los Angeles PI thing. This 1950 case concerns a libellous letter - but that's just the hard-hitting *hors d'oeuvre*.

1 *A STUDY IN SCARLET*

The cocaine-taking, fiddling (as in violin) brain-box made his brilliant investigative debut in this eventually untangled tale, impressing new buddy Watson and Inspector Lestrade - doing so well that with luck he might go on to become the world's most famous detective.

---

10 TRENT'S LAST CASE
E C Bentley · **Philip Trent**

9 THE REMORSEFUL DAY
Colin Dexter · **Inspector Morse**

8 WHISKEY SOUR
J A Konrath · **'Jack' Daniels**

7 RATKING
Michael Dibdin · **Aurelio Zen**

6 DEAD LIKE YOU
Peter James · **Roy Grace**

5 THE TROUBLED MAN
Henning Mankell · **Kurt Wallender**

4 BLACK AND BLUE
Ian Rankin · **John Rebus**

3 ORIGINAL SIN
P D James · **Adam Dalgleish**

2 THE DROWNING POOL
Ross Macdonald · **Lew Archer**

---

1 A STUDY IN SCARLET
Arthur Conan Doyle · **Sherlock**

"NO PERSON IS WITHOUT A SHADOW"

– *THE TROUBLED MAN*

TOP
10

When it comes to a Top Ten list featuring professionals, it makes sense to focus on two monumental staples of American life – medical matters and multifarious litigation. The two may sometimes interlock more quickly than you can say 'ambulance chaser', but each profession is more than capable of wobbling on its own two feet should the occasion so demand.

PROFESSIONALS

10 *DONOR*
Thinks – if ex-SAS fictional heroes are too thick on the ground, what's to do? Ah, also make him a medic, call him Dr Stephen Dunbar and turn him loose on mysterious goings-on in an exclusive Glasgow private hospital. Satisfactorily sorted!

9 *THE CASE OF THE CARELESS KITTEN*
Even if you purchase this for the title alone, you won't be disappointed as courtroom crusader Perry Mason gallops to the rescue of two clients, including long-suffering secretary Della Street.

8 *THE HOT ZONE*
A non-fiction medical book can be a bestseller, even if the subject matter concerns esoteric-sounding viral hemorrhagic fevers.

Think ebola and marburg viruses and be very *afraid* of a yet-to-be-unleashed global pandemic.

7 *PRIMAL FEAR*
Is there anything more innocent than an altar boy? Well, apart from other possible considerations, Aaron Stampler has been accused of murder (bloody knife in hand, dead archbishop). Worry you not, the intervention of unorthodox attorney Martin Vail should establish the truth of the matter.

6 *UNNATURAL EXPOSURE*
Five headless, limbless corpses have shown up in Ireland and four more pop up in Virginia. The shadowy suspect is not only messing with pathologist Kay Scarpetta's mind, but also

threatening to unleash a killer smallpox pandemic.

5 *NOW YOU SEE HER*
Successful New York lawyer Nina Bloom has a secret past, but when an innocent man is accused of murder she returns to Florida to confront the monstrous evil that caused her to flee 18 years before.

4 *THE ANDROMEDA STRAIN*
Medical mayhem meets scary sci-fi in this drama of a deadly micro-organism brought back to earth by satellite. After inhabitants of the nearest town drop dead or commit suicide, the secret Wildfire lab moves in to try and save the world.

3 *PRESUMED INNOCENT*
Public prosecutor Rusty Sabich is assigned to the case of murdered co-

worker Carolyn Polhemus. But before long it emerges that she was Rusty's ex-lover, and before much longer he's facing trial for her murder.

2 *COMA*
Student doc Susan Wheeler uncovers a deadly hospital conspiracy – op-room patients are brain-deadified so that the bodies can be used for black-market organ sales. Susan evades assassination, but then wakes up on an operating table . . .

1 *THE KING OF TORTS*
A list-topper merging featured themes, as public defender Clay Carter takes the case of Tequila Watson, random street slayer. But all's not as it seems and Clay uncovers massive medical malpractice that will catapult him to legal financial heaven. For now.

"MEN UNDER STRESS ARE FOOLS"

– THE ANDROMEDA STRAIN

TOP
10

Time to put pen to paper and create your own top 10 list of thrillers...

10

9

8

7

6

5

4

3

2

1

DAN BROWN
THE
DA VINCI
CODE

'Fascinating and absorbing . . .
A great, riveting read. I loved
this book' **HARLAN COBEN**

TOP
10

Home, home on the range – the 30-year era of cattle drives may have been relatively brief (from 1866–95, when the introduction of barbed wire closed the open range) but, with more than a little help from the books on this list, fictional fascination with the subject ensured that the gun-totin' cowboy became the iconic image symbolizing America's Old West.

RANGE **RIDERS**

10 *THE WINNING OF THE WEST*
The best-ever source for those craving the unfictionalized truth about the Old West was written by future President Theodore Roosevelt. There was plenty to recount – the telling filled six volumes.

9 *THE LONE COWBOY*
Cowboy-obsessed Canadian artist and writer Will James fled to the USA after being accused of cattle theft (he'd later be jailed in Nevada for rustling). This 1930 book tells of a young orphan learning the prairie life.

8 *HOPALONG CASSIDY*
Created in 1904 as a rough, tough, rude and dangerous antihero, Hopalong's subsequent 1935 screen incarnation (played by William Boyd, 66 films) turned him into a clean-cut cowboy – so author Mulford revised his books to synchronize.

7 *THE LONE RANGER*
Spawned by a 1933 radio series, the 18 Lone (Texas) Ranger books were penned by Gaylord Dubois (this first one) and by radio-show creator Fran Striker. Need any more be said than 'Hi-Yo, Silver! Away!'?

6 *HONDO*
Novelization by the author of his 1953 screenplay. Deserted on a remote ranch, Angie Lowe raises a son. Hondo Lane is the big man who walks in carrying his saddle. Apache chief Vittoro's people are about to rise up against the white man. Some triangle!

5 *THE SHOOTIST*
In 1901 ageing, dying gunslinger J B Books wants to go with dignity, but of course that's not a grantable wish, so bullets fly and corpses drop like flies before he pegs it. Poignantly, it was dying John Wayne's last movie stand.

4 *ALL THE PRETTY HORSES*
Young cowboy John Grady Cole rides down into Mexico with companions Rawlins and Blevins, hoping to find work. It's the start of a dangerous expedition costing John the new love of his life, and nearly life itself.

3 *BROKEBACK MOUNTAIN*
A story featuring two young 1960s wranglers, spending time together minding sheep on high Wyoming pastures. They

form an unexpected emotional and sexual bond, before going their separate ways, trying (unsuccessfully) to make new lives, but meeting periodically over 20 years.

2 *RIDERS OF THE PURPLE SAGE*
Mormon ranch heiress Jane Withersteen is coveted by polygamist Elder Tull, but tight with non-Mormon cowboy Venters and Mormon-slaying gunman Lassiter. It's powerful Western chemistry, and duly explodes.

1 *LONESOME DOVE*
In 1876, retired Texas Rangers set out on an ambitious cattle drive to a Promised Land - distant Montana Territory. The assorted characters who take part, and those encountered along the trail, make for a memorable journey.

"THE OLDER THE VIOLIN, THE SWEETER THE MUSIC"

– *LONESOME DOVE*

10 *THE WINNING OF THE WEST*
Theodore Roosevelt

9 *THE LONE COWBOY*
Will James

8 *HOPALONG CASSIDY*
Clarence Mulford

7 *THE LONE RANGER*
Gaylord Dubois

6 *HONDO*
Louis L'amour

5 *THE SHOOTIST*
Glendon Swarthout

4 *ALL THE PRETTY HORSES*
Cormac McCarthy

3 *BROKEBACK MOUNTAIN*
E Annie Proulx

2 *RIDERS OF THE PURPLE SAGE*
Zane Grey

1 *LONESOME DOVE*
Larry McMurtry

TOP 10

There's a fashion for breeding puppies that capture the best qualities of two breeds – labradors and standard poodles become labradoodles, cockers spaniels and miniature poodles become cockerpoos and more besides. So it is with this Top Ten, for the techno-thriller crosses a standard page-turner in any genre – thriller, sci-fi, espionage, war – with oodles of authentic technical detail.

TECHNO-THRILLS

10 THE CUCKOO'S EGG Another techno-thriller variant – the true story reading like fiction. It's the fascinating tale of a Californian computer manager's hunt for a hacker. After an amazing international operation, West German Markus Hess was convicted of selling hacked secrets to the KGB.

9 TEK KILL Who would have thought Captain James T Kirk of Federation starship USS Enterprise would turn out to be a writer? But so it proved, as actor William Shatner offered this among his 1990s *Tek War* sci-fi techno-thriller series.

8 ICE STATION Wow – if international corpses are your thing, look no further. The body count rockets as elite forces of various nationalities slaughter each other in, under and around Wilkes Ice Station. It may be about an alien ship that's really a spy ship, but it's hard to be sure amidst the bloodshed.

7 ARC LIGHT Is it a military and/ or political techno-thriller? Or is it just a book about World War III, as Russia and America accidentally get into a grimly detailed small nuclear war, and doves try to stop hawks making it a big one?

6 DAEMON After its programmer 'daddy' dies, computer application The Daemon starts killing everything and everyone that obstructs it. Can cybertecs Sebeck and Ross stop Daemon's dastardly dash for world domination? Possibly not.

5 THE BLUE NOWHERE Sadistic hacker Phate invades computers and victims' lives, then ensures they die. To try and stop the techno-rot, old-style homicide cop Frank Bishop teams up with freed-from-jail hacker Wyatt Gillette.

4 DIGITAL FORTRESS Disgruntled former NSA employee Ensel Tankado creates a code called Digital Fortress the agency's computers can't break, with terrible implications for national security. Then Tankado dies in Seville, and the key goes missing.

3 FIREFOX This beauty helped the then-embryonic

techno-thriller genre to fly. Burned-out pilot/spy Mitchell Gant infiltrates a Russian base and steals top-secret, super-advanced MiG-31 (codename Firefox). Gant is pursued by second MiG-31 in high-tec air chase/battle. Gant escapes (just).

2 *NEXT*
Genetic research is big business, and Frank Burnet's cells have been sold to BioGen after successful leukaemia treatment. It's the start of a roller-coaster ride featuring the likes of a human-chimp cross, humanoid parrot and complex corporate chicanery.

1 *CLEAR AND PRESENT DANGER*
The CIA's Jack Ryan almost single-handedly elevated the techno-thriller to mainstream genre. The US government is covertly directing every technical and physical resource at its disposal against Columbian drug cartels, but Jack still has to sort the mess out personally.powers effortlessly outwits stupid parents and the cruel headmistress.

"POWER . . . IT WAS ALL ABOUT POWER"

– THE BLUE NOWHERE

TOP
10

What's at the end of the authorial rainbow? Serious fiction writers might hope for a Mann-Booker, Pulitzer, even a Nobel Prize. But commercially speaking there's only one crock of gold – the serial thriller. Get 'em hooked, turn out a book a year, job done. Here are ten titles that launched their writers towards that shimmering spectrum of series success.

SERIAL **THRILLERS**

10 *OPEN SEASON*
Mix scrupulously decent game warden with deadly on-the-run Native American buddy, add incomparable Wyoming wilderness and throw in serious bad guys. Decant into a 2001 book called Open Season (when things get killed). Watch Joe Pickett go stratospheric.

9 *THE BOURNE IDENTITY*
Can three books make a mega-series? With help from Hollywood, the answer is 'you bet!'. Amnesiac Jason Bourne was well met floating in the sea when this one hit the book stores in 1980 and the rest is, well, lucrative.

8 *THE BONE COLLECTOR*
Can a quadriplegic criminologist solve one case, let alone dozens? Yup, if Lincoln Rhyme (first introduced here in 1997) hooks up with surrogate Amelia Sachs, a savvy NYPD junior officer, they'll bury the Bone Collector.

7 *THE RED DRAGON*
Who would believe a 1991 book introducing a brilliant criminal psychiatrist could commence an internationally acclaimed series? Come to think of it, if Dr Hannibal Lecter were a cannibalistic serial killer who just might help the FBI nail The Tooth Fairy, it could have potential.

6 *DEAL BREAKER*
In 1995 Myron Bolitar tiptoed towards series stardom in this opening opus that begins with a phone call from a long-dead girl, posing the sort of 'how's-that-remotely-possible?'

conundrum that became Myron's *metier*.

5 *ANGELS & DEMONS*
May 2000 saw this debut drama featuring Professor Robert Langdon (specialist subject, religious iconography and symbology – don't bother looking for a course). Series-spinning ingredients were there – secret societies, Catholicism, ancient history. Luckily, the Prof saves the Vatican.

4 *PATRIOT GAMES*
Reminding us of the prequel, CIA superstar Jack Ryan's career launch only required one backward leap from *Red October* in this 1987 biggie where he saves the Prince of Wales, his wife and infant heir (and *ergo* the British monarchy's future).

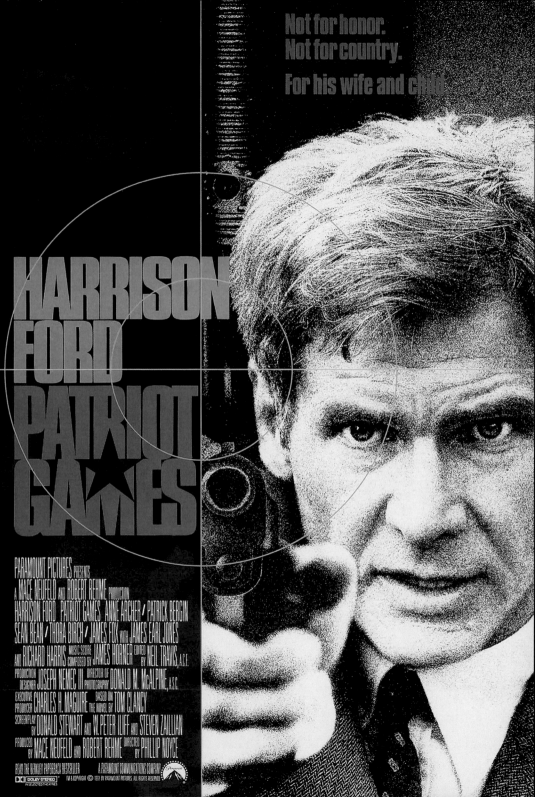

3 *POSTMORTEM*
Gore galore is a pathologist's lot and this 1990 debut for Kay Scarpetta (Virginia's Chief Medical Examiner) certainly delivered in that department, also setting a trend for pathologists who augment the day job as honorary cops.

2 *KILLING FLOOR*
A Brit named Lee Child (well, Jim Grant) harboured high hopes for his ex-US Army cop Jack Reacher when he found a publisher for this one in 1997, but subsequent megastardom for the wandering avenger probably surprised even him.

1 *CASINO ROYALE*
Leaving out automatic top-spotter J K Rowling, lauded elsewhere, Ian Fleming's estate must be way ahead of anyone else in the series stakes. The world's second-most-famous fictional character first appeared in this 1959 page-turner.

10 *OPEN SEASON*
C J Box

9 *THE BOURNE IDENTITY*
Robert Ludlum

8 *THE BONE COLLECTOR*
Jeffery Deaver

7 *THE RED DRAGON*
Thomas Harris

6 *DEAL BREAKER*
Harlan Coben

5 *ANGELS & DEMONS*
Dan Brown

4 *PATRIOT GAMES*
Tom Clancy

3 *POSTMORTEM*
Patricia Cornwell

2 *KILLING FLOOR*
Lee Child

1 *CASINO ROYALE*
Ian Fleming

"MINE'S BOND – JAMES BOND"

– CASINO ROYALE

TOP
10

The word 'pulp' somehow suggests something second-rate, and sometimes that's true. If you were a cheap publisher publishing dime crime on cheap and pulpy paper, you just might have been surprised to discover you'd hit on a winning formula that ultimately far transcended the derogatory label 'pulp fiction'. Indeed, the alternative term 'noir' is constantly being reinvented to this day.

NOIR **NOVELS**

9 *THE BIG HEAT*
When sick cop Tom Duncan dies, Sergeant Dave Bannion thinks suicide. But Tom had a hidden life and when Bannion asks questions, his wife is murdered. He doesn't take the hint and the crime syndicate feels the big heat.

8 *THE LOST WEEKEND*
The baddie's a bottle during alcoholic Don's five-day bender, as girlfriend Helen tries to stop him drinking himself to death. Don (as you do) merely contemplates killing her maid to get the drinks-cabinet key.

7 *THE BLACK DAHLIA*
Dark drama woven around a real LA slaying – that of Black Dahlia Elizabeth Short. The seedy city stars as troubled

10 *THE ASPHALT JUNGLE*
This toughie features the planning and execution of a jewellery store heist in a corrupt Midwestern metropolis that exudes seedy menace. The gang comes to grief in a welter of bad luck, personal obsession and double-cross.

cop Dwight 'Bucky' Bleichert tries to crack the sensational case.

6 *KISS ME DEADLY*
Tough private eye Mike Hammer gives a lift to a lady, but she's killed and Hammer's car goes over a cliff with him in it, her corpse beside him. He takes it badly, as the local Mafiosi discover to their cost.

5 *DEADLINE AT DAWN*
It's night-time in the soulless city. You're framed for murder and have to find the real perp in five hours, as the inexorable clock ticks down towards that deadly dawn deadline.

4 *THE BLACK ANGEL*
Kirk's on Death Row for murdering his mistress. Wife Alberta crawls after the real killer through the city's underbelly, but it

goes horribly wrong when she falls for the murderer.

3 *THE BIG SLEEP*
If you're only allowed to make music with one *noir* hero, make it with wise-cracking, cynical Philip Marlowe. Here, the LA sleuth deals with a very fatal *femme* and more double-crosses than there are fingers on a gun hand.

2 *THE POSTMAN ALWAYS RINGS TWICE*
Rural Californian diner, owned by older man (Nick The Greek) with younger wife (Cora). Drifter Frank arrives. Frank and Cora have passionate affair, determine to kill Nick and live happily ever after. But this is a *noir* classic, so it doesn't work out.

1 *THE MALTESE FALCON*
Sam Spade is *the* man, appearing in but one novel (this one) but setting the style for the subsequent hardboiled *noir* PI genre. The falcon's a figurine, body count is high, the plot is complex and at the end of it all *cherchez la femme*.

"IF THEY HANG YOU, I'LL ALWAYS REMEMBER YOU"

– *THE MALTESE FALCON*

There's something very seductive about learning secrets, but unfortunately lots of people couldn't even keep a tasty just-heard nugget of information secret to save their lives. But that's what has to happen in the murky but compulsive world of fictional espionage, where unexpected double-cross lurks around every corner and secrets are the very stuff of life – and often death.

SPY STORIES

10 *FROM RUSSIA WITH LOVE*
No list of spy fiction could ever be complete without a James Bond. This is one of the best as 007 and delectable Tatiana Romanova flee on the Orient Express with the vital Spektor machine.

9 *THE SECRET AGENT: A SIMPLE TALE*
A thoughtful early espionage novel, published in 1907 but set in the 1880s. It features Victorian spy Mr Verloc, and deals presciently with themes of anarchism and terrorism.

8 *THE MYSTERY OF TUNNEL 51*
Colourful Alexander Wilson (real life stranger than fiction) introduced spymaster Sir Leonard Wallace with this one in 1928. Think tackling threats like the Soviet Union, Empire terrorism and organized crime.

7 *EPITAPH FOR A SPY*
France, the eve of World War II. Refugee Josef Vadassy takes holiday snaps to be developed and is arrested as a Gestapo spy. He must risk everything, including his life, to unmask the real spy staying at his hotel.

6 *ABOVE SUSPICION*
It's 1939 and an English couple journey across Germany, undertaking a secret mission to meet a succession of agents with the help of a wily American reporter and a fellow Englishman. But it turns out that the Nazis are no fools.

5 *RESTLESS*
In World War II, a young Russian woman is recruited by the British secret service. She falls for boss Lucas Romer, and soon Eva and other agents are in mortal danger. What happens next? Eva's daughter pieces the story together in the 1970s.

4 *THE SCARLATTI INHERITANCE*
Washington in World War II, and a top Nazi offers to defect with vital information. But the release of the secret Scarlatti Inheritance file is the price, with potentially catastrophic consequences.

3 *THE IPCRESS FILE*
Never named in print (but Harry Palmer to film-goers), the laid-back working-class hero of this devious tale involving

smoke, mirrors and double-crossing spies helped fire author Len Deighton into the espionage stratosphere.

2 *THE RIDDLE OF THE SANDS*
An early spy classic published in 1903 (subtitled *A Record of Secret Service*) sees two Englishmen on a small yacht infiltrating the German Frisian Islands, where they unearth a Hunnish plot to invade Great Britain (duly foiled).

1 **THE SPY WHO CAME IN FROM THE COLD**
The list-topper has to be an offering from the author who elevated espionage fiction to new heights, exploring the dubious morality of British intelligence operations. Here, burned-out spy Alec Leamas must perforce go behind enemy lines one more time.

TOP 10

The greatest manager in the history of successful soccer club Liverpool FC said it all: 'Some people believe football is a matter of life and death. I am very disappointed with that attitude. I can assure you it is much, much more important than that.'. And sporting passion similar to Bill Shankly's energizes the fast-moving pages of this Top Ten.

SPORTING GIANTS

10 *THIS SPORTING LIFE*
As kitchen-sink drama swept Britain in the late 1950s and working-class heroes ruled, former pro David Storey created this grittily authentic portrait of up-and-coming Yorkshire rugby league loose forward Frank Machin. Literary and sporting drama combined.

9 *FLANAGAN'S RUN*
Inspired by the 1928 Bunion Derby, a 3,455-mile foot race from LA to New York (via Chicago), this epic novel by a former athlete gets right under the skin of gruelling sporting competition.

8 *WINNING UGLY*
Call it the combat manual for sport – as the rewards of pro sport grow ever more vast, and amateurs become ever more competitive, top ball-basher Brad Gilbert offers insider's advice on out-thinking and outplaying any opponent.

7 *THE GAME*
Any kid dreaming of a career in sport should read this memoir by a former Montreal Canadiens goal minder. It provides fascinating insight into the demands of pro sport and the realities of a professional player's life.

6 *SHUNT: THE STORY OF JAMES HUNT*
Grand prix motor racing has become a billion-dollar business, but this endearing biography recalls an era when a laid-back Englishman who liked to party and won his first GP race in a car built by an eccentric British peer lifted a world championship.

5 *INTO THIN AIR*
Mountaineering is notoriously demanding, and Mount Everest is the one they all want to conquer. But by definition that feat can't be easy, and this is the searing account of a 1996 expedition that went disastrously wrong.

4 *THE NATURAL*
Inspired by the true-life shooting of Philadelphia Phillies player Eddie Waitkus by a woman, and his subsequent comeback, this is as good a novel as the all-American game of baseball has produced.

3 *SEABISCUIT*
Rags to riches fables are compelling, but this one happens to be true. Small, knob-kneed and lazy Seabiscuit had some racing success, but when a new trainer took over he lifted

the spirits of Depression-era America by becoming a feted serial winner.

2 *THE FIGHT*
When a great American writer covers a great fight between two great American boxing champions the inevitable result is . . . a great boxing book featuring that oh-so-famous 1974 Rumble in the Jungle (Zaire, actually).

1 *FEVER PITCH*
If affirmation of the importance of sport in people's everyday lives were ever needed, this is the book to provide it. Author Nick Hornby's life and the times of his beloved Arsenal FC entwine majestically in this addictive tale of sporting obsession.

10 *THIS SPORTING LIFE*
David Storey

9 *FLANAGAN'S RUN*
Tom McNab

8 *WINNING UGLY*
Brad Gilbert & Steve Jamison

7 THE GAME
Ken Dryden

6 *SHUNT: THE STORY OF JAMES HUNT*
Tom Rubython

5 *INTO THIN AIR*
John Krakauer

4 *THE NATURAL*
Bernard Malamud

3 *SEABISCUIT*
Laura Hillenbrand

2 *THE FIGHT*
Norman Mailer

1 *FEVER PITCH*
Nick Hornby

"I HAD COME OFF THE RAILS SOMEWHERE"

– FEVER PITCH

There are two types of police detective work in the written world. On one side stands the Sherlockian sleuth, usually with a trusty sidekick, who works it out without help from the back office. On the other is the more realistic depiction of meticulous police work as it really is. This list lauds the latter, featuring ten top police procedurals.

POLICE **PROCEDURALS**

10 *GIDEON'S FIRE*
J J Maric was the *nom de plume* adopted by prolific crime writer John Creasey for his procedural series starring Gideon of the Yard, who organizes his team to probe unrelated crimes (here a fatal arson attack plus a rape and murder).

9 *V AS IN VICTIM*
A father of the police procedural, Lawrence Treat published this influential classic in 1945. A plodding third-grade detective and clever lab technician combine to link murder with a routine hit-and-run case.

8 *HELL IS A CITY*
Halifax copper Maurice Proctor acquired his authentic touch on the job, retiring only when his writing career took off.

This 1954 novel features Inspector Martineau, sorting out the aftermath of a violent jail break.

7 *NIGHTMARE*
'Queen of the Procedurals' Barbara Linington had huge success (as Dell Shannon) with books featuring LAPD detective Luis Mendoza and departmental workings. This one tackled vanishing treasure, drug dealing and law-breaking brothers.

6 *LAST SEEN WEARING*
A top-drawer police procedural from 1952, the more so because it's a very believable scenario. Focusing on meticulous police work that goes into the investigation of a college student's disappearance.

5 *THE CONCRETE BLONDE*
The title may be heavy, but the book itself is a flier, as Detective Harry Bosch gets carried away in his pursuit of serial killer The Dollmaker, with unfortunate consequences that return to haunt him.

4 *MAIGRET AND THE DOSSER*
Although the focus is on a single detective, former journalist Simenon still gave a very believable portrayal of Paris police work, and Jules Maigret always had help. Here, in a typically low-key case, an assaulted tramp's back story is revealed.

3 *THE CHOIRBOYS*
Nothing religious about these choir boys – ten LAPD patrol officers get together at the end of

their night watch for lusty 'choir practices' involving heavy drinking, bad-mouthing superiors, tall tale-telling and occasional group sex with barmaids. Over the top? Probably not.

2 COP HATER

An awful lot of authentic police procedure is covered in Ed McBain's monumental 87th Precinct series. This, from 1956, is the first of them. Detective Steve Carella puts himself in harm's way as he investigates the slaying of three fellow officers.

1 DEAD SIMPLE

Detective Inspector Roy Grace of Sussex Police may be the usual copper with personal issues, but the way he addresses his work is a super-accurate portrayal of the real thing. In this 2005 debut novel, time starts running out after an unfortunate victim is buried alive.

"I MISS MY MORNING COFFEE AND CORPSE"

– COP HATER

TOP 10

After all that grinding proper police work, we move on to the cerebral domain of inspired detectives using nothing but those (as the incomparable Hercule Poirot put it not infrequently) 'little grey cells' to defy discombobulation and in so doing get to the bottom of mysteries that are as fiendishly cunning as the devious minds of crime writers can devise.

WHODUNITS

10 *THE MOONSTONE* The English language's first detective novel, published in 1868. When a huge rock (as in diamond) goes missing after a house party, the mystery must be mastered by two very different sleuths - gentleman detective Franklin Blake and rough-cut Sergeant Cuff of the Yard.

9 *THE LEAVENWORTH CASE* Pioneering female crime writer Anne Katherine Green conjured up this case in 1878, introducing the alert Ebenezer Gryce, who soon surmises that shot-through-the-head millionaire Horatio Leavenworth didn't self-destruct.

8 *UNNATURAL DEATH* Elegant Lord

Peter Wimsey is prone to meddling, and when he overhears the story of a cancer patient close to death who nonetheless departs with unexpected haste, he's moved to investigate the three-year-old killing (for so, inevitably, it was).

7 *THE GREEK COFFIN MYSTERY* When NYPD's Inspector Richard Queen (with a little help from amateur sleuth son Ellery) deduces that a dead man's missing will is in his coffin, exhumation springs a surprise – the coffin also contains a strangled ex-con. However did that happen? Over to the Queens . . .

6 *DEATH OF A GHOST* Enigmatic adventurer-detective Albert Campion joins forces with notably named copper Stanislaus Oates to probe the possibilities when a dead painter's annual remembrance bash ends in death.

5 *VINTAGE MURDER* The fifth book to feature gentleman (brother of a baronet) police detective Roderick Alleyn. Unusually, this mystery is set in New Zealand (the author's homeland) and requires the holidaying 'tec to solve an on-stage murder.

4 *THE THREE COFFINS /THE HOLLOW MAN* This twin-titled 'tec tale (Brits and Americans speaking, as they do, a different language) is an incomparable example of the perennially puzzling locked room mystery. So who killed Prof Grimaud in his secure study and, more importantly, *how*?

3 *THE CUCKOO'S CALLING*
Would it have been a winner if the author remained Robert Galbraith? We'll never know, as a pre-publication leak outed J K Rowling (crime writer). Her almost lovable one-legged 'tec Cormoran Strike tackles the supposed suicide of a supermodel.

2 *THE MURDER AT THE VICARAGE*
Omitting Miss Jane Marple would be a crime in its own right. When detested Colonel Lucius Prothero is murdered in St Mary Mead and two people confess, the sharp spinster must sift seven suspects.

1 **THE MURDER OF ROGER ACKROYD**
Top of this particular tree must be one of the most controversial cases of the world's most famous Belgian detective, star of 33 novels. This super-clever twister sees Poirot eliminate all the original suspects.

10 **THE MOONSTONE**
Wilkie Collins

9 **THE LEAVENWORTH CASE**
Anne Katherine Green

8 **UNNATURAL DEATH**
Dorothy L Sayers

7 **THE GREEK COFFIN MYSTERY**
Ellery Queen

6 **DEATH OF A GHOST**
Margery Allingham

5 **VINTAGE MURDER**
Ngaio Marsh

4 **THE THREE COFFINS/ THE HOLLOW MAN**
John Dixon Carr

3 **THE CUCKOO'S CALLING**
Robert Galbraith

2 **THE MURDER AT THE VICARAGE**
Agatha Christie

1 **THE MURDER OF ROGER ACKROYD**
Agatha Christie

"TEA AND SCANDAL AT FOUR THIRTY"

– THE MURDER AT THE VICARAGE

TOP 10

What is it about some women who're clearly not as saintly as they might be that sends otherwise rational men weak at the knees (and sometimes somewhat soft in the head)? All right, don't answer that. But there might be a gleam of enlightenment to be found in this Top Ten involving that most dangerous of creatures, the *femme fatale*.

FATAL **FEMALES**

9 *NANA*
A girl living on Paris streets begins a career as a prostitute, aged 15. But don't pity her just yet. After a sensational stage debut that owes more to scanty cladding than acting talent, this danger woman destroys every man who pursues her (as plenty do).

8 *DERAILED*
Don't miss your usual commuter train or you might end up having an affair, being blackmailed . . . then accused of murder. Alternatively, if you do miss that train, be very careful not to sit opposite delectable Lucinda Harris.

10 *LADY AUDLEY'S SECRET*
How might a Victorian *femme fatale* behave? Well, let's start with bigamy. Have her desert a child and push husband number one down a well. Then she might plan to poison husband number two, and torch a hotel where other male acquaintances are staying. Pity she couldn't vote.

7 *TO DIE FOR*
Her husband is shot dead by her teenage boyfriend, which should arouse the merest *frisson* of suspicion that Suzanne Maretto might be a black, rather than grieving, widow.

6 *CLEAN BREAK*
Classic *noir*, as double-crossing doll Sherry Peatty discovers her husband's joining a gang that's about to knock off a racetrack's takings – and decides to grab the loot for herself with the help of her hoodlum lover.

5 *DISCLOSURE*
In a delicious reverse take on testosterone-powered CEOs who assume any employee is fair game, boss Meredith Johnson attempts to resurrect a relationship with underling (she wishes) Tom and accuses him of sexual harassment when he turns her down.

4 *GOLDFINGER*
Included more for her outrageous name than a true black heart, lesbian Pussy Galore is a challenge to 007's masculinity, but also a serious player on the team of evil gold guru Auric Goldfinger. But Pussy redeems herself in the end.

3 *DOUBLE INDEMNITY*
This 1943 novel introduced deadly Phyllis Nirdlinger, who not only manages to persuade basically decent insurance man Walter Huff to knock off her unwanted husband, but to do it 'accidentally' for a double payout.

2 *THE BRIDE WORE BLACK*
She's beautiful. She's mysterious. But one thing *is* certain – whenever Julie Killeen appears, a man comes to a sticky end. Perhaps they should have given more weight to the name.

1 *THE LONG GOODBYE*
You'd think Philip Marlowe would learn from painful experience, but no. After first trying to seduce him, naughty Eileen Wade soon shows her true colours by accusing the long-suffering PI of murdering her husband. As if.

10 *LADY AUDLEY'S SECRET*
Mary E Braddon

9 *NANA*
Emile Zola

8 *DERAILED*
James Siegel

7 *TO DIE FOR*
Joyce Maynard

6 *CLEAN BREAK*
Lionel White

5 *DISCLOSURE*
Michael Crichton

4 *GOLDFINGER*
Ian Fleming

3 *DOUBLE INDEMNITY*
James M Cain

2 *THE BRIDE WORE BLACK*
Cornell Woolrich

1 *THE LONG GOODBYE*
Raymond Chandler

"TO SAY GOODBYE IS TO DIE A LITTLE"

– *THE LONG GOODBYE*

TOP 10

The power to make people laugh is a precious gift and there's nothing more satisfying than curling up with a book that raises a smile and engenders the feelgood factor. The ten assorted titles chosen for this list all have their individual approach to humour, but the one thing they have in common is the ability to generate a laugh.

GOOD LAUGHS

10 *MOLESWORTH*
A cmplation ov wizdom ritten by Nigel Molesworth (awther). Nigel (definitely not the star speller at St Custard's School) pontificates on skool in genral and matters of moment in this entertaining 1950s prep school romp illustrated by Ronald Searle.

9 *THE VIRGIN SOLDIERS*
Malaya, late 1940s. Gauche conscript soldiers are over-sexed and under-satisfied. Private Brigg (virgin) lusts after RSM's daughter Philippa (virgin), who hooks up with Sergeant Driscoll (worldly), leaving Brigg to the tender mercies of courtesan Juicy Lucy. Not funny? Oh yes it is.

8 *WHISKY GALORE*
The *SS Cabinet Minister* (cargo – scotch whisky) runs aground on a Scottish island in 1941. Locals descend like locusts. Cargo vanishes. Cargo hunted by pompous English Home Guard Captain Paul Waggett. Let mayhem ensue.

7 *LUCKY JIM*
In postwar Britain, junior lecturer Jim Dixon charts a hilarious course through personal relationships and provincial university life. In a surreal climax, Dixon's big lecture ends in disaster as (drunk) he mocks everyone he's been trying to impress and passes out.

6 *MASH*
On one level, this Mobile Army Surgical Hospital in the Korean War does great work patching up casualties. But graveyard humour resides in the interaction of the unit's ill-assorted characters as irreverent surgeons run amok.

5 *PUCKOON*
Comedian Spike Milligan was a prolific writer. This is the anarchic tale of horizontal Irish lazy-boyo Dan Milligan in the village of Puckoon,

after it is accidentally divided by the new boundary between Northern and Southern Ireland in 1924.

4 *GOOD OMENS*
Subtitled *The Nice and Accurate Prophesies of Agnes Nutter, Witch*, this comedy is about the son of Satan and an otherworldly cast including the Antichrist and Three Horsemen of the Apocalypse (Pestilence hung up his scythe following the invention of penicillin).

3 *THREE MEN IN A BOAT*
Written in 1889 but with jokes that seem fresh today, three men (George, Harris and Jerome) and a dog (Montmorency) take a comical boat trip along the River Thames.

2 *THE LIFE AND TIMES OF THE THUNDERBOLT KID*
Crack-you-up coming-of-age memoir by humorist Bill Bryson, recalling his 1950s youth in Des Moins, Iowa. Much mirth springs from his imaginary *alter ego*, the Thunderbolt Kid (from another planet).

1 *RIGHT HO, JEEVES*
Bertie Wooster decides to sort out assorted troubles, romantic and otherwise, when he visits Brinkley Court after a spell in Cannes. His bumbling efforts have predictably disastrous consequences, and Bertie is forced to reinstate Jeeves's advisory status – after which everything's swiftly sorted.

10 *MOLESWORTH*
Geoffrey Williams and Ronald Searle

9 *THE VIRGIN SOLDIERS*
Leslie Thomas

8 *WHISKY GALORE*
Compton Mackenzie

7 *LUCKY JIM*
Kingsley Amis

6 *MASH*
Richard Hooker

5 *PUCKOON*
Spike Milligan

4 *GOOD OMENS*
Neil Gaiman and Terry Pratchett

3 *THREE MEN IN A BOAT*
Jerome K Jerome

2 *THE LIFE AND TIMES OF THE THUNDERBOLT KID*
Bill Bryson

1 *RIGHT HO, JEEVES*
P G Wodehouse

"ANY TUTTING THAT'S REQUIRED, I'LL ATTEND TO MYSELF"

– RIGHT HO, JEEVES